LIFE IN THE SADDLE

Alwyn Torenbeek grew up near the tiny Central Queensland town of Kokotunga, dreaming of riding wild horses and becoming a rodeo champion. He started his rodeo career at 14 and by 21 he was the Australian bronco-riding champion. His life on horseback includes droving cattle, contract mustering, station management work and establishing stockmanship schools for underprivileged youth. He took up endurance riding in 1967 and has several prestigious Quilty Endurance Riding buckles to his name. Alwyn is an inductee of the Rodeo, Stockman's and Equestrian Halls of Fame. Now in his mid-seventies, he lives near Rockhampton and is still a competitive endurance rider.

David Gilchrist is an Australian writer whose work has appeared in publications as diverse as *Australian Geographic*, *The Sydney Morning Herald*, *The New Zealand Herald*, *The Independent* (London), and *R.M. Williams Outback* magazine. David lives just north of Brisbane. A word wrangler, he can't ride horses or catch bulls.

LIFE IN THE SADDLE

Alwyn Torenbeek
with David Gilchrist

MICHAEL JOSEPH
an imprint of
PENGUIN BOOKS

MICHAEL JOSEPH

Published by the Penguin Group
Penguin Group (Australia)
707 Collins Street, Melbourne, Victoria 3008, Australia
(a division of Pearson Australia Group Pty Ltd)
Penguin Group (USA) Inc.
375 Hudson Street, New York, New York 10014, USA
Penguin Group (Canada)
90 Eglinton Avenue East, Suite 700, Toronto, Canada ON M4P 2Y3
(a division of Pearson Penguin Canada Inc.)
Penguin Books Ltd
80 Strand, London WC2R 0RL England
Penguin Ireland
25 St Stephen's Green, Dublin 2, Ireland
(a division of Penguin Books Ltd)
Penguin Books India Pvt Ltd
11 Community Centre, Panchsheel Park, New Delhi 110 017, India
Penguin Group (NZ)
67 Apollo Drive, Rosedale, Auckland 0632, New Zealand
(a division of Pearson New Zealand Ltd)
Penguin Books (South Africa) (Pty) Ltd
Rosebank Office Park, Block D, 181 Jan Smuts Avenue, Parktown North, Johannesburg 2196, South Africa
Penguin (Beijing) Ltd
7F, Tower B, Jiaming Center, 27 East Third Ring Road North, Chaoyang District, Beijing 100020, China

Penguin Books Ltd, Registered Offices: 80 Strand, London WC2R 0RL, England

First published by Penguin Group (Australia), 2013

10 9 8 7 6 5 4 3 2 1

Text copyright © Alwyn Torenbeek and David Gilchrist, 2013

The moral right of the author has been asserted

All rights reserved. Without limiting the rights under copyright reserved above, no part of this publication may be reproduced, stored in or introduced into a retrieval system, or transmitted, in any form or by any means (electronic, mechanical, photocopying, recording or otherwise), without the prior written permission of both the copyright owner and the above publisher of this book.

Cover design by Alex Ross © Penguin Group (Australia)
Text design by Samantha Jayaweera © Penguin Group (Australia)
Front cover photograph courtesy of Torenbeek family collection
Background cover photograph courtesy of Shutterstock
Back cover author photograph courtesy of David Gilchrist
Typeset in Sabon 11pt/17pt by Samantha Jayaweera, Penguin Group (Australia)
Printed and bound in Australia by McPherson's Printing Group, Maryborough, Victoria

National Library of Australia
Cataloguing-in-Publication data:

> Torenbeek, Alwyn, author.
> A life in the saddle: adventures of legendary horseman,
> the Kokotunga Kid / Alwyn Torenbeek
> with David Gilchrist.
> ISBN: 9781921901355 (paperback)
> 1.Torenbeek, Alwyn
> 2. Rodeo performers--Australia--Biography.
> 3. Stockmen--Australia--Biography.
> 4. Horsemen and horsewomen--Australia--Biography.
>
> Other Authors/Contributors:
> Gilchrist, David, author.
>
> 791.84092

penguin.com.au

ALWAYS LEARNING   PEARSON

To my wonderful family for putting up with me for over 50 years. A special thank you to my daughter Shayne and to Emma, Bonnie and Kelsey as well as Lyn Eather for spurring me on to write. To Yvonne Knight and Amanda Stirling for their support.
– A.T.

To my sons Benjamin and Matthew, so they might be inspired as they inspire me. To my wife Tracey – for her love, support and encouragement.
– D.G.

CONVERSION TABLE

1 mile = 1.6 kilometres

1 foot = 30.5 centimetres

1 inch = 25.5 millimetres

1 acre = 0.4 hectares

1 pound = 0.45 kilograms

1 ounce = 28.5 grams

CONTENTS

Forewords ix

Prologue: No Time to Die xi

The Birth of Myella: 1911–1939 1

War and Fast Ponies: 1938–1949 12

Becoming a Horseman: 1950–1952 21

Larrikins, Dancing and Rodeo: 1953–1955 57

Heading South: 1955–1956 69

Doing the Cross: 1957 98

A New Aussie Champ: 1957–1958 106

A Photograph: 1958–1959 132

Crossing the Ditch: 1959 145

Married Couple's Problem: 1960–1964 157

Endurance: 1965–1967 173

Allan 'Aldo' Arrives: 1968–1969 181

Death Becomes Me: 1970–1980 194

Bush Schools: 1980–1990 209

Aldo: 1991 240

Aldo's Bonnie Doon: 1992–2012 243

Acknowledgements 269

Roughrider's Lament

Beat, bedraggled and bleary.
Bruised, battered and worn.
Inconsolably weary,
Wish I'd never been born.

The bones in my back tend to rattle and crack
And the bones in my hip rub the skin.
The pain jumps about and I can't figure out
If it's greater without or within.

Sick, sad and sore-hearted.
Dirty, ragged and cold.
Figure of youth departed,
Leaving me broken and old.

My vertebrae ping like a loose fiddle string,
That I'm done you can tell at a glance.
The rodeo game spells fortune and fame,
Someone else can have my chance.

— ANON

Forewords

After retiring from gypsy life on the rodeo circuit as a rodeo champion, Alwyn needed a challenge and found it in endurance riding. He had been one of the most athletic riders I'd ever seen among the roughriders of the 1950s, he had the horses and a truck for transport, and he set out to follow the endurance rides in Queensland and interstate.

He found comradeship among the endurance riders, who rode for no prize money, but for the satisfaction of completing the journey with a sound and happy horse. By being part of a truly amateur sport of men and women with a wide range of ages, Alwyn proves one is never too old or young to participate in an endurance ride, or in life for that matter.

— Erica Williams, widow of bushman's outfitter R.M. Williams

Torrie was one of the gentlemen of the Australian rodeo circuit of the 1950s, a true champion whom I was pleased to take under my wing. He was a remarkable athlete and a front-end rider like me. The times we shared rodeoing during the 1950s were among the best times of my life.

— Lindsay Black, former Australian rodeo champion

Rodeo champion, drover, stockman and triple hall of fame inductee Alwyn Torenbeek has mustered a great number of adventures into his lifetime. We met when I travelled to his home near Rockhampton to interview him for *R.M. Williams Outback* magazine and I was immediately intrigued by his roller-coaster of a life story. I jumped on for the ride, only to find it hasn't stopped yet.

Through fire and flood, hope and happiness, love and loss, Alwyn's is a remarkable story of a legendary horseman who loves the bush and the folk who live within it.

– David Gilchrist, co-author and journalist

Prologue
NO TIME TO DIE

'Get the doctor; quick, get the doctor,' were the few words I spoke in the moments before I died on a beautiful April morning in 1975.

Let me tell you, there is nothing that focuses the mind on living quite as much as dying, especially when you are only 37 when it happens.

My wife Marion and I and our five children – Mike, Jeff, Shayne, Vonda and Aldo – lived in cattle and coalmining country 370 miles northwest of Brisbane on Woolton Station, near Theodore, a jewel in the agricultural eye of Queensland.

On this particular morning, we were all getting organised for a charity race day to raise funds for the local ambulance service. I had agreed to provide five horses for the races, and the truck that was to collect our horses was running late.

My teenage son Mike and I had risen before dawn, cooked our breakfast and started organising the horses we were taking to the races.

Just so you know, these were not trained thoroughbred racehorses that were raised on first-quality grain. They were station-bred horses raised on grass, and local landowners or managers like me provided them for these events so that the town would benefit a little. Today it was my turn to supply some horses.

Now, we'd mustered 30-odd horses to select five for a country race day. It wasn't a big problem and didn't take all that long. In fact, before the morning had grown too old, we had the horses, their saddles and bridles ready. All we needed was the truck and we'd be on our way.

There we were, as the saying goes, all dressed up with nowhere to go – or rather, somewhere to go and no way to get there. What's more, back in those days I was a little less patient than I am now; that's what you are like when you're fit, not quite 40, and still ready to mix it with whatever life sends you.

As it happened, it was ten o'clock before the truck arrived. By that time we just had to load the horses and get into Theodore.

No time to stop and yarn; very little time to stop for anything, and that was despite facing a drive of only about an hour. You see, the way it is with me, as it is with many bush folk, when you give your word to do something, well, you do it; you do it right and on time.

As soon as the truck arrived, I gave the driver a nod and Mike and I got to work. We had just started walking the first couple of horses up the loading ramp when the telephone rang up at the house.

Marion had been inside all morning and took the call. An anxious voice on the other end told her that the caller was from the ambulance service and that the race organisers were starting to wonder about the whereabouts of the horses.

Marion wasn't surprised that they were calling. We were late and there was just no getting around it. What's more, I was down as a steward for the races. Their problem was simple: no horses and no steward meant fewer funds for the service.

Now, country races, particularly charity races, are important to any bush community. That's why, in true bush spirit, the thought that something might stop me or my horses getting to the races never entered my mind. Late or not, we were on our way.

As the truck backed up to the loading ramp, I led the first horse up the ramp. Mike was hurrying along as well and led the second horse up the ramp behind me. All we needed to do was stop the truck, open the gates, walk them on, then gather up the next three and do the same again. Then we would gather our gear and we'd be off.

I don't know how often I had loaded horses onto a truck. Probably more times than I like to remember. After all, loading animals onto a truck is part of the stock and trade of anyone on a property. I had been working horses since I was old enough to ride to school, then mustering cattle, droving and, of course, working the rodeo circuit as a roughrider. Just the same, something was different this day.

On this particular day, I don't know why the driver didn't get the truck square onto the ramp. Perhaps it was because he was running late and in a hurry. It's just one of those things that I'll never know. Anyhow, he backed the truck up to the ramp slightly askew. He had swung down out of the cabin and was taking a look at the gap between the ramp and the truck, trying to decide whether he needed to straighten the truck up to the ramp, when I spotted him.

'It'll be right,' I called.

Perhaps he nodded, perhaps he answered. I don't remember.

'My horses are all broken in. They're used to trucks,' I said, trying to reassure him. Maybe at the same time I was trying to reassure myself that we'd be okay – we'd get to the races.

Whatever I may have been thinking or worried about, there

was one thing of which I was sure: my horses wouldn't shy at the sight of that gap between the ramp and the truck. It was no wider than perhaps 6 inches and not so big as to cause my horses any problem. Without further ado, I pulled the right pin on the truck gate and when the gate wouldn't budge, I reached down to lift the left pin.

To this day, I don't know why the driver jumped in the truck again or when. It is not a conversation we ever had, and I don't reckon we ever will. Time has taken its toll on both of our memories. All I know is I didn't see the driver hop in behind the wheel.

Anyway, there I was bent down to pull the bottom pin with my head between the ramp and the truck. At about the same time, the driver had reached to his left and swung the shift into reverse.

I suppose the initial rumble of the truck's engine as the driver slid it into gear probably entered my mind. It would have done. But then I had no time to react because at about that same time, the reversing truck was splitting my head into three parts as a bolt protruding from the truck gate was forcing itself into my skull on one side and a piece of rail was crushing the other. All I knew was at that precise moment blood was bursting from my eyes, ears, mouth and nose with such force that it splashed up off the loading ramp's timber floor and was spattering my knees. All I remember is looking down both sides of my body and thinking 'Wow.'

To say everything let go is an understatement; I reckon the impact was something like a Cassius Clay punch.

I would like to tell you that I remember every detail of what happened, but even now, all these years later, I still can't recall everything.

What I do know is I didn't pass out immediately. Some few seconds after thinking, 'Wow,' my mind started working again.

I had recovered from the standing eight count that followed the impact, and I thought, 'This time, old fella, you're done for.' It was then that I heard myself yell to Mike, 'Get the doctor; get your mother and get the doctor.' And then my mind and body gave in to the reality of the situation and I sank slowly to the floor. It had been a one-punch knockout blow after all.

Pushing aside the shock of seeing blood spurt out of my head, Mike bolted past the horse he had on the ramp and ran back to the house to tell his mum to call the doctor.

Although my voice was normally strong enough to rouse the station dogs or call in the horses over a good distance, it was, like the rest of my body, rapidly losing strength. Just the same, despite there being 328 feet of open space between the house and the loading ramp, the sounds of the accident, the truck, my yelling, Mike yelling, the whole commotion, got Marion's attention.

She'd only just got off the phone to the ambulance service after reassuring them that the horses would soon be on the way to the races, and quickly rang them back, explaining, 'I don't know what is going on, but something bad has happened, come quick.'

With that, she raced down to me with my 12-year-old daughter Shayne bolting after her. Well, Mike saw his mother running towards the ramp and behind her, his sister Shayne. Desperate to keep his sister from seeing her father drenched in blood and unconscious, or semi-conscious at best, Mike roared at her to get back in the house.

Shayne kept running towards the ramp. Mike picked up some rocks, took aim and started pegging them at Shayne, still bellowing at her to turn around.

No doubt Mike's actions had Shayne more confused and worried than before. Her own stubbornness kicked in and she kept coming, calling out, 'What's wrong with Dad?'

Mike answered his sister with a further bombardment of rocks, all the while screaming at her to get back in the house. I'm sure the pallid, strung-out look on her brother's face together with his incessant bombardment and screaming got the better of Shayne, and she gave up and ran back to the house in a flood of worry and tears.

In the middle of screaming at Shayne, Mike had the presence of mind to call to his mother to get the old station wagon. Marion drove the old car over to the ramp. Then, with all the courage and strength they could muster, they loaded me very carefully into the wagon.

Thankfully, Mike was raised in the bush. Many a bush kid knows how to drive from a young age and Mike was no exception. He slipped in behind the steering wheel and Marion crawled into the back with me, placing her hands on each side of my head as Mike slowly and carefully pulled away.

Although it was not a topic Mike, Marion or I spoke about over the years that followed, I'm sure neither Mike nor Marion thought of anything except getting me safely to hospital – Mike worried only about the driving, while his mother concentrated on keeping my skull in one piece.

There she was, the woman who had been part of my life during most of my rodeo days, who had lived rough on numerous stock routes droving cattle, the mother of my children, the woman I loved, sitting in an old shirt and shorts beside me, cradling my crushed head, as our 15-year-old son drove to meet the ambulance 6 miles down the road.

But those 6 miles would not be the end of the trek to hospital. After that, there was still another 12 miles to the Theodore Hospital and a two-hour drive in the ambulance that would blow out to four hours as we made our way to Rockhampton.

Mike drove as carefully as he could on the dusty and rutted track that passed for a road in those days until we met the ambulance.

Blood filled my ears and prevented the sound of the approaching ambulance from entering my mind. Then, as they moved me from the car to the ambulance, the most remarkable thing happened: I was suddenly sitting with my father. He had passed away some years beforehand, yet here we were, sitting somewhere above the ambulance. I felt no pain; I was just quietly enjoying Dad's company again. It was the most remarkable feeling and one that lingers with me still.

Although it was wonderful sitting there, pain-free, with my father, after a while I knew Dad was trying to tell me to go back, not to stay with him.

There was a certain gesture Dad used when he was worried. And without saying a word, he made that gesture. Right there and then, I knew it was time to go back. It wasn't my time to die. Dad wanted me to live and that was exactly what I intended to do. Moreover, I intended to live long and live well.

Getting back into my body was not painless. It was a miserable process; I felt pain and plenty of it.

Nonetheless, taking on the challenge to live and meeting it meant, as far as I was concerned, not letting a single memory escape my mind. I had to fight to remember everything and to keep those memories, because each of them made me who I was, and who I would become. To live, I needed to remember.

Chapter One
THE BIRTH OF MYELLA: 1911-1939

Friesland, a northern province of the Netherlands, brought the world Frisian cattle and horses, the spy Mata Hari, artist M.C. Escher, its own language and provided a home to Egbert Torenbeek and his family.

If family lore is correct, this son of a Dutch pirate loved the land so much that in the early twentieth century, rather than take up life on the seas, Egbert chose a farmer's life. He toiled as a dairyman, producing milk for the folk of the Friesland capital Leeuwarden.

Unfortunately, however, Egbert's penchant for spruiking his political opinions attracted the attention of the local authorities, who threw him into prison for three weeks. Once out, he left home for Germany, where he picked up dairy work, and met and married Luise Lutz. It was 1904; Luise was 19 and Egbert was 30.

In 1910 Egbert collided with German officialdom and decided it was time to leave Europe for good. As his brother Bartel had left for Australia some years earlier, he followed him. Egbert, Luise, their young family – Wilhelm (six), Ruard (five) and newborn Gustav – and Egbert's 33-year-old sister Ybeltje headed for a new life aboard the Norddeutscher Lloyd line's S.S. *Zieten*.

For the Torenbeek family, their two-month trek from Germany through the Suez Canal, to Batavia and Papua, and along the outer rim of the Great Barrier Reef ended on a dirty, dusty Brisbane wharf, where they were greeted by the pungent odour of rancid blood and offal that wafted from the meatworks upstream and mingled with the smell of putrid mangrove mud.

Once on the wharf, they navigated through a jumble of immigration and customs officials, baggage handlers and delivery personnel, then onto the mail train for the final 12 miles to the Immigration Depot at Kangaroo Point, in the heart of Brisbane. This was to be the Torenbeeks' first home in Australia.

Brisbane still had no sewage system, was only just discussing its public transport needs, and rats infested much of the riverside areas, but the Immigration Depot was welcoming, clean and comfortable.

There was dormitory-style accommodation that looked out across the river, a kitchen, dining room and scullery. The new arrivals slept in neat rows of beds furnished with tidy brown calico bedspreads and had the use of clean, green nightstands. Their small world included a garden containing roses, a large Poinciana and ornamental shrubs. Between the garden and the gate lay an avenue of camphor laurel and weeping figs.

The Immigration Depot must have had an air of romance, because Egbert and Luise soon added two more sons to their brood: Egbert and Gerard. Then, in 1913, the family pulled up stakes, waved goodbye to the manicured garden and moved to the tiny town of Dalby in the fertile Darling Downs, 130 miles northwest of Brisbane.

Life for the Torenbeek family now meant surviving in a hut in the middle of a silver-grey acacia mosaic punctuated by prickly pear, under a roof of rust-red corrugated iron that shaded those on the inside from a breathless, pitiless sun.

A timber slab door opened from the outside and rough bunk

beds ran along the interior walls, with a crude hearth in the far corner, black as pitch and just as sooty. Hessian divided the hut into spaces for cooking, eating and sleeping, with nothing spare.

Beyond the snakes and lizards, hot sun, and unimaginably hard environment, their lives also changed to accommodate the banal peccadillos that are such a large part of outback life. Even their names changed: Egbert Torenbeek became Charlie, his son Wilhelm became Bill, Gustav was Gus and Ruard was called Snowy. Young Egbert became Bert and Gerard was Whitey.

Their European manners were also Australianised. Occasionally, locals riding by the Torenbeek dairy would bid the Dutchman a hearty, drawn-out 'G'day'. Charlie, with an eon of polite Saxon heritage behind him, would smile, pause his work and doff his hat. Inevitably, the passer-by would respond with, 'For Gawd's sake, leave yer hat on, Charlie. You're in Australia now.'

Amid the myriad changes to which the Torenbeeks had to adjust, they found few things in the outback more heartbreaking than drought. In their first ten years on the Darling Downs there were two significant and prolonged droughts. The dairy struggled during the droughts, so Charlie hitched his horse Snifter to the dray and, together with his sons in a Model T Ford, cut and carried timber to load the train at a nearby siding. Usually Gus, Bill and Snowy would shoulder much of that work.

By the time they'd moved into a four-room cottage complete with two bedrooms, a front veranda and a sitting room, it was 1923 and the rains came. They turned the Queensland plains into a sea of waving green and filled the rivers until they were 'running a banker'. However, by 1924 the Torenbeeks were broke.

Then, in the midst of their economic malaise, a little luck came to Charlie and Luise. A friend offered the family a share of a dairy by the bayside town of Redcliffe, near Brisbane.

A year later, however, their stint in Redcliffe came to an end as

Charlie and Luise separated and Charlie and his sons returned to the Queensland outback.

It was there that Bill, by now a quietly spoken young man, fit and ready to start his own life, met, fell in love with and married Agnes Saxelby. Diminutive Agnes, with her shock of dark wavy hair and impish smile, was willing to join Bill in whatever adventures life sent.

Agnes didn't have to wait long. Soon after the wedding, Bill, Agnes and Bert moved to Kumbia near Kingaroy in Queensland's South Burnett region, 124 miles northwest of Brisbane.

They survived the Depression by cutting timber and selling it for the ovens and factory furnaces of Brisbane. With the money they earned, they built a small timber house and Bill and Agnes started their family. In 1930, Agnes gave birth to Gwenda and they continued battling to put a little money aside so they could build their own farm. Seven years later, the Torenbeeks had added Daphne (four), Wilma (two) and newborn baby boy Alwyn to their family. Bill and Bert had also managed to scrape together the £10 they needed to secure a Brigalow Belt property in a Central Queensland land ballot.

Central Queensland's fertile Brigalow Belt, west of the region's capital Rockhampton, was at that time still covered in sometimes almost impenetrable thickets of belah, gidgee, lancewood and bendee trees. For those like Bill and Bert Torenbeek, who were willing to clear and work the land, it offered the promise of a good living from cattle, wheat, citrus, cotton or dairying, courtesy of good rainfall and close proximity to markets.

In 1937 the brothers drew a block that would be called Myella. This made them part of a community that lived in and around the tiny town of Kokotunga. Not much more than a school, a general store that included the town's public telephone, a recreation reserve for the cricket and football clubs and a spattering of houses, Kokotunga was a very active frontier town – an outpost in a Brigalow wilderness.

These were the days of community picnics, children's races, tug-of-war, ice cream, soft biscuits and cakes, watermelon and sweets. Yet with no boundary fence, no yards, no house, and no permanent water, life on Myella wasn't an easy ride.

Making a go of it meant long days grubbing trees with pick, shovel and axe to clear a homestead block, then putting a trace harness on a horse and drawing in all the logs for building yards and sheds or piling them to burn in the stove. Then there was the problem of needing a home.

Bill and Bert's housing solution was simple but laborious. The brothers still owned the house at Kumbia near Kingaroy, 310 miles to the south, and they set about taking it apart board by board, numbering each board in succession. They loaded the dismantled house onto the freight train and the train delivered it to Kokotunga; then they carted the bits on Bill's Model T Ford, piece by piece, trip after trip.

The brothers used most of their money on moving the house, so they had nothing left with which to pay for lining the inside, and the home remained unlined for a dozen years as building and working the dairy took all their time and resources.

As far as Alwyn's sisters were concerned, leaving the house unlined just meant an opportunity to play. They'd climb up into the ceiling cavity and dance on the rafters – at least when nobody was looking – and their laughter echoed through the house and out across the Dawson Valley.

Throughout the valley, however, and on Myella in particular, menace lurked. There, among the mulch and leaf litter on the ground, lived the quickest and most vicious attack snake: the death adder. The locals called it Kokotunga, a name borrowed from the Aboriginal dialect of the Wuli Wuli people. Whatever the name, the snake had enough neurotoxic venom in its gob to knock off a beefy stockman in no time, let alone a wee lad like Alwyn.

During the wet season it was common for two or three snakes to slither near the house every day and sometimes come inside. Nigger, the family dog, was always vigilant and would bail up a death adder and growl and bark until Agnes had time to grab her 0.22 calibre rifle, which she always kept handy.

Agnes was a crack shot and seldom missed at any distance up to 180 feet. The few times she did miss, her hunt was permanently recorded with bullet holes in the walls or windows from where she'd taken a pot shot at an indiscreet snake.

Having dispatched the snake, or perhaps a dingo or goanna, she'd carefully rake and sweep the area immediately around the house so she could easily see the tracks of any wayward dangerous animals.

One time, before the family had electric lights, when Alwyn was still very young, Agnes was doing the washing in the dairy about 300 feet away from the house. It was getting dark.

Alwyn toddled into the dairy. Along the way, he slapped his little foot down on something unusually soft that didn't quite feel right. The boy squirmed, shivered and quickened his pace, right to his mother's side, then looked up at her and said, 'I stood on something that went plop.'

Agnes put down whatever she was cleaning, rolled and lit a piece of paper that was lying nearby to make a torch, and started looking around to find what her son had stood on. She found it easily. In the flickering firelight, only a few feet away, was a death adder.

The young mother didn't miss a beat. Before her son could utter another word she swooped on her rifle, aimed and fired, killing the serpent instantly.

On the upside, apart from the deadly snakes and plenty of lizards, there were wallabies and a good supply of brush turkeys on Myella. If the family was short on meat, Bert, who was also handy with the rifle, would often bag a turkey for dinner.

Wallabies weren't on the menu; they were slayed for their skins. However, the two eldest girls rather liked watching the wallabies, so they would follow along behind Bert and, when he wasn't looking, pull his snares to save the roos.

Of course, a young family can't live on beef or turkey alone. In the early years, Agnes would bake bread and make homemade butter in a wooden churn. However, the butter had to wait until they bought their first herd of dairy cattle a year after moving onto Myella.

From then on, life on Myella revolved around the early-morning muster of their cows to a chorus of 'Come on, Hilda; move on, Jenny; steady, Daisy', as they called in each cow for milking. Eventually, the Torenbeeks were able to afford milking machines. After that the novelty and excitement of milking never returned.

What did return was the goods train. It came by Myella twice a week, bringing mail and groceries from the grand emporium Thomas Brown and New Zealand Loan in Rockhampton to Baralaba and western communities. Among the groceries were tins of prunes and fresh fruit and vegetables. These were essential, as regular droughts made growing their own vegetables near impossible.

Every four months or so Agnes would post an order to Thomas Brown and New Zealand Loan for many non-perishable necessities. Her order would arrive at Kokotunga on the night train the following Friday to be collected early on Saturday morning.

Every six months, the sound of clattering pots and pans and the rumble of an old Chevrolet hawker's van would announce the arrival of Mr Clarkson the travelling salesman.

Mr Clarkson would pull up outside the Torenbeeks' house as all those inside would race out, keen to see the latest nice things he was touting – anything from buttons to cottons, dresses to food colourings. A late visit inevitably meant that Bill and Agnes would invite Mr Clarkson to stay over, which meant more time for their girls to sift through his van to find something extra special.

Getting groceries from the train, on the other hand, meant the possibility that Agnes might have ordered some dried fruit to make one of her fruitcakes. There was nothing more alluring than the smell of fruit, sugar, flour, eggs, milk and a little spice baking to form a mouth-watering cake fresh out of her wood-fired oven. She'd then ice it to perfection.

Sometimes the family needed to get away from the farm for a day, so early in the morning before sunrise they'd hurry down to the lower paddock that bordered the train line and when they saw it rattling towards them, puffing great clouds of grey smoke, someone would strike a match. That tiny light was the only signal the driver needed to stop the train at the Myella back fence. They'd jump on board and arrive in Rockhampton about mid-morning, just as the Central Queensland humidity pushed the barometer from dry to intolerably uncomfortable.

As the train crossed each intersection, the Torenbeeks saw large shop windows that displayed every manner of 'modern convenience' from below the shade of sidewalk awnings or second-storey verandas with ornate turned-timber balustrades.

Inside the shops, shopkeepers in starched, stiff aprons waited patiently by long hardwood timber counters to sell them the latest bric-a-brac that Rockhampton had to offer. One such store was Kelly's General Warehouse. You could get anything you wanted from Kelly's, a large warehouse with a brick façade sporting tall second-storey windows.

If not Kelly's, there was the New Zealand Loan Warehouse or the Walter Reid Building. These riverside merchants offered a world of goods and chattels essential to bush living. The Torenbeeks would spend much of their time in town within these warehouses, selecting the goods they needed, especially new boots and clothes or dry foods, and ordering other things for delivery to Myella by train.

After shopping, the family would head to a favourite café called Ricketts near the grand old sandstone post office. Ricketts was all about sodas in tall glasses, comfortable booths, and warm, smiling service.

Other things broke the humdrum of the dairy routine. There were more serious distractions – usually emergencies, and they happened often enough. And that meant tackling the 'roads' – in reality little more than tracks – that crisscrossed the district. It needed to be a real emergency before anybody would take the risk of a high-speed dash to the Rockhampton or Baralaba Hospital.

Among the Torenbeeks' neighbours was a thin, lanky and weather-worn man by the name of Reg Hutchinson. Reg had a love for life and a heart as wide as the state of Queensland to boot.

There was an Aboriginal family who lived on Reg's property and worked as farmhands to pick his cotton. One warm Central Queensland evening, just as the sun fell below the horizon, one of the Aboriginal boys came running up to the homestead. Covered in a lather of sweat, he burst into Reg's kitchen and blurted out, 'Missus bin finished up pretty quick now.'

Reg knew what that meant: Mrs Daylight, the boy's mother, had gone into labour. Reg's face went pale and his hair stood on end as he gathered his thoughts. Calming himself, he looked directly at the lad and asked, 'How long Missus been?'

The boy looked at Reg quizzically and said, 'All day, last night.' Reg's eyes grew as big as dinner plates and he leapt into action. The problem was, in those days, there were no phones and few vehicles. Reg had the problem licked, though. He ran outside, threw his leg over his pushbike, and in a rhythmic cycle of push and pant, as if demonstrating solidarity with the 'Missus', pedalled the 5 miles to Myella.

By the time Reg arrived, it was pitch dark and he was dripping with sweat. He threw his bike to the ground and raced to the front door, calling for Bill to come quick.

Bill threw his clothes on, gathered his round-rimmed glasses and a torch and raced out the door to Reg. Still struggling for breath, Reg explained the situation to Bill and the two of them hurried to Bill's Model T Ford truck.

Bill adjusted his spectacles as if to gather his thoughts, gave the flivver two swift turns of the crank handle and, when the thing had sparked into life after giving out its customary whirr and sputter, bundled himself in beside his mate. The old Ford puttered through the bush, muttering them along the track back to Mrs Daylight's camp. A booming flatulent backfire from the truck that set off the station dogs and saw the horses galloping into the nearby bush announced their arrival.

Bill had barely stopped when Reg raced inside. Needless to say, Mrs Daylight was by this time well into her labour and quite distressed.

They made her as comfortable as two men could manage to make a woman in labour, laying her in a swag on the back of the truck before hurrying towards Baralaba Hospital, 16 miles away. The old car put in a splendid performance, skipping and sliding around every dusty corner, ricocheting off every bump, pushing the 20-horsepower engine as hard as it would go, striving for a glorious 40 mph and finding something less.

Reg sat bolt upright behind the wheel peering into the night while Bill tried desperately to calm Mrs Daylight, who was paying Bill Torenbeek the same attention she would any man given the circumstances – none at all.

When they arrived at the hospital, the two men were politely told to wait patiently in the waiting room. Before long, as the new day dawned, a healthy baby girl was born and christened Dawn Daylight – and the bush telegraph sprang into action.

Just so you know, the bush telegraph is a marvel of bush communication, then and now. It doesn't use wires or electricity. All it needs is one neighbour to bump into another and say, 'Did ya 'ear what happened the other night . . .?'

The story of how Reg and Bill had driven the rough track to Baralaba Hospital, how Mrs Daylight held on stretched out on the back of the flat-top, and how a short time later Dawn Daylight was born flew around the bush telegraph quicker than any news had before.

Chapter Two
WAR AND FAST PONIES: 1938–1949

Alwyn remembers – strangers in the bush

Considering the isolation, the limited resources, the lack of access to the amenities that town folk enjoyed, happiness should have been hard to find. It wasn't.

For me, however, that feeling of happiness started to change in 1942. My first fair dinkum memories go back to that year. I was five, and our farm was doing well. It was the year that Japan threatened Australia.

With war in full swing and the threat of a Japanese invasion very real, we spent a great deal of time doing air-raid drills at school and were joined by youngsters from the coast, who had been billeted in bush communities to escape the invasion threat. Sometimes, entire families moved west and lived in makeshift huts just outside the township.

Another wartime change was rationing. Rationing made the otherwise straightforward everyday tasks a challenge. And that wasn't the worst of it.

Fear. It was a mark of the times and it sat in our minds every day, especially after my uncles joined up.

Uncles Gerard, Bert, Harry, Jack and Peter saw the horrors of Kokoda and Tobruk and were among the many young men from rural Australia to sign up. Between them they fought in some of the worst battles of the Pacific, including Milne Bay in August–September 1942. The horrors of Milne Bay haunted Uncle Jack in particular; he suffered from shell shock and bouts of malaria for the rest of his life. New Guinea so damaged Uncle Harry that he never shared his war memories with his family. Uncles Bert and Peter were among the Rats of Tobruk who held the Libyan port of the same name against the German Afrika Corps.

But war also meant strangers in the bush. Myella was right in the path of the occasional AWOL digger or GI determined to escape the war – if only for a little while.

Sometimes, when we were riding to school we would see one or two AWOL soldiers on the road. When the often weary and frightened men saw us, they would disappear within seconds, as if the bush had swallowed them. The sight of the men would cause us to catch our breath and then smile and ride on. There was no chance we were about to give them up.

But there were other things that occupied our minds more than soldiers in the bush, things that took my mind off my uncles at war.

That was when the floods came. Lives were lost in families right across the Dawson and Don valleys. Cattlemen, their families and their stock died. Cattle carcasses were seen in tree canopies 25 feet above the ground and were still there a year later. Yet we were spared. The flood waters went down and then, I remember, it happened. A great misery began.

It was called school.

* * *

On Sunday, 3 September 1939, the Australian Prime Minister Robert Menzies said in an address to the nation, 'It is my melancholy duty to inform you officially that, in consequence of the persistence of Germany in the invasion of Poland, Great Britain has declared war on her; and that as a result, Australia is also at war.'

With those words the lives of thousands, including the Torenbeek family, were changed. Fear and anxiety became part of their daily existence until 1945.

Years later Alwyn would reflect, 'You have to understand that no matter where the Japanese Army was, they were not that far from Tropical North Queensland. That meant, for us, the war in the Pacific was at our doorstep. Amongst those that lived anywhere from Rockhampton north, war was a very tangible thing. We felt it.'

The ever-present fear of invasion, combined with the occasional sighting of AWOL soldiers, meant that few things relieved the Torenbeek family of worry about war. Mother Nature was one of those things.

In February 1942, a thunderclap heralded the arrival of rain. Soon the Brigalow folk heard the glorious sound of rain drumming on their roofs.

The rattle and patter of the rain grew quicker and louder and more violent until nobody could hear themselves talking and it spread south to flood the central highlands, Maranoa and the Darling Downs.

The storm that broke the drought in 1942 dumped between 6 and 8 inches of rain across the district over a week. Myella collected a whopping 12 inches in the first two nights.

By the end of the week, one local dairy had water running over the roof, and had lost their windmill and some of their best stock. Another family had to take shelter under a tent fly strung up between trees on high ground as floodwaters rampaged through their house further down the hill. The rain swamped the railway station and rose to the top floor of the hotel at nearby Rannes. Several families still living in bark huts, as many of the early pioneering families were, lost everything.

With the Don River on one side of Myella, the Dawson River on the other and the homestead on the high ground in between, the Torenbeeks were able to sit out the deluge, albeit trapped on an island.

Even when it'd stopped raining the waters took a full two months to drain away, allowing the slow-flowing coffee-coloured floodwater to make the road unusable and gouge out the train tracks, stopping the train. Luckily, supplies weren't an issue as the Torenbeek cupboards were full.

However, after the floodwaters had receded, it wasn't long before the family remembered how close they were to the front line of the war with Japan. The Central Queensland of Alwyn's childhood was a key location in the Pacific War, and the establishment of Camp Rockhampton in 1942 was a powerful reminder of this. Thousands of Allied troops, including the US 41st Infantry Division, were based in or near Rockhampton on their way to action in New Guinea.

The floodwaters receding meant more than an opportunity for the defence forces to secure a new base; it meant Alwyn had to go to school and face his 'great misery'.

Though Alwyn's older sisters had initially been home-schooled, when Alwyn started school the four siblings began riding to the Kokotunga school. It was quite an experience.

The ride to school was not far, just 4 miles. Nonetheless, anyone watching the Torenbeek children would not always have seen a harmonious gang of children calmly trotting to school. From time to time, things got fiery.

In the middle of squabbling over this or that one sister or another would lose her cool and give the other's horse a great whack on the rump, causing the beast to bolt. Not that the girls' cantankerous horses needed much encouragement to give their riders a harum-scarum ride. The old mare Janet, in particular, was a shocker. Every mile or so, she would decide it was time to shake up the kids and try her luck with a few solid kick-ups. Sitting behind Daphne, all Alwyn could do was hang on until the old mare decided to settle down. And with each kick, on each unpredictable ride, his love for rough-riding and tough horses grew.

Sometimes they would travel to school by sulky, the three girls riding along on the single bench seat while Alwyn rode in the buggy's small tray behind the seat.

The girls would hand their little brother their pencils to sharpen on the way to school and Alwyn would sharpen them on one of the sulky's iron tyres as they rattled along. While he was busy, the three feisty girls were likely to break out into tiffs that would last until they lost control of the buggy and had to compose themselves and their horse to head the sulky straight once more.

For a small town, Kokotunga had what seemed like a great school, especially when it came to sport. It had a tennis court, cricket pitch, rounders court, high jump portables, tumbling mats, a medicine ball, baseball bat and ball, a lumber-room, an air-raid shelter and five well-grassed acres for horses.

At Kokotunga, as at many bush schools, there was one class, and the solitary classroom was the entire school. That meant just one teacher taught 25 kids in five different grade levels.

Unfortunately, Kokotunga School was missing two important things: enough students to make the most of the facilities, and a teacher of merit.

Alwyn's school experience left him with what became a lifelong set against teachers, and helped cement his desire to be anywhere except at school. By the end of the first day Alwyn was thinking, 'If this is school, someone else can have mine.'

Alwyn sat at his desk beside his mates 14-year-old twins Fred and George Pegge, like three crows on a perch, waiting to find out what this school thing was all about, when the teacher called Fred and George to the front of the room.

The bastard they called Sir, took out a bamboo cane and flogged them without explanation – three cuts on each hand, one on each leg and a whack on the backside.

They say, what goes round comes round. The twins vowed to take their revenge. They were capable of handling themselves; all they needed was the right opportunity to present itself. When it did, they waylaid the teacher and gave him a belting that saw the twins ousted from the school and the teacher sacked. On hearing that the brothers had belted the teacher, Alwyn felt a sense of justice. As far as he was concerned a bastard of a teacher had got what he deserved, although he'd miss his mates. His sense of justice didn't last, though. The next Kokotunga teacher was good and kind, but didn't stay long. Then came Wally, and all signs of justice vanished.

Wally was the final nail in the coffin as far as any chance of Alwyn enjoying his formal education in Kokotunga went. He was a brute. He took joy, Alwyn reckons, in being 'an absolutely perverted bastard almost without interruption'. And he disliked Alwyn from the very first moment they met, and went about caning him every day after that, etching the phrase 'On the floor, Alwyn, to receive six of the best' into his young mind.

In 1947, two years after the war, Bill and Agnes had another son, Lester; by then the three sisters had left school and 11-year-old Alwyn was riding to school by himself.

He'd rise early each morning, have breakfast, do his morning chores, flip three or four somersaults for his morning exercises, believing they kept him strong and improved his balance, and ready a horse to ride to school.

The young boy saw the ride between Myella and Kokotunga as

the 'four miles of freedom' that enabled him to plan his revenge on Wally. Or ignore school altogether and go horseriding.

At least once a week, Alwyn would catch a snake, carry it to school in a calico sugar bag, plant the serpent in one of the toilets or some secluded place, then arrange for a mate in the know to find the thing. During class the mate would ask to go to the toilet, happen across the snake and run back to report the problem to the teacher.

Wally, horrified at the thought of having to deal with a snake, would order Alwyn and two of his mates to catch and dispatch the intruder. The boys would simply take their time to do the task and so relieve themselves of the burden of schoolwork.

One morning, Alwyn spent a while catching a 4-foot-long brown snake and hid it under the tumbling mats just before the physical education session with Wally.

The class was lined up and ready to start tumbling. One of the students was asked to go over to the pile of mats and spread them out. Just as the boy moved the first mat, he went pale and yelled 'snake' as loud as he could manage. Wally rushed over to save him and also turned pallid on seeing the large brown snake. The class was convinced it was a death adder, and chaos promptly broke loose. From that day on, as word got around amongst classmates that Alwyn had brought the snake that many believed was a Kokotunga or Death Adder to school, Alwyn collected the nickname 'The Kokotunga Kid'

Sometimes, Alwyn's father would keep him away from school so he could help move cattle from neighbouring properties to the Kokotunga slaughterhouse. As they rode their horses between properties Alwyn learnt to ride with hands, heels, balance and posture.

In 1949, the year after the last Torenbeek boy, Ralph, was born, Alwyn and his father were moving some cattle towards the nearby town of Baralaba when a couple of drovers came towards Kokotunga with a mob of horses bound for the slaughter yards.

A beautiful bay mare came out of the mob and trotted over to Alwyn's father. Bill took a good look at her. Rather than see this beautiful mare go off to the slaughterhouse, Bill bought her from the drovers for nearly £4.

Bonnie, as the little mare was known, was a rogue. Every morning she taught the future rodeo champion a lot about riding rough horses. He'd get her saddled and hop on when, out of sheer bloody-minded cussedness, she'd buck, twist and turn until he took control. The lessons she taught were rough, but just the same, she helped 13-year-old Alwyn win three local campdrafting competitions.

A campdrafting competition is all about speed and agility as the rider and horse cut a beast from a mob of cattle in the yard or 'camp' and block and turn it at least two or three times, then weave it through a series of gates. Alwyn loved the sport and savoured the thrill of victory. Yet, he still sought out other opportunities to compete.

While Bonnie was great for campdrafting, Alwyn would ride his second-favourite horse, Minstrel, a three-quarter grey Arab mare with a lot of pace, up a nearby gorge called Ghost Gully for a very different sort of competition.

As he waited at the top of the gorge, a low, shrill wail would catch Alwyn's attention. Soon he would hear the cadenced chuffing of the Friday-afternoon steam train as it rattled along the track, growing closer.

Eventually, the large black form of the engine would loom tall over them and as it did, Alwyn would let out a roar, shift his weight forward ever so slightly, lift his reins and grip a little more firmly with his legs. Every movement of his body was subtle, gentle and unequivocally told his mare that the contest was on – a 3-mile race to Myella's front gate, horse versus train.

There was no echo of the lash of a stockwhip to wake the gully ghosts. Alwyn didn't need a whip; he just let out a whoop and his body talked to the mare. Minstrel responded easily, bolting along the gully as the fireman stoked the boiler and the pressure rose steadily on the gauge.

Alwyn could feel the wind in his hair. He heard his heart beating, his horse breathing steadily, the rapid pound of hooves on hardened earth, the metallic clash of iron wheels on steel tracks and the rhythmic chuffing of the engine. Riding fast and close to the train, he smelt the grease and coal, hot oil and tang of the steam.

Across the rough and broken ground they galloped, the boy never shifting in his seat and the horse staying steady, never losing her footing as her rider let her have her head. To the right of the mare the silver-grey blur of eucalypt and Brigalow rushed by; on the left, the metallic shimmy of the train and the roar and rumble of its mighty engine. Reverberating all around, the ever-quickening syncopated drum of hooves pounding on sun-hardened earth.

Then, when the 3-mile race was run, in a cloud of sandy white dust, and with a face blackened with soot, the boy let his reins go, stood in his stirrups and threw his arms in the air as the engineer allowed the shrill sound of the whistle to soar across the valley, signalling that the boy and his mare had won. Minstrel answered with a triumphant neigh.

Alwyn often won and when he didn't he'd just ride harder and faster next time. For Alwyn, there was always another time, another ride, another race, another chance to win.

Chapter Three
BECOMING A HORSEMAN: 1950–1952

Alwyn remembers – waiting for the gate to open

By 1949, Dad had been watching me for a while as I was working around Myella, taking stock of what I was good at. So he gave me charge of the horses, saying, 'Looks like you're going to be a horseman.' Then, thinking of the work involved with building and keeping a workable team, he added, 'But don't get too many.'

He would give me a hand to start a young horse and the rest was up to me. After a few rides I would take them quietly to school; they'd have a good spell through the day then move out beautifully on the way home and I had a well broken-in horse within two weeks.

As for me, Dad insisted I learn to ride well. He'd insist that I watch my posture, and always ride properly with hands and heels. That meant using skill and technique to encourage my horse rather than a whip and spurs.

The horsemanship skills my father taught me were priceless. They helped me so much when I got my first taste of stock work.

One day, while looking for stray calves, I happened to meet

two Aboriginal stockmen, Tim Albury and Claude Solomon. They were top bushmen and cattlemen, and our neighbour Rolo Davey was paying them to ride out on his property to bring home any strays.

Those Aboriginal stockmen had a lot to teach me about stock work; it wasn't surprising that we teamed up together as often as possible to get our work done. Unfortunately, I could only go out weekends as I was still going to school. Nonetheless, the experience I gained from those old bushmen was not lost on me.

By 1951, I was heading towards 14 years old and, when not helping Dad, I was picking up work on nearby properties.

I remember Bill Nott. He employed me on Bardia Station, an outstation of another of his properties, Cooper Downs, on the banks of the Don River. Before taking up my job on Bardia, I had been doing some casual work at Clayfield for Bill Ferguson, who wasn't the best horseman. He did know how to breed fine-looking horses though.

Curiously, he didn't breed any particular bloodline. He just bred the sort of horses he liked the look of. He was especially good at breeding golden or creamy-coloured horses.

Bill's neighbour Noel Roberts owned a golden creamy stallion called Dadda that Bill was sure would make a good mate for his mare. Noel agreed to allow Bill to put this mare to Dadda and the result was a beaut golden-creamy foal called Yellow Lad.

Bill pampered Yellow Lad and fed him on Clayfield's lush pasture of Rhodes grass; by the time he was three years old he had grown into a mountainous horse – over 15 hands tall and all muscle. Then, Bill had a go at breaking his beautiful pet.

Unfortunately, Bill's mollycoddling had taught Yellow Lad that the horse rather than the owner is boss.

Anyway, Bill was convinced the horse wouldn't be a problem. So he threw on his slouch hat, saddled up the horse and got on.

As if giving him the okay to ride, Yellow Lad stayed nice and still. Bill encouraged him forward but he refused to move. So Bill gave him a slap on the shoulder and Yellow Lad responded with an almighty jump forward.

With that, the rim of Bill's slouch hat flopped down and before he managed to flick it back out of the way, he found himself clutching a handful of grass rather than his horse.

This encouraged the cattleman to bring in some well-respected stockmen; over a period of a few months a series of good horsemen attempted to get Yellow Lad rode. Over the next two years, rider after rider tried and failed on the monster of a horse. He had become Clayfield's cur to all those who tried to turn him into a workhorse.

Bill knew I had a passion and ability for riding rough and tough horses and was keen to see his horse ridden. So, he put a proposition to me. 'If you can get him in work, he's on the market and half the money's yours.'

I accepted Bill's challenge, saddled up my workhorse and led Yellow Lad the 5 miles back to Myella.

Riding along beside Yellow Lad like this was more than a matter of convenience. It put the rider above the horse, which is paramount in getting an unbroken horse to behave.

The next day, in the cattle yard, I walked quietly over to Yellow Lad and held out the back of my hand for him to smell. The horse took a tentative sniff and then I went to work, gently and slowly slipping on a bridle and getting him saddled.

Yellow Lad had no problem with this, because other riders had taken him that far before. He just stood quietly as I placed the saddle on him. I gathered up his reins and quickly mounted.

Now, it's important to understand that a buckjumper is like a highly trained athlete and, like any athlete, he is always ready to show you his moves.

Although I had shown Yellow Lad I was in control by leading him beside my workhorse, actually riding him was another thing altogether.

Even the toughest horse in peak condition can only buck for around 15 seconds. That's because every time he bucks then lands heavy, he expels air from his lungs. He soon pumps out more air than he can get in and so he has to settle just to catch his breath.

Yellow Lad gave me a solid workout for 15 seconds and then settled down with me still in the saddle. That meant first round to me. So I dismounted and gave him a good rub-down.

Every day for three days, I took him for a ride. Each day he gave me a bit of a shake around until he finally settled down. After each round, I gave him a good rub-down, just like the day before. Then, on the fourth day, he was ready to behave. Trust had arrived and bound us together. What's more, it was a trust that meant he was now a one-man horse.

All the while, Dad had stood by the yard watching, ready to step in and help if I needed a hand. After every session, my father's look of pride was immense, but he saved his best until after the final ride. On that day, he was beaming.

Having accepted the new job at Bardia Station, I loaded Dulcie the packhorse with my gear, and then saddled Yellow Lad. The gelding was as quiet and gentle as a kitten. I checked the stirrup length and he just stood there and waited. I looked over his girth strap and made sure his bridle and buckles were secure. He waited.

I gathered in his reins and mane, placed my left foot into the stirrup, grabbed the cantle and, before he could change his mind and misbehave, sprang up and balanced for a moment over his withers. Nothing – he didn't blink. I eased myself around and gently into the saddle. He couldn't have cared less. I knew that

I had his respect and he had mine.

Yellow Lad rode along beautifully and I can tell you the Bardia stockhands' eyes were popping out at the sight of that attractive horse trotting along happily with a lightly built boy of around 14 on his back, as natural and easy as could be.

No sooner did I arrive on Bardia Station than Alec McKinley – the manager of Wileen Station – who had happened by, sauntered over to me and said, 'Is he for sale? I want him for my son Lex.' I said, 'Yes, £25, but your son better be able to ride.'

It was a serious warning, but the old man must have reckoned I was showing a little too much pride for a young Kokotunga lad. He looked at me with disdain, as much as to say, 'You cheeky young bastard, if you can ride him and lead a packhorse, my boy will have no trouble.' So Yellow Lad changed hands and I was £12 10s in front before I even started work on Bardia. I was smiling – which was more than I could say of McKinley's son after Yellow Lad gave him a good roughing up.

Fifteen years later, I came across Lex McKinley and had to ask if he remembered a beautiful yellow horse. Lex responded that it was a 10-metre ride he'd never forget and that Yellow Lad never saw a saddle again.

Working on properties like Bardia, I reckoned I was in the money. Life was good. And more important than having some cash was the feeling of freedom. I was working at what I loved and spending time by myself. I remember liking the loneliness and the going from place to place moving cattle or horses.

When I became a rodeo roughrider I used all those lessons I learnt from working for people like Bill Nott, taming wild horses on properties like Bardia.

When my rodeo days started, I found my own routine, just like I did when working for Bill. I'd rest or sleep behind the chutes until about 30 minutes before my ride. Then I'd get up and start pacing, reminding myself I had to ride 'front end'. That means riding forward on the saddle.

As I put my gear on the buckjumper I'd say to myself, 'I'm going to ride this fella, we're not arguing about it. I'm going to ride him, not hold him.'

When your horse is drawn and your name announced, you approach the animal in the chute and look him in the eye. He looks you in the eye and you talk to him before he's haltered and saddled. To this day, I don't know how to describe the feeling of sitting up on a bronc waiting for the gate to open, when you're ready to go and he's ready to go.

The gate opens and you're off. It's fantastic, and then you get off him. If you and the horse have entertained the crowd, the hair stands up on the back of your neck. It doesn't matter if there are 4000 people watching or just four – you're a horseman, roughrider, entertainer. At that moment, rodeo has you bitten and it doesn't let you go. You just want another ride. I remember them all and how it all started.

* * *

Warm and unrelenting, the summer rains came early to Kokotunga in 1950. They fell as the new year dawned and continued into May.

The western roads from Townsville, Mackay and Rockhampton turned to mud, the grass grew high in the fields and the sky regularly changed from dirty grey to clean blue and back again. During the lee-times between storms the air was fresh and sweet, fragrant with pollen and eucalyptus.

The coming of the rain meant that the vast channel country to the southwest, on the edge of the desert, became a lush mosaic of emerald grasslands and golden wattle. Even the land north of the channel country, the agricultural area around the Torenbeeks' Central Queensland home, changed – but not just from the rain.

Two years earlier the British and Queensland governments had formed the Queensland–British Food Corporation (QBFC) and communities right across the Brigalow Belt were sent into a spin as the Queensland government bought up vast properties. The quiet backwoods pastoral lifestyle was disrupted as more tractors, ploughs, flat-top trucks and other heavy machinery flooded the region – a steel and diesel armada. On some properties like Peak Downs, further west than Myella, the horizon was thick with dust haze as the corporation built new roads.

The QBFC had arrived to transform those empty acres of the Central Queensland landscape into vast fields of waving grain, to fatten pigs on the harvest and cattle on the stubble. The Downs country was alive – especially in the Clermont and Capella area.

However, the haste to produce food was so great that no forethought was given to storage. Large open sheds had been built at Bajool and the grain was stacked in corn bags at 14 bags to the ton to await transport to England. It didn't take too long for spontaneous combustion to set the sheds alight and turn them into a smouldering disaster.

Although crops flourished in 1950, the constant rain turned dirt roads to quagmires and harvesting was almost impossible. Then the mice plague came. Fields of squirming grey mice, wriggling black and tan mice, short, fat and round mice, rodents of all sizes turned freshly harvested grain bags into dust in the fields, ravaged saved grain already in storage and even invaded houses, rampaging through bedrooms and kitchens.

In the end, so great were the difficulties of 1950 that QBFC's last grain consignment was not loaded until 21 July 1951. Out of the chaos came a poor harvest and limited pig production; only cattle showed a profit.

Some of the poor-quality grain was sold for stock food. The Queensland–British Food Corp's disaster saved stock for a lot of farmers, including the Torenbeek family.

With the Myella stock benefiting from QBFC's poor business results, the dairy was doing well and Alwyn was able to think of other things. The idea of becoming a rodeo rider began to ferment in the mind of the young Kokotunga Kid and he started getting around the local rodeos, keen to see his heroes in action – although he was never truly just a spectator. Many rodeos included an associated campdraft competition, which Alwyn couldn't resist. His mare Bonnie was agile and quick – a perfect campdraft horse.

Among Alwyn's heroes at these rodeos were champion riders like the irascible Dally Holden. Dally was built like a jockey with an ego inversely proportional to his size, and rightly so – he was one of the best all-round rodeo riders of the 1950s.

Then there were the Woods brothers, Alan, Wally and Norman. Alan was a gentle man and one of the best saddle bronc riders on the circuit, as was Wally. Norman, or Normie, was a real hard-case larrikin, but as a rodeo roughrider he lacked the class of his brothers.

Wally Mailman and Lindsay Black were two Aboriginal riders of the 1950s who caught Alwyn's attention. Like many riders, Wally and Lindsay were stockmen who loved the thrill of the rodeo. Unlike white roughriders, who as stockmen earned as much as £9 per week, Wally and Lindsay came to the sport after doing stock work for no more than £5 per week, and for a long while as little as £1 per week. For black riders, the rodeo ring was an egalitarian haven where they found the same opportunities as white riders and enjoyed the same rewards.

Wally Mailman was born under a coolabah tree in the low, flat red-dirt country in western Queensland near Augathella. He was a gentle Bidgeree man ready to ride anything that bucked.

Lindsay Black was among the best riders of his era; in his own justifiable opinion, 'there was no Aboriginal rider that had done what I had done'.

Wally, Lindsay and scores of top riders gathered at the Rockhampton Industrial Fair and Rocky Round-Up of 1950. There in the massive crowd an excited young horseman named Alwyn Torenbeek dreamed of joining them.

These champions like Holden, the Woods brothers, Black and Mailman were made of sturdy stuff. Without protective vests, helmets or mouthguards, not a single piece of protection except long leather chaps, they rode in enormous arenas that were sometimes unfenced, at least at one end. The earth was hard; no soft fall in the 1950s. The crowd would sit or stand right up to the barrier fence, with some even sitting on the top rail.

In those days the champion riders knew that there was no chance of pick-up riders catching them if their bronc bolted. A tough nut like Lindsay would flash his usual broad-faced smile at his pick-up riders, point two fingers at them as if he were holding a pistol and pretend to shoot in their direction – as if the whole episode was just one big laugh. Blackie, as he was known, was an entertainer and had been since he kicked off with rodeo in 1945.

By the 1950s, Lindsay Black certainly pulled a crowd, especially at Rockhampton. And what a crowd it was. At some of the rodeos, Rockhampton in particular, spectators from all over central and northern Australia would turn up, perhaps 20,000 or so, keen to cheer on their favourite roughrider.

First among the roughriders at Rockhampton's Rocky Round-Up of 1950 was Dally Holden. He had already won the Rough Riding Championship of Australia the year before, so he was out to protect his title. Alwyn stood ringside as Holden survived a high-kicking ride on a firebrand of a horse named Red Ruby in the first of the buckjumping heats.

The finals of the Queensland buckjumping championship rides

were breathtaking as eight roughriders pitted their skills against crafty and vicious horses. Alan Woods scored a re-ride after taking on a brutal gelding called Woombi, then rode a mare, Deanna Durbin, who fought like a mass of clock springs wound the wrong way.

Another rider who inspired Alwyn was a champion from South Australia called Alan Bennett. Not only did he beat a lively bullock, but he bent down and collected his surcingle, the belt that normally ran under the belly of the beast. Then, with the ride done, Bennett leapt off and kicked up a handstand of his own – twice. The bullock ran away to the far end of the arena, shivering with indignation.

Young Alwyn was not to know that the fates were about to intervene – at the upcoming Kokotunga Rodeo, where Alwyn was an amateur campdraft junior competitor.

Alwyn was checking on his four campdraft horses, which he had secured in the shade by a small stand of brigalow, when he noticed another competitor standing nearby among his own horses.

The competitor was a muscular, fair-haired stockman with a worse-for-wear look about him despite being just six years older than Alwyn.

Always ready to turn a stranger into a mate, Alwyn sauntered over, held out his hand and introduced himself with a hearty 'G'day, Alwyn Torenbeek'.

Taking the kid's hand, the softly spoken bushman replied, 'G'day, Bob Kelly.'

The two yarned about horses and rodeo and how Alwyn went to school with Bob's sister Maureen. It turned out that Bob had also entered the Kokotunga Rodeo in one of the more daring events: the pole-bending races.

Pole bending is pure excitement, an event that draws audiences' hearts into their mouths as a line of four horses thunder along a slalom course, zigzagging between six tall sticks.

Alwyn watched Bob in action in a pole-bending race, working

his horse at speed with effortless precision. That elegant display of horsemanship ensured the two young riders would remain friends in rodeo – friends for life.

Before rodeo, however, Alwyn needed to finish school. During the spring of his final school year, 1951, his health broke down. Headstrong, self-reliant, athletic and perhaps just a little wild, he had spent much of the winter enjoying the life of a latter-day Huckleberry Finn.

Instead of going to school he'd play hooky, catching snakes, skinning wallabies and snaring and scalping dingoes. The dingo scalps were worth £1 and wallaby skins fetched £1 for eight skins. This was handy money for a young fellow and much more fun than going to school.

Unfortunately, the draw of earning money and the excitement of chasing down snakes, wallabies and dingos lured him out into the cold night too often, and come October he was hospitalised with infected kidneys. The long three-month recovery put paid to any chance of sitting the scholarship exam. It didn't matter, though, he was just happy to see the end of his school years.

That year, the skinny 14-year-old started working stock, horses and cattle, earning £1 per day on a property with the ill-omened name of Journey's End and then on Bill Nott's Clayfield Station and Bill Beazley's Perch Creek also.

That's how Bill Nott came into Alwyn's life. Bill Nott already had a reputation as an amateur boxing champion, First World War hero, grazier and businessman when he met up with Bill Torenbeek in the waning days of 1951 and invited Alwyn to work on Bardia, an outstation to Cooper Downs, for the grand sum of £10 per week.

Bill Nott was a tough man in a rough world. Yet the old digger was fair-minded, had few vices and didn't suffer fools easily. Alwyn met his expectations – he was hard working, a non-smoker and non-drinker, and had a remarkable affinity with horses.

Back then, most of the land from Rannes, 90 miles southwest of Rockhampton, to the tiny village of Banana, around 30 miles north, was the property of Bill and Fred Nott. By 1952, Bill Nott had had to curb his involvement in some of the more demanding aspects of station work due to a mustering accident that had occurred two years earlier.

Bill had been out mustering when he came across a dingo and fell while riding hard and fast in pursuit. It was little wonder he went hard, as dingos were the curse of cattlemen from the coastal plains right through to the harsh Tanami Desert. Just the same, after months in full-body plaster Bill rode slower and that meant he needed extra help like Alwyn to work his horses.

The story of that mustering accident and Bill's subsequent determination to get back to work provided Alwyn with a lesson in the merits of endurance and patience, one that would serve him well in later life.

Over the years, Bill Nott's property had attracted men of all sorts – decent blokes, lonely coves and rogues. Alwyn Torenbeek was a fresh-faced kid among some bush-hardened stockmen.

There were blokes like Harold Smith, described as 'the whitest man you'd ever find'. He stayed loyal to Bill for three decades. Then there was the station hand that made it his habit to always carry a sawn-off 0.22 rifle wherever he went. He cared so little for Nott's horses that on one occasion he walked out from his quarters and shot four horses stone dead, saying nothing more than, 'That is another one less,' with each horse he killed. Other men tried their hand at stealing horses or beef or anything else that took their fancy.

On another occasion, one of the young boys who worked on Cooper Downs left his loaded rifle lying around in the shed. Incensed by the boy's casual disregard for safety, Bill, who was still a mighty man, picked the weapon up and snapped it in half, saying in a calm, cool voice, 'That will teach you a lesson.'

Alwyn didn't need any lessons of that kind. In fact, when it came to manners, bush sense, bushcraft and stockman skills he needed few lessons. And so he began his career as a horse tailer and horse-breaker.

Among his duties at the time, Alwyn was in charge of feeding and grooming three magnificent thoroughbred stallions called Crown Solicitor, Turon and Hendra Lad. He also had to manage 160 workhorses. His task was to make sure that there was a plant of around 20 horses exercised and ready for work when the stockmen needed them.

As it turned out, Alwyn's old campdrafting and pole-bending chum, 20-year-old Bob Kelly, also worked on Bardia Station. He would break the young horses, ride them twice to make sure they were right and then hand them to Alwyn, whose job it was to give the newly broken horses up to 10 rides in what was known as the kitchen's yards before making them available to the stockmen.

Apart from his time with Bob Kelly, Alwyn's work on Bardia often had him living and working alone. The conditions would have been tough for anyone, especially a stripling like Alwyn, but he loved it.

He lived in a tiny timber and tin hut with a small table and six beds crammed into a single room probably not more than 18 or 20 feet square. Although the other beds were set up for the other stockmen, Alwyn was often left at the hut alone, day in and day out, while the stockmen were camping out, mustering.

It's possible that Alwyn's isolation from the other stockmen kept him out of trouble, for Kelly and the others were typical bushmen; they worked hard and drank hard – especially when they had the opportunity to drink ice-cold beer.

The Kokotunga butcher had a sizable cold room that he kept stocked with beers from the Rannes Pub. Kelly and his mates kept their beer cold in the butcher's cold room too, and on any given evening, they'd travel into Kokotunga, sit back by the cold-room door and proceed to empty whatever beer stores they'd socked away inside.

They'd while away the hours talking about the latest rough horse they had on the property, or perhaps the two New Zealand lads who were touring North Queensland on a motorbike at the time, or maybe the story they'd read in the paper about how Brisbane girls were taking to motorcycles in steadily increasing numbers.

They might yarn about the amateur rodeo riders whose time in the saddle was limited, as they tended to spend most of their rides going up and then coming down. Inevitably, about the talk would turn to Gladys Gill, Australia's leading woman roughrider of 1950. During her ride, Gladys would remove her coat while her horse was doing its best to throw her into the dirt. There wasn't a horseman anywhere in the central highlands or beyond that didn't admire her skill and dexterity.

Given that the sessions by the butcher's cold room often went well into the night, it was little wonder that there were many mornings when Bob Kelly would turn up on Bardia Station a little worse for wear.

But seedy mornings didn't bother Alwyn. Those cold-room sprees were for the older blokes. Fresh and clear-minded, he'd rise before the sun, dress, then retrieve some bacon or beef from his Coolgardie safe, which was little more than a little box made of wire mesh and hessian, and cook his breakfast outside on the campfire.

After working until well after sunset, he'd settle into his small tin shed alone, with nobody and nothing for company except the glow of a slush lamp and his own thoughts.

Despite the isolation, Alwyn felt lucky to be working with older stockmen and he respected them for their experience. One day, he had the opportunity to show them the stuff of which he was made.

Alwyn was riding a bad young colt in a small yard. He called for someone to open the gate so he could ride him into a bigger yard. Well, stockman Ollie Watt, a former prizefighter with a face like weathered granite, swung the gate open just as a wiry stockman called Mick Coyne opened the next yard gate to turn out the horses in that yard. And things turned to custard.

Alwyn was stranded riding at full tilt in the middle of a mob of around 100 horses hurrying to their spell paddock and his young colt bolted, galloping with the mob. Between them and their spell paddock a railway bridge arched across the paddock. Under the bridge was a mud hole.

The mob, with Alwyn wedged among them, rampaged through the archway, pounding into the mud and water. Crossing the mud wasn't the end of the madness. Alwyn's colt hit the dry ground and decided to buck, high, hard and fast.

As far as Alwyn was concerned, this was real good or at least a lot better than riding a runaway. The colt kicked and leapt, stiffened his legs and arched his back and threw his head this way and that. Alwyn held his balance and eased him down, nice and calm. Then he turned him round and calmly rode back towards the bridge and the yards.

The waiting stockmen had seen the mob sweep the colt and the boy away under the bridge and out of sight. They'd not seen the shenanigans beyond the bridge, but just the same they reckoned that the young lad was prostrate in the mud by now and that it might be time they decided which one of them would retrieve his broken body.

Then they heard the clip clop of a lone horse cantering through the archway. As the boy and the colt rode out into the sunlight, each of the stockmen, horsemen of renown every one, gave up an almighty cheer – a hero's welcome. The boy rode tall in his saddle; the colt cantered back into the yard like a show pony in a dressage ring. It was one of the wildest trips Alwyn ever had in the saddle.

Alwyn's brief time on Bardia Outstation gave him the opportunity to pursue another equine ambition: becoming a jockey.

If you've never been to a country race meeting, you've missed seeing the heart and soul of outback Australia. Imagine a wide horizon slung low below a brilliant blue sky, broken only by a shoulder-high white post-and-rail fence set in a ring roughly a mile around. Put beside it a tall structure of timber and iron and call it the members' stand, for good measure and a sense of respectability. Plonk beside that an open yard next to a shaded stand for the general punters and you've got your average country racetrack. In the shed there's a bar, and within the shade by the rails, a wooden deck provides a place for the bookmakers.

As it turned out, Bill Nott had a son-in-law called Len Stevenson. Len was a kindly sort of bloke and like his father-in-law had few vices, except he did love the races and often entered the three thoroughbreds Crown Solicitor, Turon and Hendra Lad in country race meets.

Len knew Alwyn was skilled at handling the stallions, so he'd often take the boy with him to work as strapper. A strapper is sometimes called a groom in more lofty circles. It's the strapper's job to make sure that the horses, usually thoroughbred racehorses, are clean, and to feed, groom and rug them when necessary, then saddle them for track work or on race day. This was fine work for Alwyn, who loved being in the vicinity of well-bred – or, for that matter, rough – horses.

Sometimes, when the races were a little lower class, Len would leave the stallions at home and take rougher horses, and Alwyn'd go along as jockey. In fact, the local race steward often would not allow the rougher horses to start without Alwyn as the jockey.

For those brief moments on the country tracks, for all the punters cared Alwyn Torenbeek could have been renowned 1950s jockey Gordon Richards or 'Scobie' Breasley.

Truth was, the sort of horses Alwyn rode at these country races were beyond rough. They'd drop their heads at the barrier and kick and carry on, desperate to see their rider dredge up the track with his chin.

Alwyn loved the thrill of racing. The field would ride up to an elastic rope, steady their rides; the starter's pistol would fire, the rope would fly up and it'd be all in and anything goes to see which horse possied up to take the win.

With horses putting on tantrums that'd make a triple-jumper green with envy, some jockeys found themselves sitting in the dirt; others just gripped on for dear life, grabbing mane and reins, gritting their teeth until they crossed the finish line. But the Kokotunga Kid would ride them out, in near-perfect balance right from the jump. He'd have the horse's measure and ride along as if at one with it, striding towards the finish line.

Alwyn knew if he grabbed the front, his horse might do three or four good bucks as the field passed him by, but by then the horse would settle and he'd be racing. Then it was just a matter of running the other horses down – hopefully before the winning post. He got a few good rides like that and got a few past the post as well.

Occasionally, Alwyn would be asked to ride as a race carnival pick-up rider, where he'd be on the lookout for any tearaway that would keep on running after the finish, terrorising its jockey.

At the starting gun, Alwyn'd take off, striking out at full gallop across the infield to be in front of the field at the finish. Then he'd grab hold of the head of any runaway horse to help slow them down.

It was all good fun for the horseman. There were, however, potentially dangerous times, especially when chasing down a runaway horse that had worked its tongue over rather than under its bit. The pain of a misplaced bit is considerable, and no horse in that predicament will stop when a jockey pulls the reins. Instead it'll work itself frantic in a high-speed run – unpredictable and dangerous.

But Alwyn would be waiting at the end of the track. Unflinching, he'd ride quickly across the track, cutting the runaway off before it got past him, stopping the miserable animal and rescuing the jockey if need be. Sometimes he'd settle the racehorse and relieve it of its bridle while it was still moving, or readjust the bit to get the horse back to the stable.

Unfortunately, Alwyn's weight rose and put a stop to his jockeying days. Although never overweight, Alwyn bulked up naturally as he grew, putting him beyond the ideal for a jockey. Nonetheless, he still managed to pick up occasional rides when lighter jockeys couldn't be found.

In 1952, after Alwyn had been working for Bill Nott for around three months, Bill Torenbeek arrived at Bardia Station, looked around his son's camp, which seemed as lonesome as a bush undertaker, and insisted he come home.

Although Alwyn left Bardia, he wasn't keen for dairy life either. He had heard the siren's call of the rodeo circuit.

The teenager knew if he was going to try the rodeo circuit he'd need to practise. So he got busy building horse-breaking yards. With hand tools and Myella timber he crafted a round yard, crush and chute. Impatient to get going, he started practising as soon as he had 'enough' yard built, rather than wait until the whole project was standing. That meant he only had two middle rails in place around the yard.

Mostly he had no one with whom to practise. He didn't fret. He'd saddle his ride, swing the gate open while on top of the horse, then tackle the bucking bronc alone and unassisted.

Bob Kelly, the horse-breaker from Bardia, had also heard the call of the rodeo. He came by Myella on his BSA motorbike and suggested that the two of them 'get on the bike and do some rodeos'.

Bill Torenbeek said, 'I don't mind if you ride buckjumpers but stay away from bullocks, there is always someone getting hurt riding bullocks.' Then he relented, realising his headstrong son was keen to give bullock riding a go. Perhaps Bill hoped that a good fright on a bullock ride might settle the boy and he'd pass over bullock riding to stick with riding broncs or buckjumping.

But of course Alwyn was already well and truly sold on the idea of buckjumping – wild horses were his tea, damper and scones.

It had happened in the spring of 1951 at the annual Rocky Round-Up. There, Alwyn had watched as rodeo hero Tom Willoughby drew the bay gelding Woombi. The horse was a wall of muscle and gave Tom a harsh ride, shaking every bone in Willoughby's body as he bucked high then hit the ground like a jackhammer. Willoughby took a pounding, but showed the crowd an unforgettable ride.

Tom Willoughby and Woombi had met before at the 1949 championships and the horse had thrown the wiry Willoughby into the dirt a full five seconds short of the 10-second ride he needed to score.

But Willoughby was not going to be beaten this time. After all, he had contested every Australian buckjumping championship since 1944 and, although he had often reached the final, he had never won the event. With each near-win the veteran rider had become increasingly determined to take out the championship and Woombi wasn't going to get in his way.

Willoughby readied himself in the chute, determined to make this ride his. The chute opened and Woombi vaulted into the ring, kicking, diving and jumping. But the roughrider held on.

The bronc gave a mighty twist at five seconds and the rider held his balance. A lunge and a kick at seven seconds from Woombi still didn't unseat Willoughby. By the 10-second mark he was holding on with all the strength and balance he could manage until the bell rang, marking a full ride.

Then, just before the pick-up rider could help Willoughby off Woombi, the horse gave a couple of vicious kicks that had the experienced roughrider in trouble. He lost one stirrup, yet stayed on for another four seconds before the bay gelding tossed him to the dust with a goodnight kick. Willoughby rolled over in the dirt and offered a grin, which acknowledged that while he'd won the ride, the mighty Woombi had had the last word.

Before he left the ringside Alwyn watched the great Alan Woods come to the chutes. Alan had made a name for himself as an incredible roughrider. On this day he was taking on Tokyo Rose, a wily 14-year-old outlaw of a ride that many roughriders said was the toughest buckjumper in Australia. The ride was every bit as tense as Willoughby's ride on Woombi, yet the apparently shatterproof Woods took out the win. With the images of that Woods-Tokyo Rose ride still dancing in his mind, Alwyn made his way to sideshow alley.

Sideshow alley was just off to one side of the rodeo arena at the bottom of a steep hill. The hill acted like a buffer to the noise of the rough-and-tumble of the rodeo and to Alwyn it felt like wandering into a different world.

A showman beat his drum, calling all about to come by his big tent. 'Come on, men and boys, roll up, roll up and try your skills in Dolly Baker's Snowy River Stampede.'

Dolly Baker's Snowy River Stampede was a dirty khaki canvas palace with a floor of straw that allowed cocky young men who fancied themselves as roughriders to get in and have a go. They'd battle the first bucking bull ever seen in a tent – a nasty big Brahman ready to terrorise anyone who wanted to give it a shot. All in a ring that was around 20 feet across.

Tents like Dolly's inspired would-be roughriders with the idea of becoming part of the lore of the rodeo world by perpetuating stories of legendary horsemen. Typically, the punter might hear how he'd be riding in the same tent as 'the stockman who taught John

Wayne to walk like a cowboy' or a man who 'had ridden with Teddy Roseville's roughriders back in 1901'.

There was at least one rodeo tent yarn that held firmly to the truth, however. It told of a tent rider whose life took him from the wild Australian outback to a small town in New Zealand. He was Queensland Harry. Dubbed Prince of the Great Never Never, he was celebrated as a horse-tamer and showman extraordinaire. Many a young boy in the Brigalow Belt and beyond, including Alwyn, had heard of the breathtaking horsemanship of Queensland Harry. It was legends like those associated with Harry that gambolled in Alwyn's imagination as he stood outside the massive tent.

Of course, Dolly's was not the only tent doing the country show circuit. There were many others, like Lance Skuthorpe's Wild West Show, The Gill Brothers' Rodeo Circus, Bibby Brothers' Circus and Buckjump Show and Thorpe McConville's Wild Australia.

Alwyn took up their testosterone-filled promise and relished their adrenalin-pumping action – although he never let on to his father that he rode in the sideshow rodeos. His old man would have known it was likely, in any case.

The only trouble was that the show folk didn't really play fair. That first time in Dolly's tent they put him up on a chestnut mare with no stirrups and no head rein. He had only a breast strap and his own balance. To say it wasn't easy is an understatement, but Alwyn thought it was 'jolly nice', just the same.

The tent showmen had another trick if you didn't look like falling: a bloke in the middle of the arena would pull on the horse's flank rope, getting the horse out of sync and sending the rider into the sawdust.

Alwyn didn't mind. His philosophy was simple – 'They didn't play fair but that didn't matter. You knew that before you went in. You knew that whatever ride you got it wasn't going to be a fair ride, but it was going to be one hell of a ride.'

For a little while, Alwyn couldn't keep away from the sideshow tents. He was still trying them in 1956 when he strolled into Larry Delahunty's tent during the Clermont show one morning.

Delahunty was a showman from Charters Towers who often travelled through northern Queensland and the Northern Territory. On this occasion, he had a real good mare that had never been ridden. She was called Black Angel.

Champion roughrider Lindsay 'Blackie' Black had been offered a ride on the mare as a drawcard for the afternoon. That morning, Alwyn put his hand up to ride Black Angel, not realising Blackie was keen to give the mare a go. By that stage, Alwyn had been around the rodeos for a while and had started to gather a bit of a reputation as a handy rider, so he'd figured he had a pretty good chance with Black Angel.

As he strode confidently up to the boardwalk, the showman yelled out to the crowd, 'Here we have a local lad who's going to have a go; climb up onto the board, lad.'

Alwyn clambered onto the boardwalk without a hat and in borrowed riding boots. Then he was called into the ring. He had mounted Black Angel and was ready to go when Blackie strode up to the showman and said, 'What have you done? I'm supposed to be riding the mare this afternoon and this little fellow's goin' to get her rode.' Worried that he'd miss out on having a champion like Blackie ride his mare, the showman marched over to Alwyn to implore him to get off the horse. 'Lindsay tells me you can ride this mare and wreck his afternoon,' the showman said.

Alwyn offered a cheeky smile and replied, 'You give me three quid and I'll make sure that I don't.' So that's what happened. He went round a little bit then let the mare get away from him.

To this day Alwyn believes he should have had a proper go on Black Angel, because by the time Blackie had his ride he came clean off the mare himself. At least Alwyn came away with three quid;

to him that was the main thing.

Away from the sideshow tents, back at Myella, Bob Kelly and Alwyn packed their gear in Bob's black BSA motorbike and hit the open road, in search of the fair dinkum rodeo. Their first stop was a rodeo in the Central Queensland town of Dingo. It was 12 April 1952 and the first time Alwyn had entered a rodeo that was an official Australian Rough Riders Association (ARRA) show. At the time ARRA was the governing rodeo body in Australia. All professional riders out to earn prize money rode at ARRA events.

Bob Kelly steered his bike up and over the unforgiving tracks that were known as the Don River Road, dodging and ducking the bumps and dips until they were beyond the salmon-coloured cliffs of the tablelands. In the saddlebags slung over the tank were the boys' reins, bull ropes and a single change of clothes each. It was a long trek, and by the end Alwyn had concluded that if the brand BSA stood for anything, it was 'bloody sore arse'. Eventually, however, Dingo lay before them.

Dingo was then a railway and cattle town with very little to recommend it, save an excellent-quality sawmill, a hotel and a rodeo ring. A rather large rodeo ring. While riders found an enthusiastic crowd of up to about 800 keen spectators, plenty of able competition, and fine stock on which to ride at the Dingo Rodeo, as far as Alwyn was concerned 'the arena was so large that if you got thrown off on the far side, you had to make sure you had a packed lunch to walk back to the chutes'. Also, the open-air grandstand could only hold an audience of around 75; most spectators would whoop and holler either from their cars, which they'd parked around the fence line, or from the grassy areas nearby – often while they enjoyed a picnic.

The duo pulled into Dingo and Bob brought his bike to a stop outside the Dingo Hotel. The pub was handy to the rodeo ring and arguably the best spot to camp for a night. It was a single-storey hotel with a good wide veranda out the front and a sign over the door announcing that a Mr So-and-so was the licensee.

It was the sort of pub where stockmen, station managers and roughriders alike would walk in from out of the swelter and find their places at the public bar, lean against the counter and watch the cool amber-coloured Cairns Draught climb the walls of their glasses as the publican poured their beers. Then, when they'd finished that one, they'd casually hand back the sudsy glasses to have them refilled.

Bob and Alwyn strolled into the bar to ask the publican if he minded them staying the night. The publican looked quizzically at Bob, gave Alwyn a sideways glance, then returned his gaze to Bob and protested.

The publican was used to roughriders landing in town for the rodeo, chatting up the local girls and then getting into a melee with the local boys over it. He was used to blokes like Bob Kelly, who'd drink hard and play hard. However, that wasn't the Dingo publican's concern; it was Alwyn's age that caught his attention.

'Look here, Bob,' he said in a low sort of snarl, pointing his stubby index finger directly at the lad. 'He can't come in here. He ain't even had his first shave yet.'

The horse-breaker just gave him the sort of look he'd level at a temperamental pony that didn't realise it was ready to be rode, and the publican gave in without another word.

'Fine,' he said, 'but you and the lad will have to sleep out on the veranda.' Then he organised a couple of mats for the boys to use as bedding, explaining that they were welcome on the proviso that they didn't upset the other patrons, the boy stayed out of the bar and they paid 10 shillings each for the use of the hot shower. Bob responded by buying a beer or two. It seemed to Bob like the sort of thing a cove ought to do to repay a publican's hospitality; besides, he didn't really need an excuse for a drink.

Eventually, down at the rodeo ring, Alwyn readied himself in the chute for his first bullock ride – and his first official rodeo ride. He checked his bull rope, took a deep breath, relaxed and gave the rodeo boss a nod. The gates flung open and the Kokotunga Kid was off and riding.

The bullock started across the arena, spinning in a frantic circle at a breakneck pace one way and then the next, kicking hard into the air between each change of direction. The seconds ticked by. Five seconds, six, and seven as the beast spun tight, fast, continuous, then kicked high and hard, landing with a body-jarring blow each time, in an attack that would have most riders unseated. Alwyn held on, his balance perfect, moving in unison with the raging bullock. Eight seconds, nine, ten and the pick-up rider helped him step off the beast.

As the creature indignantly strutted across the grounds and back towards the chutes, Alwyn Torenbeek, the Kokotunga Kid, was grinning broadly – he had smelt success and inhaled the glorious tang of victory. He was living his dream.

The thrills and spills of his bronc ride came next, followed by his bareback ride. All the while he was mixing with the many riders that had swarmed into Dingo from as far as Springsure, almost 200 miles further west. Better still, he got through his rides completely unscathed – unlike the eventual winner of the bullock ride, who was a large, pretentious sort of cove called Chilla Seeney. Chilla scored well enough on his rides to collect the prize money and took some lacerations on his arms for the trouble.

Fellow rider Lindsay Black thought Chilla was a good bloke, but 'you wouldn't leave your money lying around if he was there'. Although Chilla had been riding for about two years by then, Alwyn had put up a close challenge, turning in a respectable second to Chilla in the bullock ride.

By the end of the weekend, Alwyn had picked up his first rodeo ribbon, a small amount of prize money and 'was walking 10 feet tall', ready to head off to the rodeo ball.

Every rodeo put on a ball and the Dingo rodeo was no exception. The Dingo folk held their ball in the closest town with a ballroom – the tiny hamlet of Bluff, another railway and cattle town, which was 18 miles away from Dingo on the worst road you ever did see.

Bob and Alwyn dressed up in their spare, 'going out' clothes and bummed a ride off someone to be among the 300 rodeo ball-goers kicking up their heels. If Alwyn's memory serves, the hall was really humming thanks to an orchestra coming all the way from Rockhampton.

Young, athletic and somewhat cocky, Alwyn had no trouble attracting the attention of the local young ladies. That, unfortunately, would often attract the attention of the local young men, who found it more than a little vexing that 'their girls' took notice of the roughriders. Sometimes the local stockmen would express their displeasure with their fists. And the ensuing free-for-all could be quite something.

At the Dingo rodeo ball a number of the local blokes thought that they needed to show the roughriders what was what when it came to chatting to local ladies, and the hall erupted, with roughriders and locals going blow for blow, including the women. At one stage Lindsay Black caught sight of his mate Les Whyte. Years later, Lindsay recalled, 'I was standing back out of it and this woman was hitting Les on the head. Les had no hair on his head and there she was belting him on the head with her high-heeled shoe.' Lindsay couldn't stand by and watch a mate take a whopping, not from anyone. So he wound up and whacked her, putting Les's assailant firmly on her backside. Or as Lindsay remembered the tussle, 'I bloody flattened her.'

Having survived the Dingo rodeo, Bob and Alwyn covered many

of the nearby Central Queensland rodeos. They'd arrive on the back of Bob's motorbike, find somewhere to camp for a night or two, then head off to the rodeo secretary's office to register.

More often than not, the rodeo secretary would cast a cautious eye over the young rider and then, almost as if Alwyn wasn't present, turn his attention to the older rider and ask, with just a hint of condescension mixed with curiosity, 'Is this kid with you?' Then, anticipating Bob's reply, he would add a lazy, 'I suppose he wants a junior steer ride?' Bob would say, 'No, the same as me – the three open events.'

The secretary would stare long and hard at Bob, then say, in that long drawn-out way only bushmen can manage, 'Come on now, he hasn't had a shave yet.' But by the end of the rodeo, Alwyn had more often than not removed any doubt about his ability, thanks to his remarkable displays of riding. With each ride the fledgling Kokotunga Kid was building on his rodeo skills.

Ridgelands, just 20 miles northwest of Rockhampton, was celebrating its fifth rodeo when Alwyn and Bob arrived in 1952.

It was Saturday 19 April. The air hung heavy and humid, stealing the spirit of the bucking broncs and bullocks. Nonetheless, a keen crowd gathered in record numbers below a grey sky. The show had attracted riders from across Central Queensland, New Zealand and New South Wales.

Although the first few rides lacked lustre, as the day grew older it cooled just enough to pick up the vim of Ridgelands' stock and the intensity of most of the bullocks and bucking broncs increased quickly and dramatically.

One hapless spectator, who had waited patiently to see a half-reasonable ride, moved eagerly to the rails as a bronc surged out of the chute and thundered around the ring. The spectator whooped and hollered and, overcome by the moment, leant in towards the rails so as to get a better look at the contest.

That was until the beast, while leaping past the fan, flung his hind legs so high that they cleared the ring's top rail, kicking the man in the face. Although the horse's rider managed to hang on to score a successful ride, the spectator had seen the only decent ride he was going to enjoy that day. Instead of watching more bucking bullocks and buckjumpers, he came to in the back of an ambulance bound for Rockhampton Hospital.

It was the bullock rides that caught the attention of many who were there that day. The rodeo organisers had decided to give some Zebu bullocks a go.

Cattlemen had introduced Zebu into Queensland cattle stock to help them overcome the state's regular droughts and crossed them with British breeds. While it turned out to be a good choice for the industry, it had some unpredictable consequences for the rodeo ring.

While they were normally docile and slow to rile, once their dander was up, these fearsome beasts took to the riders like no other bullocks before or since, sending most roughriders who cared to take them on into the dirt almost from the jump.

A silver-blue Zebu heifer gave one rider a thorough drubbing, spinning like a corkscrew. Another rider didn't even make it out of the chute. The creature threw him, then crashed down on top of him, his full weight landing on the roughrider's stomach. Another Zebu blasted from the chute, then threw itself on the ground. Yet, the rider stayed with the beast when it scrambled to its feet.

The buckjumping saw some promising rides. One novice rider who went by the name of Rocky Ridge spurred on a horse called Power to ride all the way to the bell. A New Zealand rider flew from the chute on a fiery bronc called Spitfire, the two landing and taking off time and again.

Nevertheless, the bulk of the rides were disappointing and few riders scored points, no matter how much they spurred their animals on. Then, just as things seemed bleakest and felt as though they couldn't get worse, the heavens opened and down came the drought-breaking rain the district had wanted – just not that weekend. Considering the relief it brought to parched paddocks, it's hard to know if it was heralded as a blessing or a nuisance.

Although Alwyn didn't come away with a win, it didn't matter; the thrill of competing was all he needed to want to rodeo all the more. Next up came the Rocky Round-Up and then Mt Morgan.

The Rocky Round-Up was the ultimate event on the rodeo calendar and attracted riders and spectators from far and wide. It also moved at a pace unmatched by other rodeos. The secretary of the Rockhampton Agriculture Society, Rex Pilbeam, was a man who got things done and that meant making the rodeo hurry along at a cracking pace. It was Pilbeam's way.

Rex, who was also the city's mayor, insisted that riders didn't dally. In the bullock riding alone, he got through 70 riders in 50 minutes. His recipe for speed was simple. The chute boss would call a competitor's name three times and was almost guaranteed each rider would be ready by the third call, each call being made in quick succession. Should a tardy rider miss the third call, there'd be no fourth call, and he or she would be removed from the competition with no chance of an appeal.

What's more, chute boss and competitor Dally Holden enforced Rex's rules to the letter. As the name implies, the chute boss had absolute power. No matter who the rider was, champion or new chum, the threat of expulsion from the rodeo was a dire one.

Holden was not the only competitor to take on the task of chute boss. Ray 'The Fox' Crawford was another rider who'd often vie for the position.

Crawford had earned his nickname in and out of the ring. He was cunning and knew an opportunity when he saw it. He was known to stroll, as casual as you like, into rodeo committee meetings and smooth-talk his way into the job of chute boss.

The story goes that he'd waltz into a committee room and offer the members a hearty 'good morning'. Then they'd talk about the weather for a while before getting down to rodeo business, at which stage the committee would inevitably come around to the problem of finding a chute boss.

Ray Crawford might talk a bit about being busy in training and how he wouldn't have time for it himself, until the committee, unanimously believing they'd cornered him after a long debate, would offer him the job. To which 'The Fox' would reluctantly agree, as if he'd never spent a minute thinking how handy it might be to have that role in one or two of the tougher rodeos.

Reflecting on Crawford many years later, Lindsay Black explained why the opportunity to be chute boss was sought after: 'If you could land being chute boss,' he said, 'you could rig the draw.' Lindsay reckoned that 'you'd always think the draw was rigged' when Crawford and another rider called Bonnie Young were running the show.

Nonetheless, it was Holden in charge at Rockhampton and Pilbeam's speed strategy worked as the almost 10,000 spectators who surrounded the ring roared and cheered at the fast-paced thrills and spills.

An enthusiastic roughrider named Punch was the first out of the chutes on a buckjumper, yet tasted the arena dirt well before riding a full 10 seconds. The next rider, called Barber, had a close shave with disaster when he burst out on a rough ride called Rocket, who took just two seconds to cut Barber down to size. Then came an excited Jack Atherton. He'd drawn a big, strong, rough-looking beast that landed the cowboy in the dirt in three seconds with such a heavy thud that Atherton coughed up gravel for days afterwards.

Seeney was the last rider. Now, Seeney had ridden well in other events, yet was not really well liked. He had a reputation for being self-centred to the point of arrogance. He'd take a ride wherever he could get it and was even recorded by a local newspaper as having ridden and won novice events when he was no longer a novice. Just the same, Seeney held his ride for a full 10 seconds and took the win.

Rockhampton was a big rodeo and that meant it attracted riders of all types, each competitive in their own way. One New South Wales rider was somewhat different to the typical 1950s roughrider. While many would wear their suits and fine gear to each rodeo ball, during the rodeo most riders wore workmanlike gear – simple cotton shirts, bush hats and trousers covered by leather chaps. Not Les Whyte.

Whyte was called 'the Gentleman' because of his smart-looking suits. He was the very model of sartorial elegance. Les would turn up at rodeos wearing tight-fitting trousers, a plain champagne shirt, a bright bow tie and a pork-pie hat.

In 1952 the Gentleman drew a fractious horse but he took control all the way to the bell. Then, perhaps he lost concentration; perhaps he was beaten by a crafty horse – whatever the reason, just as the bell rang his horse bolted.

The horse, realising this was his chance to ditch his rider, galloped across the arena, heading straight for the side fence. Well, the momentum sent the Gentleman clear over the fence where it ran by sideshow alley and the horse followed him, hurdling the top rail with ease. There was a steep drop from the ringside down to sideshow alley and Whyte plummeted all the way to the bottom.

The crowd waited, hushed and fearful that the Gentleman might have ridden his last ride. One minute went by and nothing was seen of the unlucky rider; by five minutes the crowd was perfectly still, quietly hopeful that the Gentleman would return.

Then Whyte limped back up the hill and waved at the spectators, declaring, 'It's a long way up that hill.' The crowd let out a collective sigh and exploded into spontaneous applause so loud it was probably heard in Brisbane, 400 miles to the south.

For Alwyn, watching a runaway horse send the likes of Les Whyte careering over the fence added to the atmosphere and excitement that was rodeo. He witnessed another memorable ride when crowd favourite Lindsay Black took to the arena. Black was among the best at the 1952 Rocky Round-Up. In fact, he was probably among the top ten riders for the best part of a decade from the late 1940s.

Black leapt from the chute on a large grey horse that bucked high and fell on its side. A tenacious and skilled rider, he stuck to the horse as it rose with him still on its back.

The horse went to buck again and it stumbled. This time it didn't tumble but stood favouring one leg, which it had broken. Lindsay slid off its back. The crowd fell silent. The horse was led gently back to the crush.

Then, out of the silence that sat still and heavy across the crowd, one sound burst. It was a noise nobody wanted to hear – the sound expelled in the infinitely small moment as a bullet shattered the animal's skull. For a while, the sadness among those present, especially Lindsay Black and the other riders, was palpable.

The roughriders and those who followed the rodeo circuit, for the most part, thought of their mounts as athletes – equals in the ring. Losing a good horse in an accident was almost like losing a mate.

Even after retiring, Lindsay Black would still think back and lament the loss of an occasional good horse. 'When a good horse had to be put down – well – that was a horse that you'd miss,' he'd say.

The respect the riders had for each other was no less strong. Despite the fierce rides and equally furious competition, there was a sense of incredible camaraderie among the roughriders.

This was on display when Wally Woods was crowned buckjumping champion at the Round-Up after riding a feisty mare called Touch'n'Go. The taffy mare was a good horse for Wally to pick in the finals. He reckoned that although she kicked like a Moulin Rouge showgirl, she rode like a grandmother's rocking chair. She was the horse every roughrider wanted to draw for a final.

The enthusiasm for Wally's win was unbounded and Bob Weick, a sinewy-looking bloke with a face like old saddle leather, and Lindsay Black lifted Woods high on their shoulders, all three with broad silly grins wedged on their faces. Black and Weick carried the triumphant Woods to the side of the arena and posed for a photograph. The three mates were jubilant. Little wonder – Black and Weick had picked up second and third place.

After the thrills and spills of Rocky came Mt Morgan, which served up a rollicking rodeo with a flavour all of its own.

Mt Morgan, around 25 miles inland from Rockhampton, was not an agricultural town. It was a rough-and-tumble mining town established on an ore body of 400 000 tons of copper, 300 tons of gold and 40 tons of silver.

So much wealth came out of this single mountain that it funded oil exploration in what was known at the time as Persia and led to the establishment of the multinational company BP.

Mt Morgan was no place for the faint-hearted. The miners worked hard and played hard. Theirs was a spirited rodeo with first-class stock and game riders as its hallmark.

Among the competitors was a Victorian rider called Wally Woods, who stole the show with his skilful riding.

At the end of the first round Woods was in front of fellow competitor Wally Plowman by just three points. Plowman was a no-nonsense sort of bloke and every bit as competitive as any of the best roughriders.

The thing is, winning a rodeo is a combination of the luck of drawing good stock and the athletic ability of the rider and the beast. As it happened, a local horseman called Dave Morgan had supplied a mob of horses that'd make even the sturdiest veteran rider draw a thoughtful breath before he entered the arena on one. They were rough to the core.

Woods drew one of the best on his next ride. Woods's mount went out hard, determined to teach him what high kicking was all about, yet the roughrider made riding the outlaw horse look easy. Importantly, it gave him the lead he needed over Plowman.

Then, Atomic Bomb came to the chute. This was a horse with a reputation for being as mean and fiery as his name suggested. Still, Woods rode him easily and added another tough scalp to his tally.

Nonetheless, the best ride of the final went to Bob Weick. A good all-round rider who could ride a saddle horse or wrestle a steer with the best of them, Weick hailed from The Caves just north of Rockhampton and was as game as they come.

Weick boomed from the chute on a wild beast called Golden Flash, who pounded, twisted and bucked all the way to the middle of the arena. Once there, Golden Flash thundered and gyrated, bucked and kicked like a demon until the pick-up rider galloped over to rescue Weick.

The third man out was a willing rider called Charlie Newton who rode a firebrand of a horse called Myall, and he held on tight to the bell. Then Wally Plowman took to the arena on Jet Bomber, who strafed round the ring. It was said at the time that the horse was 'a bad 'un', and for Plowman on that day there was no doubt about it. The Bomber simply shook Plowman to the ground, before the bell.

Plowman should have been off and safe; however, he got tangled up in the straps as he fell and Jet Bomber dragged him by one foot. As if that wasn't enough, the horse then pulverised the ground all around him for several seconds, which must have felt like hours.

Before the Bomber could hammer the rider beyond recognition, to Plowman's eternal gratitude a pick-up rider cut him free of the tangle and he fell back in a mix of exhaustion and unutterable relief.

But nobody was going to carry Wally Plowman off that ground. As steady as you like, the rider stood up and strode triumphantly back to the chutes.

Perhaps the feistiest ride of the rodeo was when 19-year-old Cliff Minter, a stockman from Coff's Harbour in New South Wales, took a hard lesson in roughriding.

Minter's mount bounced like a rubber ball from the moment the chute door swung open and his grip was jolted loose – so he flung up both arms and, amid yells and cheers, went within a second of riding-out time 'no hands'. From then on, when riders would tell the story of Minter's ride they'd talk in respectful tones about the roughrider they called 'Acrobat'.

But Mt Morgan wasn't finished with Minter. The young rider won a draw to attempt to ride the feature horse. This wasn't a horse with which to be trifled. He was a brute that stood tall, perhaps more than 15 hands. They called him Rumbling Billy.

A buzz flew around the arena like a dingo with a burr under its tail that Minter was going to try to ride the infamous Rumbling Billy. Someone started to pass around a hat to make sure that the boy had a chance to win a decent purse, on the off-chance that he did ride that snorting, grumbling, bad-tempered mountain of muscle on four legs.

The challenge for Minter was simple. If he were to win and ride Rumbling Billy for a full 10 seconds, he'd collect more than £12. However, in the event of a win by the horse, the money was slated for charity.

The time came. Minter was primed and ready to ride. The rodeo announcer went to work, spruiking Rumbling Billy's reputation; saying, as if he had money on the horse, that Rumbling Billy had 'never been ridden'. Then, to balance things, the announcer apprised the crowd of Minter's no-handed ride.

Rumbling Billy was readied and in the chute. Still the horse's fearsome reputation had the lad unmoved. Minter was clearly a horseman of stoic stuff.

The chute flung open. Minter gave it his all for four bone-shaking seconds before he went over Billy's head. The horse spun, chopping out clods of earth around the fallen rider, dancing a fandango above the rider's head. Then, Rumbling Billy struck Minter with a kick that lacerated the cattleman's head. Minter had to be carried out of the arena and taken to hospital, but that wasn't the end of the tough roughrider. He was back in the saddle at the very next rodeo putting in a first-class performance on the buckjumpers.

Minter wasn't the only rider to suffer the punishment a wild bronc could pass out that day. After all, Dave Morgan had gathered some of the toughest and roughest horses he could. A wicked beast called Black Imp threw Wicky Marcon over his head, sending the rider spreadeagled into the dirt.

Then Starlight, in a fit of anger, threw himself and his rider Keith Lindley to the ground. That secured Lindley a re-ride on a horse called Scottie. Lindley swaggered up to his chute, full of confidence. That confidence stayed firm until Scottie hit the arena with a sharp jump and twist that put the rider on the wrong side of the fence. The bronc joined a company of several horses that had made their riders hurdle the rails that day. One in particular gave the pick-up men a wild chase right away from the arena and off across the neighbouring paddocks, screaming with delight as it galloped up a faraway hill and stood thrashing and floundering in the bracken.

The sight of horses dancing on the heads of roughriders or renegade buckjumpers hurling roughriders over fences didn't worry Alwyn. He just shrugged and reckoned that those unfortunate riders had used up all the bad luck, so good luck was sure to come his way.

Chapter Four
LARRIKINS, DANCING AND RODEO: 1953–1955

Alwyn remembers – Madame Butterfly

In early July 1953 Bob Kelly took Dad and me to a charity rodeo in nearby Baralaba. I was only 16 years old and few people had seen me ride at a rodeo.

The manager of Redcliffe Station, on the eastern foothills of the Dawson Range down by Mimosa Creek, had organised a number of fine horses and bullocks for a rodeo campdraft and bullock-riding competition in aid of the Baralaba Ambulance Committee.

Among them was a feared outlaw called Madame Butterfly. She had given many of the better riders on Redcliffe Station a taste of the Dawson Valley dirt.

The Madame was a beautiful dark-brown thoroughbred with a high star on her forehead, clean-legged, bright and lively.

Queensland champion roughrider Bennie Boson was among those at the Baralaba Rodeo that year. Bennie had retired from rodeo and had taken up work as head stockman of Fairfield Station beyond the Expedition Range. Bennie was sure I was just the sort of young wannabe to give the Madame a go.

He watched as the mare was brought into her chute. The arena announcer called for any rider game enough to take on the horse. Boson strutted over and stood firmly in front of Dad and me and, staring at me, demanded, 'Don't you think about getting on Madame Butterfly, she'll be far too strong for you and probably for anyone else here today.'

I turned to my father and said, 'Do you mind if I put my hand up?' Dad just asked me, 'Do you think you can handle the task?'

I'd already looked her over and said to Dad, 'She doesn't look to have any dirt in her, she's clean-cut. She can only buck me off or maybe I'll walk off her if she's too tough.'

Dad had seen me take on rough horses before; he knew I could judge the risk this horse presented and he knew that I was skilled enough to walk off her neck if the going was too tough. He immediately nominated me for the ride and got about the task of saddling the mare with a Davidson & Smith saddle.

Relaxing in a Davidson & Smith saddle was a great way to end a ride – there was nothing on them to catch you on the way out. Usually the Davidson & Smith saddles were made for, and were the exclusive property of, the Australian Rough Riders Association, but I was friendly with Jo Gray in Rockhampton. He got hold of a busted one and passed it on to me.

Once at the chute, I nodded for the gate. Madame Butterfly jumped from the gate and we both got down to business. I was able to straighten her head out square into the arena and took control of the ride.

Her leaps and bounds were high and long. The height of the buck didn't matter too much but the fact that she leapt long meant I had a split second longer than when on other broncs to settle and keep my seat.

Ten seconds is a long time to withstand a ferocious onslaught, but I rode her out to time. On the first ding of the bell I relaxed all my muscles and ignored the urge to react reflexively to her movement.

That allowed her to throw me over her front end and me to land safely on my feet, which made everyone think I jumped off. It was a little trick I practised over my entire rodeo career.

Anyhow, no sooner had I stepped off Madame Butterfly than two of the Baralaba footballers, the team captain Tiger Slater and vice-captain Shorty Campton, bolted into the arena, lifted me shoulder-high and carried me triumphantly off the field of play and back to the chutes.

When I got back to the chutes, two of the older riders strode over to me, not to offer their congratulations, but to let me know that 'if you keep pitting yourself against those odds we will be riding over the top of you by the time you're 20'.

By the time I was 20 they had the tut-tars – that was, their nerves had made them unable to ride – and I was riding over the top of them.

As I write this, at 75, I'm still waiting for the tut-tars to seep in. As far as I know, when Madame Butterfly was retired she had only one defeat against her name – mine. This is a memory that can never be taken away.

* * *

It was raining in Central Queensland, almost constant, heavy rain. By the end of January 1953, the Comet River was at 29 feet and running over the road bridge. The Mackenzie River at Dingo was beyond 36 feet and rising three-quarters of an inch an hour. Swamps and lagoons that had been dry for months were full and they made up an unbroken stretch of water.

Then, as if the rain hadn't brought enough gloom, a state election was called following the death of the popular premier Edward

Hanlon, putting the Labor government at risk after eight continuous terms in power. However, for Bob Kelly and Alwyn Torenbeek neither the impact of drought nor the whirlwind of politics put them off their game. For them, things couldn't have seemed better.

Bob Kelly had gathered enough prize money to trade in his worn-out BSA motorbike for a second-hand Singer Tourer. The £600 for a new one was just a tad steep at the time.

With the Singer roaring, Bob and Alwyn motored off on another adventure. Never shy of driving fast, Bob would get the Singer into top gear, listen as it responded enthusiastically and hold on as he steered it along the rough and rutted roads, hurling it around the corners, tyres squealing like day-old piglets.

They set a cracking pace, top down, rambling along the country roads, thudding and grunting through potholes. If faced with a climb, Bob could count on the Singer to get them over the top; the overhead camshaft four-cylinder had all the get-up-and-go they needed to take the Dawson Range or just about any other range reasonably easily. And all the better, they could carry more gear in the Singer than they ever could on Bob's old BSA.

By 19 September, a bright spring sun shone over the Rockhampton Showgrounds on the first day of the 1953 Rocky Round-Up. All the stations from near and far had rounded up their outlaw horses; together they tallied up around 350 wild rides, ready for a breakneck rodeo.

This particular rodeo found a prominent place in Alwyn's memory because it was the first time he won prize money at the Round-Up – the rodeo he esteemed most of all. By the end of the weekend the rooky roughrider was jam-packed with pride.

There he was, in front of thousands of spectators, standing at the presentation ceremony receiving his first major rodeo ribbon. This was the stuff of which his dreams were made.

The third place had put him alongside his rodeo heroes like

Dally Holden and other top riders. Just the same, Alwyn thought he had better remain humble. He reckoned being too boastful would see the veteran riders shun him.

Alwyn was so overjoyed at winning a major rodeo event that he forgot about picking up his prize money. He hadn't even asked anyone where he could collect it. He and Bob Kelly simply packed up their gear and went straight on to the next rodeo.

As the sun rose on 1954, Bob and Alwyn were red-hot keen to hit the circuit again, but massive floods crept across the Central Queensland landscape, keeping them at home.

By February floodwater had isolated 5000 homes in Rockhampton and the water was still rising, leaving the entire city an island. And, for some royalists like Alwyn, another fear lingered. The Queen was set to tour the region in March and that tour was now in jeopardy as an enormous quagmire of bubbling mud and surging brown water oozed through Rockhampton's streets.

The 1954 flood was at its height and running down the Dawson River when three Kokotunga men, Alwyn's roughriding mate Bob Kelly among them, decided that the abundance of water had made them a tad thirsty.

The flood had backed up into Benleith Creek, southwest of Kokotunga, and the inundated creek was the only thing stopping the stockmen from curing their thirsts with a good cold beer.

Even in flood the Benleith was economical in its movement, and the men knew it. They had acquired an old Royal Australian Air Force belly tank, or jettison fuel tank, and had left it and some paddles down by the creek just in case of such a predicament. Typically, the belly tanks were large cigar- or canoe-shaped objects whose halves made ideal flood boats during the monsoon. And this time it really came into its own.

Bob and the boys rode their motorbikes to the banks of the swollen creek. Then they enthusiastically launched their boat into the flooded Benleith and started paddling – striking out across the deluge, mariners on a mission.

Astonished by their own cleverness, they made it to the other side, a journey of a few hundred yards.

That left the lads with a brisk walk of about an hour to reach Baralaba, where they strolled onto the veranda and into the public bar of the weatherboard single-storey pub. Happy as could be with their achievement, they moseyed up to the timber bar wearing self-satisfied smiles.

The publican was amazed. Before him stood three triumphant, yet very wet and muddy, young stockmen. He smiled, shaking his head at the sight, and poured three schooners of Cairns Draught, placing one before each of them.

They downed the schooners and promptly ordered enough beer to see them right for a few days once they were back on the Kokotunga side of Benleith.

However, the return trip wasn't quite the easy cruise they'd experienced on the way to the pub. Their boat, now laden with beer as well as three burly stockmen, didn't take too much to start rocking. The whole kit and caboodle swung like a pendulum and down she went, dumping the boys, their beer and their pride into the turbid creek.

Bob and his mates were of a mind that they'd get back later and rescue the boat, so they took off their shirts, tied them together and used them to secure the boat to a pole that was almost completely underwater. The pole just happened to be a telephone pole, and the floodwaters were high enough to lift the boys up near the wires. In need of somewhere to stow their paddles, the cowboy sailors hoicked them over the wires for safekeeping – promptly shorting the wires and plunging Baralaba into a communications blackout.

The local police sergeant, Tony Shick, was not in the best of humours when he had to travel along the line to find the short circuit.

The word is, Shick gave Bob and the other Kokotunga lads a roasting over that adventure – one they'd never forget.

By the time the floodwaters had receded and travel by road was again the preferred option, rodeo had got under Bob and Alwyn's skin so much that they would stay away for two or three weeks at a time, hitting rodeo after rodeo. Staying away for longer stints also meant less time toing and froing on those rough country gravel roads, and that was worthwhile.

Eventually they'd head home and get back to working 'around the farm' breaking horses, sometimes picking up a droving trip or taking up the occasional offer to cut a few hundred fence posts. Cutting fence posts was always a good money-spinner and it kept them fit.

In between jobs, Bob and Alwyn went off to the Dingo Rodeo, where they came across a young rider called Peter Poole. He was a young Pom with very little gear and virtually no experience but enough enthusiasm to become somebody in rodeo.

When Peter bucked off his first bullock within two seconds then his second in around three seconds, he swaggered into the chute area claiming, 'I'm learning rather quickly, this is the sport for me.' He meant it too; later Alwyn and Bob would bump into him at that year's Rocky Round-Up.

By the time the 1954 Rocky Round-Up opening-day procession paraded through Rockhampton the worries and hardship of the floods were almost forgotten.

Hundreds of people lined the route to watch the parade, which stretched out up to a mile long. Floats of all sorts rattled and rolled, rumbled and roared along the streets. Way out the front, eight of the best roughriders, or at least the eight with the most moxie, sat or stood on a struggling Massey Ferguson tractor. Another mob of roughriders covered an open-top Land Rover, beaming from ear to ear.

Somewhere along the length of the parade that snaked through the city, among the steady stream of station hands and stockmen wearing ten-gallon hats, a young Kokotunga Kid rode. The 17-year-old was joining 102 other roughriders who had nominated in the many different rodeo events scheduled over the next three days.

The rodeo kicked off as a crowd of 8000 packed into every available space around the arena. The Rocky Round-Up of 1954, as usual, was a whirlwind, a hurly-burly of riders working as stockmen or pick-up riders before becoming roughriders once again when their numbers were called.

Spectators sat mouths agape at the sight of crowd favourite Dally Holden flying over his horse's head only five seconds after leaving the chutes. And Holden's wasn't the only surprise. One buckjumper left its rider in the ring, then startled the audience when it cleared the fence and leapt into the seats at the front of the grandstand, then scattered drinkers at the bar as it found its way through the crowd and into the outer grounds.

Another surprise for Bob and Alwyn was meeting up with Peter Poole again. Alwyn and Peter were competing in the second division bronc ride for younger boys. Peter drew Red Terror in chute three. The horse was everything his name suggested and had thrown champion rider Ray Crawford the day before. Peter nodded to the chute boss, the gate opened and from the back of what must have felt like a towering inferno Peter launched into the air, landing on the edge of the trotting track.

No sooner had Peter's bum hit the dirt than Rockhampton mayor Rex Pilbeam, who ran the Round-Up with a no-nonsense attitude and had his chute boss working in overdrive, turned to Alwyn and called, 'Ready in chute four.'

The horse Alwyn had drawn was a horror called Snip that had busted Dally Holden into the dust the day before. Alwyn nodded and the chute gate exploded open. The timekeeper had only just started his stopwatch when a swift kick sent Alwyn flying through the air to land in a heap beside Peter, who was still recovering from his ride. Well, the crowd erupted. The future rodeo champions shook themselves off, 'took their bows' and hurried out of the ring.

Of course, the rough-and-tumble wasn't left up to wayward buckjumpers and their broncs. The bullocks showed the 1954 crowd what riled beasts could do to their riders.

The Round-Up that year used Zebu-cross bullocks and they made their presence known even before they ran twisting and twirling into the ring. They kicked, stomped and snorted, putting their handlers on notice while still in the holding yard.

In the arena the belligerent beasts sent 40 of the 60 or so riders into the dirt well within time. In fact, they sent several riders to hospital with head injuries in what seemed more like a battle than a rodeo. One of those who suffered the worst was a young farmer called Charles Doon. Doon hailed from the tiny coastal town of Carrawal just 20 miles or so to the east.

Full of ambition, Doon took on one of the fiery beasts, was thrown, hit his head hard on landing and then the Zebu kicked him while he was out cold in the dirt. He went home with head injuries, concussion, broken ribs and shock.

Thankfully, not all the high kicking was done in the arena. Alwyn, who at that time was riding as Allan Torenbeek, enjoyed the traditional rodeo balls almost as much as the thrills, spills and danger of the ring. He'd dance and kick up his heels well into the wee hours. Of all the rodeo dances, he loved the ones at Baralaba and Kokotunga the most – and between them Kokotunga was his favourite.

The Kokotunga dances were about having a great time listening to anything from old-time dance music to rock'n'roll. The hit band at the time was a local group from nearby Mt Morgan called Mould's Orchestra. When they played a good-sized crowd would line up at the ticket office by the front door, eager to dance until dawn.

Some of the Kokotunga dances turned out to be quite eventful. One evening some years earlier, the Baralaba police sergeant had put on his best blue dress uniform, blue serge tunic and trousers with a royal blue pinstripe running down the side of each leg. He squared off his cap, and carefully mounted his horse to ride the 16 miles or so to the Kokotunga Hall. On arrival, he dutifully took up his post by the door, on the lookout for any potential troublemakers.

As the evening went on, everything was quite peaceful, so the sergeant retired to the ticket office with Bill Torenbeek and two other Kokotunga locals, Reg Hutchinson and Henry Abbott – none of them above a bit of a lark.

Thanks to a good supply of rum, it wasn't too long before Bill was wearing the sergeant's jacket, Henry had on the officer's hat and the sergeant was handcuffed. Unfortunately, despite having donned his dress uniform with such care before leaving for the ball, the sergeant had left the keys to his handcuffs in the Baralaba police station.

The local dairymen shuffled the officer into the only car that was at the hall that night, Reg Hutchinson's trusty Model T Ford, sat him up in the passenger's seat, and Reg drove back to the Baralaba police station to remedy the situation. Then the two men motored back to Kokotunga to rejoin the revelry.

Alwyn often went to the dances in 1955. They were all the more interesting if they offered the chance to meet Marion Sainsbury, a young lady who'd become important to his future.

Marion's family were latecomers to the Brigalow Belt. Like the Torenbeeks had done years earlier, they'd drawn property that they called Iron Bark in a land ballot in 1954. The Sainsburys had moved from dairy country further south and arrived as monsoonal rain saturated tropical North and Central Queensland, causing destructive floods throughout the Fitzroy Basin around Rockhampton and the Dawson River catchment, including the area near Kokotunga.

The family camped on the Kokotunga town common to wait out the flood. The Sainsbury camp consisted of Marion's parents, six children (the three eldest had already married and left home), a small bondwood caravan, a station wagon and the water-drilling truck the family ran to supplement their dairying income.

Marion was busy helping her parents establish the camp when, as luck would have it, Alwyn Torenbeek happened to be passing by – and he was taken.

The young roughrider watched as she went about her work. Although he lingered only briefly, it was long enough for him to think, 'Hey, that's not a bad-lookin' girl.' Soon afterwards they met on the dance floor at the Kokotunga Tennis Club dance.

The brash young roughrider must have made an impression on Marion. She went home that night and told her mother that she'd met the boy she was going to marry. From then on they met regularly at dances.

The trouble was, a poor mail service and no telephone meant organising rendezvous was a tad tricky. Luckily, Marion's brother Richie and Lester Torenbeek were still going to school and caught the same school bus. So Lester and Richie became couriers for the couple – carrying notes between Alwyn and Marion, passing them back and forth on the school bus.

If the school-bus note shuffle didn't work, Alwyn would saddle his horse and ride the 15 miles to Marion's house, arrive about dinnertime and return home by midnight with his answer.

Alwyn fell in love with Marion at one Kokotunga dance back in 1955. Somehow that dance was different. Alwyn took Marion for a walk outside the hall, he looked into her eyes and told her that he'd decided to head south to try his hand at other rodeos.

Marion looked back at him and with a hint of melancholy asked,

'Why are you going away?'

She wanted to know why he felt the need to be more than the top rider in the Dawson Valley. He told her he wanted to be national champion. And that was that.

As they stood in the moonlight out the front of the Kokotunga Hall, Marion gave Alwyn a small passport-sized photograph of herself. It was sort of like a friendship ring shared between them. And in the years to come, whenever another young girl decided to get to know Alwyn, if things looked a little too serious, he'd show them Marion's photograph and that was that.

Chapter Five
HEADING SOUTH: 1955–1956

Alwyn remembers – big arenas, no bull

Heading south eventually meant discovering that Dad was right when he had suggested I stay off the bullocks and bulls. Let me tell you, they're more likely to hurt you than the buckjumpers.

I can't remember a buckjumper sending me from the arena to spend a night in hospital. I've had plenty of nights between starched white sheets from those other critters though.

It's not surprising, really, considering that back in the mid-1950s right up until about 1968, we were still riding in big arenas. Back then, the arenas were too big for the rodeo clowns to work the bulls in. That meant a rider could be stepping off a bull perhaps 180 feet from the chutes. The upshot of that was that he'd be on his own. All that was needed was for the bull or bullock to feel somewhat offended by the presence of the rider and it would be on for young and old.

Sometimes they would herd each animal into the middle and then continue with other rides. Believe me, that could end up very scary if you were on top of one beast and then had to get off while you were surrounded by bulls. It made it very hard to get away in one piece.

Nonetheless, I preferred the large arenas. When it came to buckjumping, I reckon the horses preferred the bigger rings also. Of course, it was a boost to your confidence knowing that the pick-up men knew what they were doing.

But beyond mixing it in the rodeo arena with tough stock and fellow roughriders, there were the rodeo balls and town dances to look forward to. Heading to them was one of the highlights of the rodeo circuit. After all, there was what I call the 'new broom' effect.

When young, popular rodeo riders like us would arrive in town, the local girls would all take an interest because we were like the new broom – we swept in and brushed aside all before us. But first we had to get there. And when I was heading to Melbourne that was quite a journey.

I recollect Kevin Beirton's old Ford Anglia carried us, chugga, chugga, chugga, up hill and down dale all the way to Melbourne.

Melbourne was an amazing place for young boys from the bush. There we were in this great city, about to make camp on the hallowed turf of Flemington Racecourse, the home of the Melbourne Cup.

* * *

When a rider puts on their hat, jeans and boots, then straps on their chaps at a rodeo, he or she is about to take a chance on some wild horse or bullock giving them the ride of a lifetime for just a few seconds. In those few seconds, each one its own heart-pounding eternity, winning means a pay cheque; failure means the possibility of broken bones, shattered dreams and no cash in the bank.

A dependable and skilled pick-up rider can't make the ride wilder, or help the roughrider stay on to win, but they can help prevent the broken bones. In the rodeo ring, the pick-up man is simply the difference between a rider leaving in the back of an ambulance or surviving for another ride.

As far as Alwyn was concerned, Queenslanders Alex Smith and Stan Beazley, together with Ray Davis from New Zealand, were among the best pick-up men. At any given rodeo, when the timekeeper rang his bell to signal time, pick-up riders like Smith, Beazley and Davis could ride swiftly to the side of the roughrider, and haul the rider off a horse even if it was still thrashing and kicking high and hard. They'd lug the rider over their pommel, then, on manoeuvring the pick-up horse away from the thrashing outlaw, they'd set the rider down safely onto the ground.

The best of the pick-up riders were so good that many spectators would find a ringside seat just to watch them work. They were poetry in motion, at one with their horse.

Despite the skill of the Queensland pick-up riders, by the end of 1955, Alwyn reckoned he'd try his hand further afield and the vast array of rodeos between Rockhampton and Melbourne seemed just about right for the up-and-coming rodeo champion. He was keen for other challenges – southern challenges.

Apart from opening up the chance to take on a larger rodeo circuit, driving to Melbourne had something else to offer – 1956 was the year of the Melbourne Olympic Games.

Alwyn broached the subject with Bob Kelly to see if he was up for a rodeo jaunt around the southern states. For the first time in a long while, Bob said no.

Bob had heard the puff about the Melbourne Olympics and the usual flim-flam about whether or not they'd be ready on time; he no doubt knew that 1956 represented the best opportunity to experience the southern rodeos, but he remained steadfastly unmoved.

Bob had decided to go 'drovin''. Droving work offers a certainty and appeal that that no rodeo circuit can match. For experienced ringers and drovers like Bob, the droving life, riding alongside lowing cattle, camping under the stars of the Milky Way, held a particular attraction that townsfolk could never understand. The bright lights of any big city were, for many bush-bred boys, dim by comparison to a wide horizon or a star-filled night. So Bob wanted to stay with his droving plant out on the plains where life was as simple as the horizons were wide.

Although disappointed, Alwyn wasn't short of potential travelling mates. Kevin 'Keg' Beirton was a schoolmate, a year or two older than Alwyn and working as a Baralaba stockman.

Kevin was a fine sportsman when it came to track and field events – one of Kokotunga's best. Like Alwyn, he was mad keen on roughriding and tried real hard for years, but despite his sporting prowess, his undoubted courage, his ability to display great dexterity in athletic pursuits, when you looked at his riding skills from head hoop to bunghole, he didn't quite have what it took to be a roughrider. As time went by, it was clear that the skills he needed for rodeo didn't and wouldn't ever come to him.

Kevin would follow the rodeo circuit until well into the 1960s, still trying to master the art of riding broncs and still bucking off. Word has it that in a long career, poor old Kev only ever collected six ribbons. After he'd won them, whenever the roughriders were camped at any rodeo for more than a day, Kev would mount his ribbons on a tree or post near his swag – such was his joy at those modest victories.

He kept that tradition until one day, while in a rodeo camp near Maryborough on Queensland's Fraser Coast, someone thought they needed them more than hardworking Kev Beirton and lifted them off his 'bedpost'. The poor man never saw them again.

A good hand on a quiet horse, Kevin's horsemanship wasn't any better away from the rodeo arena. Kevin once joined Alwyn on a droving trip as the cook, as he was nursing an injury. One morning he decided to lend a hand by bringing the horses in closer to camp.

Alwyn had a beautiful black mare hobbled nearby. So Kevin strolled over to the mare, took her hobbles off and put a halter on her; then he slipped on her back. Well, before Kevin had too much of a chance to get his plan into action, the horse bucked and flicked him into the dirt.

He stood up, scratched his head and as he staggered back to camp, he called over to Alwyn, 'I thought your horse'd be nice and quiet. I went over there a little stiff-legged and came back a bloody sight stiffer.'

However, by around Christmas 1955 Kevin was keen as ever to prove himself as a horseman and he reckoned that his best chance at rodeo success was only a telephone call away.

By this time, Myella was connected to the world via the telephone and the wires were sagging low in the heat when the phone rang in the house. Alwyn answered.

'Alwyn,' Kevin said, his voice crackling along the phone line. 'I hear you want to go down south.' The bush telegraph had got the word to Kev that Alwyn was on the lookout for a ride to Melbourne and Kev wasn't willing to let the chance go by. He knew that this would be his opportunity to gather tips from champion riders and gain invaluable experience in the assortment of rodeos around Australia's southeastern corner.

And as if to make the deal sweeter, the ever-enthusiastic Kev offered his Ford Anglia Tourer for the trip, which would take them through New South Wales and Victoria to Melbourne, arriving in Melbourne in time for the Moomba Festival rodeo.

Moomba Festival was still an infant, having only come into the world in 1955. The canny business-folk of Melbourne had invented Moomba as a city drawcard that they hoped would rank alongside famous international civic highlights such as the Pasadena Tournament of Roses, the Edinburgh Arts Festival and the Nice Battle of Flowers. Having decided to hold a festival, they then chose the name based on the city's Aboriginal heritage. An Aboriginal leader, Mr Onus, came up with the name, saying, 'Call it Moomba. Moomba is the name of a gathering of the tribes; not secret and mystic like the corroboree, it's joyous and open-hearted.' Smiling, he added, 'It means get together and have fun.'

At the festival's heart was a grand parade through the drab, grey centre of the city down Swanston Street. Along the way hundreds of thousands of people would cram into central Melbourne just to watch the glitzy and glamorous pageant livening up the normally lifeless city. And in 1956, Moomba was set to strive for more opulence and more razzamatazz than its inaugural year. This year the festival would include an impressive big city rodeo.

It was Boxing Day 1955, and the blistering summer sun had not risen far above the horizon when Kevin Beirton picked Alwyn up from Myella. Alwyn loaded his gear into the car and the Ford's throaty engine roared to life. With wide grins, the two young men waved at Alwyn's parents, who were standing outside Myella's little weatherboard house to wish them farewell.

The car rumbled down the track in a small cloud of dust. Bill and Agnes watched as they drove into the distance, then Bill gave Agnes a cuddle and said in a gentle voice, 'Don't worry, dear, he won't be gone long.'

It was a momentous time in many ways. Not only were the Olympic Games due to arrive in Melbourne, but television was also about to enter Australian living rooms for the first time, where it would stay for evermore. Australian troops went into action for the first time against Communist terrorists in North Malaya; Lorraine Crapp broke 18 world swimming records in training; Lew Hoad beat Ken Rosewall in the first all-Australian Wimbledon final since 1919; a reclusive Jørn Utzon won the prize for his design for the Sydney Opera House; and Alwyn and Kevin were on the road.

Kevin's Ford Tourer, with its slick wheel arches and sporty cloth top, was ideal for a couple of young men touring Australia's eastern states. There were a few problems with it though; the poor old flivver had little in the way of brakes and even less by way of lights. So they drove during daytime only. All the way the boys had to steady her down the hills and around corners as much as possible without using up too much of the brakes or overly taxing the engine.

The Ford was, for all that, a fine motorcar and with a little coaching and judicious use of the brakes it carried the duo the 500 miles or so down the track into the Southern Darling Downs village of Killarney. It was New Year's Day and most of the best riders were in town.

The rolling foothills, deep secluded valleys and dramatic waterfalls that form the landscape around Killarney were a far cry from the hot, humid land under Capricorn from which they came. Killarney was then the furthest Alwyn had ventured from home.

At the camp down by the showgrounds, the boys had rolled out their swags by the car and were just settling in and yarning about how much softer the arena ground looked here than in Central Queensland and thinking they ought to make some lunch, when a rather smart-looking young roughrider came by their camp.

With a warm smile he asked, 'Are you blokes going south after here?' Then he added, 'I'd like to come with you to Parkes,' still wearing the same smile. His name was Tommy Cannon.

Cannon had been out droving and mustering on the wide Central Queensland plains, and had gathered enough of a bankroll to feel it was time to head home to his parents' property at Parkes in central New South Wales.

Considering Kevin and Alwyn's entire plan was nothing more elaborate than to spend New Year's Day in Killarney then travel south to any Australian Rough Riders Association rodeos in New South Wales and Victoria, with perhaps a quick trip across to Lucindale on South Australia's Limestone Coast, there was no reason for them not to give Cannon a lift.

Besides, it's not the nature of the people of the bush to turn down someone in need. So Alwyn and Kevin teamed up with Tommy 'Shotgun' Cannon.

Shotgun, active, good-looking and as wild as they came, was a strong rider. Throughout his rodeo career he usually managed to find himself placed among the winners, but constantly missed out on taking out the bigger championships.

The desire to drink rarely tormented Shotgun, but there were irregular and infrequent occasions when the call of liquor became unbearable. On those occasions he really put it away and kept drinking until he had, as they say, written himself off – usually on a half-bottle or so of methylated spirits.

At that moment in Killarney, however, Tommy's benders were still a surprise waiting to be sprung. Nor did his smiling face give any clue as to his high-quality riding. Any rodeo fan of the 1950s would have had to go a long way to find a competitor as solid or with such a never-give-up attitude.

There were many stories about Tommy's endurance and determination as a roughrider. One involved Tommy riding in Western Queensland at a rodeo called the Springsure Young People's Rodeo. The day had started warm and pleasant enough, yet storm clouds gathered as Cannon mounted his ride. Then it started to rain, constant beating rain that wouldn't let up. But like any good show, the rodeo continued.

Up until Cannon's ride, the leading rider at Springsure was Lindsay Black, who'd met his match when a wild thing called Crazy Jane threw him in the finals after barely moving out of the chute and going into a spin that'd put any tornado to shame.

Cannon came to the chutes. He was already nursing an injury from a rough ride at an earlier rodeo. Cannon's chute shot open and his mount stumbled and fell on the rider's crook leg.

Ambulance officers and fellow riders raced to Cannon to find the rider hobbling to his feet, scowling in great pain. 'You'll have to give it up, Tommy. You'll never hold on with a leg so damaged,' said the St John Ambulance officer – a sentiment that many of the roughriders gathered by his side echoed. But Cannon just shrugged it off. He was determined to ride, and ride to win.

Instead of withdrawing, Shotgun just grimaced and took a spell behind the chutes until his re-ride was ready. Then, he hobbled over to the chutes, mounted the fresh bareback buckjumper and the gates flew open. Cannon held on; poised and balanced, he took out the ride for a win, stepped off his mount and hobbled to the chutes while all around him tried and true horsemen, all household names of the day, like the Black brothers Lindsay and Gordon, Possum Hutchinson, Keith Barber and Bryan Young, stood in utter admiration.

For a small town, Killarney knew how to hold a rodeo. Not only did it give Alwyn a chance to team up with 'Shotgun' Cannon, it also gave him the chance to ride one of the best-known horses, a bandit called Good Oil.

Roughriders would say Good Oil would steal a win from you with very little encouragement and throw you all round the arena while doing it. He was a thoroughbred with a rough, tough action that carried Alwyn into second place behind a lean, small-hipped rider called Johnny Roberts.

Roberts' blasé approach to roughriding was fabulous. He was known to say, 'A good man can make £1200 to £1500 a year moving from rodeo to rodeo.' Roberts took the whole thing as a bit of a lark – as casually as a game of croquet – saying, 'Orr, there's not much risk. It's over-rated. You break an ankle now and then, but that's nothing.'

Alwyn's ride to time on Good Oil gave him ample confidence to pull off a win on the bullock ride as well.

Later that night, with a few good rides behind them, the boys got dressed in their best gear and went to the Killarney Rodeo Ball.

Apparently, there hadn't been a 'new broom' sweep into Killarney for some time. Kevin and Alwyn had only just arrived at the ball when one local girl who'd made her mark as a Sydney model and was home for the New Year celebrations set her sights on Alwyn, a fresh young fellow just out of the bush. She strolled over like a filly on heat, saying she wanted to dance. Alwyn agreed, but her attention embarrassed him so much that he went beetroot red and fell mute for the whole time they were dancing. He could have lit a campfire from the heat pouring out of his cheeks.

All through their dance, the young roughrider racked his brain for an excuse to leave, and as soon as one presented itself he scrammed straight back to their camp at the showgrounds – well before the night was over.

They were back on the road bright and early the next day and any lingering awkwardness Alwyn may have been feeling gradually faded. In order to spare the little Ford, given the increased burden of an extra passenger, the team reduced their travel to 200 miles a day. That meant making slower time, but it also meant more camps in more little towns and, ironically, more time to find local dances.

Making those distances meant dedication, determination – and a driver's licence. Kevin wasn't too committed to the idea of driving, and he'd left his driver's licence back in Central Queensland.

Tommy and Alwyn were both athletic, both filled with the need for adventure, and for them driving was another thrill. Alwyn had picked up his driver's licence by virtue of the fact that he'd driven his mother to the Baralaba police station just so the sergeant could acknowledge the young man knew how to drive. And Tommy, well Tommy loved to live life, so it was little wonder he was keen to take his turn behind the wheel.

It was, therefore, natural that Tommy and Alwyn saw their

opportunity and convinced Kevin, a far more reluctant driver, that he should leave the driving to them so as not to run the risk of falling foul of the law.

As well as not driving, Kev didn't go in for any nightlife either. That meant Tommy and Alwyn felt honour bound to shoulder that responsibility also.

Consequently, wherever the three amigos spent a night on their way to Parkes, Tommy and Alwyn would usually borrow the car and head off to whatever local dance or ball they could find. In doing so, they felt they'd relieved their mate of the problem of driving and taken the load off his shoulders when it came to socialising, secure in the knowledge that their camp was in safe hands with Kev.

Perhaps Kev got sick of being left in camp – to this day nobody knows what spurred him into action – but it wasn't too long before he got his licence sent down to him.

Arriving in Parkes meant the opportunity to relax for a while with Tom's parents, who lived a little further along the track on a property at Peak Hill. Then the day came when Kevin and Alwyn reckoned it was time to go. So they jumped in the little Ford and were waving goodbye to Tom and his parents when Tom spoke up, saying, 'I'm going too.' So the three of them set off for Young.

The town of Young, once known as Lambing Flat, nestles in a lush green valley that provides a good supply of Australia's cherry and stone fruit between mid-November and late December, with the stone-fruit season usually continuing until the end of March. However, the trio of roughriders didn't want to rely on picking fruit for their income; they were out to win prize money at the rodeo.

The Young Rodeo was the usual flurry of dust, hooves and horns. Unfortunately, none of the three mates managed to draw any prize money from the rodeo.

Always ready to find work whenever he needed it, Young was a worthwhile stopover for Alwyn. As well as the possibility of picking fruit, he found there was a good income to be earned on the backs of horses outside of the rodeo ring.

The owners and trainers of local harness-racers needed their horses exercised off harness and were keen to see Alwyn saddle and ride several of the trotters. They explained that riding was good for the trotters and they would do it more often except finding competent riders was hard. So Alwyn was doubly rewarded. He loved the idea that he was being helpful. And because the owners were desperate to find competent horsemen they were prepared to pay handsomely. There wasn't a roughrider who couldn't do with a little extra cash.

Apart from the work with the trotters, there were more social reasons that made it hard for the three roughriders to leave Young. As soon as they arrived they were an absolute hit with the local young ladies. They were, as Alwyn put it, the 'new broom'.

However, as all good things must end, so did Alwyn's stay in Young.

It happened one day when the boys were in their favourite Young café having a chitchat. They had become proverbial milk bar cowboys, having invested considerable time in the café with a few of the local girls.

In walked Lindsay Black. Lindsay didn't like to see young fellows waste their time and it was clear to him that Alwyn in particular could do better than sit around in a milk bar.

Lindsay stared at Alwyn. 'Come on, Torrie,' he said. Lindsay always called him Torrie – a lot of his friends did – even when he'd lost his patience with him. 'You're out of here – you're coming with me.'

Lindsay was Queensland bronc-riding champion at the time, so Alwyn felt he owed him respect and he did what he was told – right there and then. He got up, leaving Tommy and Kevin behind, and headed off with Lindsay Black.

Perhaps the real downside of leaving Young was the fact that Alwyn had gotten to know a young girl called Joany. Lindsay's stern words meant a quick bye-bye to Joany. Alwyn kept in touch with Joany for a year or so after that, but they never met again.

Although he'd left out of deference to Lindsay, the champion had reminded Alwyn that he was happiest as a roughrider, not a cowboy in a quiet country town. It also taught Alwyn to never lose sight of his goal of becoming a champion rodeo rider. Lindsay taught him that it is much better to remember your dreams and follow them than to waste time and do nothing but dream.

Lindsay Black had been touring with Dally Holden, but Holden had left him behind to attend a rodeo. That left Lindsay travelling with Alwyn – especially as the experienced roughrider could see that the up-and-coming champion was perhaps losing his way.

Lindsay and Torrie caught a bus to Berry, in the rolling green hinterland south of Sydney. Although they were surrounded by some of the most beautiful country in New South Wales, Lindsay and Alwyn weren't there to enjoy the pastoral setting. After their bus took them across the bridge on the outskirts of Berry into town, they headed straight to the showground and signed up for the rodeo.

There, Alwyn took several rides, resting quietly behind the chutes between rides, then approaching each horse, quietly talking to the beast and then giving a nod for the chute to open. By the end of the rodeo, he had picked up some prize money with which to travel, and he and Lindsay Black were on the road again.

In the meantime, Tommy and Kevin had fired up Kevin's old flivver and got down to Bega and then Dalgety, sitting in the rain shadow of the Snowy Mountains near the Victorian border. By hopping trains and buses, Lindsay and Alwyn had also made their way to Dalgety. Here Alwyn rejoined Kevin and Tommy on the Monaro Plain, where cold, harsh winds blew across rolling hills that rose to the rugged peaks of the Tinderry Mountains and fell into the shallow valleys of the Upper Murrumbidgee.

This was Snowy River country, where, according to Australian bush poet Banjo Paterson, 'the pine-clad ridges raise their torn and rugged battlements on high, where the air is clear as crystal, and the white stars fairly blaze at midnight in the cold and frosty sky. And where around The Overflow the reed beds sweep and sway to the breezes, and the rolling plains are wide.'

But even as Kevin, Alwyn and Tommy were riding wild horses at Snowy River country rodeos, the country around them was in the process of being changed forever.

The roads, towns and tiny villages in the region were all busy as an international mob of hundreds of workers grafted away in the Snowy Mountains, working to change the face of the river in the belief that they were harnessing the forces of nature to benefit a nation.

In 1956, they were still in the early years of a vast project that was then scheduled for completion in about 1980, at a total cost of more than £400 million. The Snowy Mountains Hydro-Electric Authority employed thousands of workmen from 30 countries to divert the waters of the Snowy River to the Murray River by a series of dams and tunnels to provide power for industry and water for irrigation.

In among these extending fingers of industry the boys blithely caught as many rodeos as possible, winning some and missing out in others. As usual, if funds were a bit tight they'd pick up work here and there if need be.

Kevin and Tommy were keen to travel to a rodeo at Kyabram, while Lindsay chose another direction. Alwyn decided to stay with his original travelling companions and so they motored onward along the southern byways.

Kyabram, in the rich agricultural lands of the Goulburn Valley around 130 miles north of Melbourne, had a reputation for holding a remarkable rodeo so robust that it had been filmed in 1951 for a Hollywood documentary. In fact, such was Kyabram's reputation that the rodeo of 1956 lured roughriders from as far away as Cairns in Far North Queensland and Darwin in the Northern Territory.

On 12 March 1956 about 250 mountain-bred cattle and 200 outlaw horses gathered to the high post-and-rail fence of the arena to test the cream of Australia's horsemen.

Among them was Alan Woods, triple Australian titleholder and favourite for the buckjumping title, the incorrigible 'Shotgun' Cannon and the ever-enthusiastic Kevin Beirton.

Despite putting up quite a show, the Kyabram Rodeo reminded the trio that winning at a rodeo takes skill and the luck of drawing good bucking stock that really know how to pump. Between them they had the skill but no luck with the mountain-bred stock. So the three roughriders filled their wallets, not with prize money, but with money earned picking fruit.

From Kyabram they bumped over to Deniliquin on the edge of the Riverine Plain down by the Edward River, a branch of the Murray that runs through what is probably the flattest land on earth. Once again, the trio didn't buck off, but the Deniliquin stock, like their Kyabram cousins, didn't want to put on too much of a bucking show.

After Deniliquin, they made reasonable time all the way to Lucindale in South Australia and then back into Victoria and on to Melbourne, in time for the Moomba Festival.

But for all the effort they took getting to Melbourne, getting through the city to their campsite at Flemington Racecourse was another thing altogether.

There they were in Kev's Ford Anglia, with the brakes worse than ever. They had to push the car to get it started and pray the brakes would hold to stop it.

They chugged into Melbourne and hooked up with two other

vehicles – fellow roughriders – one car in front of Kev's and one behind to escort him through. If the lead car, a Land Rover, got too far in front, Kev would give his car all she had to keep up and risk running red lights in the effort. Their mate in the third car would do the same for fear of being left behind and lost in Melbourne.

Relief washed over all of them as they rolled onto the racetrack, which was to become a rodeo arena for the duration of the festival. The roughriders were flabbergasted to be camping on what they, and the Australian racing fraternity, considered to be hallowed turf, the home of the Melbourne Cup.

The Moomba Festival of 1956 began with a non-stop, 12-hour carnival at the Melbourne Showground and finished on Saturday March 17 with what was optimistically called an international rodeo.

Governor Sir Dallas Brooks, a Gallipoli veteran and keen sportsman, opened the festival, which was slated to feature the biggest rodeo ever staged in Australia, including American roughriders, an Aboriginal corroboree, the crowning of the Moomba Queen, pigeon races, boxing, wrestling, cycling and a fireworks display.

Meanwhile the Australian National Theatre presented opera, ballet and drama at the Alexandra Gardens. The Alexandra Gardens became the centre of the festival during the final weekend, holding the Henley Regatta, speedboat racing, and water skiing.

Among all of the Moomba activities, the rodeo was the only event that caught the attention of some of the so-called wowsers of Melbourne. One critic writing in *The Argus*, a local Melbourne newspaper, sniffed, 'So we are to witness a rodeo round-up at the Moomba Festival on Saturday . . . Is that the best the Moomba committee . . . can find for the fun of the fair?'

But the vast majority of festivalgoers loved the spectacle of rodeo – a phenomenon few city folk had the opportunity to enjoy. They especially enjoyed seeing the roughriders from the USA.

Moomba crowds were told that Chester Brittain and Alfred Cox – two cowboys from Texas – were 'roughriders with a difference'. The word was that Brittain and Cox had paid their own airfares and planned to raffle their saddles after the show to raise money for Australian charities.

Most Australian rodeo riders earned their living cattle-droving on big stations and then chased danger and the smell of dust and sweat in the ring, but these two Texas cowboys didn't 'ride the ranges herdin' cows'. They owned their own ranches, and rode the outlaw horses just for fun. As Melbourne's *Argus* spruiked, 'They're the Hopalong Cassidy type of cowboy. They're quiet spoken, they don't drink or smoke. But as soon as they straddle a saddle all their gentleness is gone – and they ride as hard as the best of them.'

The Argus also implored children who might have a cowboy outfit to wear it at the rodeo because the Americans were going to present prizes for the best-dressed cowboy and cowgirl.

Alwyn and his mates Shotgun and Keg were keen to ride up against visiting American competitors. Unfortunately for the Texans, however, Australian rodeo saddles were much smaller than the saddles they used in the USA, and they found it quite difficult to ride in them. Accordingly, the US roughriders' performances were below par.

While the Americans fared poorly, Alwyn came away with a small amount of prize money. However, it wasn't the money that meant the most to Alwyn; for him the greater thrill at the Moomba Rodeo was hearing the ringside announcer call out his name, or at least the name under which he was riding, to an enormous crowd of roaring and cheering spectators. Back then, Alwyn always nominated as Allan Torenbeek, believing that Allan was easier for the crowds, officials and other roughriders to pronounce.

There in front of the chutes at the Moomba Rodeo he heard neither Alwyn nor Allan. Above the din of the crowd he heard the announcer call him 'the Queensland Boy Wonder – the Kokotunga Kid'. Nothing could have been more perfect. That had been the way ringside announcers had introduced him at many rodeos between Kokotunga and Melbourne. But at that moment, in front of that crowd, he realised it didn't matter really whether it was said over the microphone at a small turn-out like Bega or the Moomba Festival in Melbourne, hearing those words made him feel proud.

Moomba came and went, and although most of the Queensland riders went home empty-handed, Alwyn didn't mind. He'd attracted the attention of a large audience and gained invaluable experience. Things couldn't be better.

There was another bonus too. Apart from the admiration of 80,000 spectators, a Cloncurry boy named Jimmy Kennedy and Alwyn had also caught the eye of a couple of nice young girls and they arranged to meet them under the clocks at Flinders Street Station the day after the rodeo, to do some sightseeing around Melbourne.

The four whirled around the city, seeing all the sights Melbourne of 1956 could offer, including the new Olympic Stadium that was still under construction. Then, around midnight, Jimmy and Alwyn started thinking it was time to head home, Jimmy to 'The Curry' and Alwyn back to Kokotunga – a bushie can only put up with so much city livin'. The two lads looked at each other and said, 'Queensland now.' They promptly piled their gear in Jimmy's 1937 Chevrolet Roadster and after some quick goodbyes were on their way, belting along the many single-lane rough bitumen and gravel tracks. As daylight lit the landscape, the duo had made remarkable time despite the roughness of the roads and hauled the Chevy Roadster across the New South Wales–Victorian border.

However, they didn't know that ahead of them a flood criss-crossed much of eastern Australia.

In early March the weather had dumped misery onto several

towns in Queensland's far north, with hundreds of people needing evacuation from their homes as treacherous flooding followed in the wake of Cyclone Agnes.

Agnes cut a 350-mile-wide swathe of devastation from the eastern coast between Cairns and Mackay through almost to the Gulf of Carpentaria. Beyond the tropics the miserable weather continued heading south.

By mid-March, Melbourne flooded. Torrents of water swung parked cars sideways as the floods turned city streets into raging rivers. By that stage Jimmy and Alwyn were well and truly on the road and had managed to sidestep a flood in the New South Wales midwestern town of Dubbo.

Dubbo had seen what was then labelled as the worst flood in history. The entire town had been evacuated and the Royal Australian Air Force had dropped in sandbags to help build levees against the floodwaters.

Beyond the New South Wales border, Jimmy and Alwyn found heavy rains had fallen in western Queensland and caused flooding through the channel country and into the Murray–Darling system. By the time the floodwaters hit Morgan in South Australia they were reported as peaking at more than 39 feet, with the Murray River spreading 62 miles beyond its banks in some areas.

Such were the magnitude of the various floods that engulfed eastern Australia that Movietone newsreels of the time described them as 'swirling floods rising every minute until they've engulfed every building'.

Ahead of Jimmy and Alwyn, 200 miles to the north, scores of small towns lay almost completely isolated thanks to the Manning River flooding to near record height. Floodwaters had cut many roads including the Pacific Highway to Brisbane, and landslides north of Newcastle had stopped rail traffic on the main northern line to Brisbane. Northwest of Newcastle, the government had deployed the Army and Royal Australian Air Force to help save the homes of more than 2000 people threatened by flood.

Regardless, Jimmy and Alwyn inched on northward in the Chevy and managed to avoid any significant flooding until they reached the outskirts of Parkes late at night.

Jimmy drove to the top of a hill on the outskirts of town; before him the lights of Parkes shone bright into the night sky. Between them and the town below, a yellow sign sat beside the road. It read, 'Flood waters for the next 3 miles.'

Still unaware of the devastation that had befallen much of eastern Australia, Jimmy and Alwyn just looked at the sign, then at each other and decided that the sign was an old one left abandoned on the side of the road.

Jimmy smiled at Alwyn and Alwyn returned the consideration with a nod. Jimmy revved the Chevy's engine and sped forward – straight into the floodwaters just a few feet in front of them, hidden by the dark night. From that time on, they made progress a little less blithely and picked a steady path through the floodwaters only if they thought they'd be able to cross safely.

Eventually, after a 200-mile detour, Jimmy drove his red Roadster into Brisbane, only to find that the roads west and north of Brisbane were impassable. That was the last straw for Jimmy Kennedy. He decided that Brisbane was the place to stay.

Determined to get home, Alwyn looked for an alternative and chose to fly to Rockhampton rather than sit out the flood in Brisbane. The weary horseman then caught the rail motor to Kokotunga and walked the two and a half miles to Myella to arrive home 'to a hero's welcome' as his family sat down to dinner. It also meant that he was back in among the familiar and testing Queensland rodeo circuit.

Despite the floods making getting around the Central Queensland rodeos difficult, Alwyn and his old travelling mate Bob Kelly were determined to give it a go. So they battled the odds, crossing swollen and boggy roads and rivers to get to Dingo.

At Dingo, Alwyn drew the fearsome Domino. This was a bronc with a formidable reputation – yet Alwyn reckoned the draw was lucky. The wild horse was as fierce as any bronc the roughrider would ever ride, and kicked and spun like a gymnast.

The Kokotunga Kid got on Domino in the chute, looked the horse in the eye, said a few soft words to him and then gave a nod to let the chute boss know he was ready.

The chute doors burst out and Domino with them. The horse sprung high then landed like a pile-driver time after time. He'd turn this way then twist the other, then suck back and land where he'd taken off. Then he'd start all over again until the timer rang his bell. That roller-coaster, bone-shaking ride landed Alwyn the Dingo Rodeo bronc ride and was Domino's first defeat.

Beating Domino and winning ribbons at Dingo put a smile on Alwyn's face that was fit for sharing – and Marion was the someone special he wanted to see.

As for Bob, he was happy to have watched Alwyn's win and was keen to see a particular girl also, Doreen. Both young women were at Kokotunga.

That meant that instead of heading to the nearby rodeo ball at Bluff they'd hurry to the Kokotunga Ball, which was on at the same time. Trouble was, Kokotunga was more than 100 miles away via Baralaba across some of the most wretched roads in the Brigalow Belt.

Nonetheless, they climbed into Bob's Austin and hit the potholed narrow back tracks leading to Kokotunga. By about six or seven that evening the roughriders were making good time, despite battling mud, high water and bad light, and were only a handful of miles short of Baralaba.

Then they heard a thud as they scraped bottom on a deep pothole and knocked out the car's sump plug. Out poured a stream of oil.

Very soon the engine's high temperature and a solid knocking sound told them that the car was in trouble. Rather than risk destroying the engine, Bob stopped the car. Although their hopes of catching the Kokotunga dance should have run as dry as the car's oil pan, the bushmen just stepped out and started walking, determined to make the dance.

The night air was cold and the town dark and quiet when they walked into Baralaba just before nine that evening. Then their luck returned. Alwyn's father Bill was in town and happened to be motoring down the main street as the boys waltzed into town.

Always accommodating, Bill shuttled the boys between Bob's place, Myella and Baralaba so they could clean up, sort out what they needed to get Bob's car moving, collect the car and return to Kokotunga. Once there, Bob went on to the dance and Alwyn dropped his father home, arriving at the Kokotunga Hall on the stroke of midnight.

The young roughrider sauntered into the hall glowing with excitement and made a bee-line for his group of mates. There among them was the girl he wanted to see the most: Marion. He told her of his success at Dingo and they danced in each other's arms until the ball ended at around one in the morning. For Alwyn and Marion, it was a magical hour.

Dingo was the start of another Queensland rodeo run that put up plenty of tough stock. All the big rodeos north and west of Rockhampton boasted 250 to 300 of the meanest broncs a roughrider could ever hope to come across. Among them were broncs with intimidating reputations – great hulking beasts called Yarra, Woomby, Sugar, Windmer-Wirlwind or Egg Shell. They were the wildest, cleverest and most unforgiving broncs, and they wouldn't give a second thought to pounding any rider into the sawdust.

These top few were the broncs that were mostly put up in feature rides – the rides where the rodeo organisers would draw one rider from the top ten riders at any particular rodeo and then put up a purse of £20 to £25 to be won if the rider stayed in the saddle for a full 10 seconds. The crowds flocked to see these great beasts and those riders willing and able to take them on.

The enthusiasm for those thrill-a-minute feature rides was a reflection of the athleticism of the horses and the roughriders, and in a perverse sort of way a reflection of the general sense of optimism in rural districts across Australia in 1956. Rural folk identified with the battle and the win that might come at the end.

The sense of optimism was mainly due to excellent wool prices in the opening years of the 1950s, and a boom in the early months of 1956. Even in dairy and cattle towns like Kokotunga, money was flowing like rivers of honey and that economic upturn and the sense of affluence that went with it continued into 1957.

Throughout the remainder of 1956 Alwyn stopped competing as Allan and took on rodeos as Alwyn. As he travelled, he saw the hallmarks of rural wealth – new cars were shining in the sun on the main streets of every outback town. What's more, as people found themselves with more disposable cash, the crowds at the rodeos steadily grew.

But rodeos do more than just bring crowds to country towns. For the riders, rodeos weld friendships. At the beginning of his 1956 western rodeo run, Alwyn met a young woman who became very important to him over the following two years. She was fellow roughrider June Mossiter.

June was among a posse of impressive women roughriders that included Nora Holden, wife to Dally Holden and 1951 women's buckjumping champion of Australia, Madge Bratby, who was acclaimed as a champion lady roughrider, Kitty Gill, who her showmen brothers promoted as 'the world's champion lady roughrider', and buckjumping champion Nora Vickers.

June Mossiter had her own truck, camping gear and a beautiful campdrafting mare called Brownie. Beyond campdrafting she rode buckjumpers if given the chance.

Blonde and athletic, the young lady roughrider had an undeniable charm and beauty. June and Alwyn felt an immediate bond – an intangible tenderness that rose beyond friendship and stopped short of romance. Theirs was, as far as Alwyn was concerned, a relationship in the style of that shared by the closest brother and sister. The two never travelled in the same vehicle, but shared the same camp area whenever they rodeoed together. Together, they felt safe. They would go to a ball or dance together, but as Alwyn explained, 'If either found a take-home partner that was quite okay.' It was a wonderful relationship that lasted until 1958.

Among the towns to which Alwyn travelled, Longreach was one of the farthest away – 700 miles northwest of Brisbane, 400 miles west of Rockhampton and 1180 miles east of a town named Alice, in the hot, dry heart of Queensland.

The Longreach Show had been scheduled for early May in 1956, but torrential rains that had made the roads impassable had postponed it until 22 May.

That's not to say the town's elders couldn't have held it earlier than that. It was just that the folk of the outback, ever mindful of the need for a celebration, didn't want to risk missing the nearby Barcaldine Show scheduled for 8 and 10 May. So the date of the Longreach Show was moved, and late May saw Alwyn Torenbeek making his way down the wide, dusty streets of the town that since 1921 had been the home of Australian airline Qantas.

Around the arena, 8000 people gathered and watched Alwyn and the other roughriders take on some fierce stock. The sheep and cattle farmers of Longreach had put together an electric rodeo that stirred the hearts and minds of the visiting roughriders almost as much as the 80,000 spectators that had turned up to see the Moomba Rodeo in Melbourne.

The Kokotunga Kid picked up some lively stock and put on quite a show for the rowdy crowd. But 1956 was not to be his year at Longreach. Instead, his mate and mentor Lindsay Black came out best. Blackie had won the Queensland championship at Winton the year before and was out to keep the title that year at Longreach.

At the end of the first round, the Kokotunga Kid was among the points with Blackie in second place to New Zealand rider Jim Olsen. Blackie returned to the chutes for his second ride. That ride stepped out into a lively little dance, but Lindsay was a skilled rider and he polkaed with the horse for 10 seconds. The timekeeper's bell rang and Lindsay, always the showman, swung his leg over the horse's neck and stepped off his mount, but stumbled as his feet hit the hard ground, and fell. The problem was, the horse hadn't realised the dance was over.

Still riled, all 15 or 16 hands of horse continued to dance over him, smacking Blackie in the back of the head. There the rider lay, silent, still. And he stayed that way for some minutes, with the crowd in stunned silence. Then, with a circle of roughriders gathered around him, the champion staggered to his feet, lifted his head and limped to the side of the arena.

The hit that Blackie took added to the injured back and ankle he already carried and altogether made him a very sick man. But the ride had gained him a clear lead of five points. That was the tonic he needed. He was back in the saddle for the final, and an excellent ride on a good buckjumper clinched his victory and the Queensland championship. Alwyn came in second and went away with an even greater thirst for victory. With the thrills and spills of Longreach behind him, he made his way to Cloncurry.

Born as a northwestern frontier mining town, 'The Curry', as it is known, is the birthplace of the Royal Flying Doctor Service, the first Queensland School of the Air and the arrival point of the first Qantas paying passenger flight from Charleville. It is also situated in the native homeland of the warrior Mitakoodi and Kalkadoon tribes.

No town with that sort of background was about to offer a gentle ride for up-and-coming rodeo stars. On the contrary, The Curry offered one of the toughest, roughest, most ornery rodeos anywhere and not just because they put up some sizzling stock.

Rodeoing at Cloncurry meant battling the stock, fighting the heat and doing it while risking being bucked onto a ground that wasn't just hard, but littered with broken glass. The arena had been built over a reclaimed refuge tip, and while hitting the sunbaked earth mightn't have hurt too much, a rider would find that lacerations from countless broken bottles sure did. Survive that, and there was still the fine dust that each ride kicked up. One way or the other, there was no getting away from harm at a Cloncurry rodeo. Riding at The Curry would draw blood, bruise bodies or force lungfuls of suffocating powder down even the most careful riders' throats.

After Cloncurry, to the relief of many riders, came Winton. This was a small town that held a place in many an Australian bushman's heart. Every bushman raised in the outback, then and now, would know that Winton is a town of folklore, home to Australia's unofficial anthem 'Waltzing Matilda', which was first performed in public at Winton's North Gregory Hotel.

Winton, like Cloncurry, was a hard-hitting affair. This was the fair dinkum outback, where just a couple of years earlier the rodeo had seen rather a remarkable turn of events in which a bullock fell dead in the arena and was then butchered on-site to share among the roughriders – free.

It was at Winton that Alwyn met bushman R.M. Williams. By this time Williams was already something of a celebrity, a legend of town and country lore. It was a meeting that the roughrider never forgot.

The young roughrider was sitting quietly on the riders' stand, awaiting his ride call, when a man with the bow-legged swagger of a horseman, a fine felt hat tilted just so and a stylish grey moustache approached him. Alwyn recognised the bushman from photographs he'd seen in *Hoofs and Horns* magazine. This was no ordinary fan.

As the man approached, he offered Alwyn a shy smile and said, 'I'm R.M. I've been watching your progress for some time.' This was quite a compliment, coming from a man so highly regarded in rural Australia.

Williams had been born seven years after Australia was proclaimed a federation. He'd taken to the bush in his teens, lime-burning and building in stone on the goldfields of Victoria and Western Australia.

Then a missionary explorer called William Wade came into his life in the late 1920s. Williams had signed on with Wade as a camel boy to trek across Australia's central western deserts, where he learnt the lore of the bush and the local Aboriginal people taught him how to survive. It was while with Wade that he honed his stock-handling and bushcraft skills from the stockmen of the desert fringe cattle stations.

When the Great Depression of 1932 hit, R.M. camped out in the Gammon Ranges of South Australia with his young family, barely making a living digging wells. Out there in some of the most godforsaken territory on earth he met an itinerant saddler named Dollar Mick.

Dollar Mick was a self-taught leatherwork genius and he taught Williams all he knew. It wasn't long before R.M. was selling his own handmade boots, and eventually he sold a pair to cattle king Sidney Kidman. That connection gave Williams the exposure he needed and he went on to establish his first factory and eventually one of the most recognisable bushman's outfit brands in Australia.

The future rodeo legend and the outback icon talked about rodeo, cattle properties, droving and more. Alwyn told him he was thinking of making his way into the Territory. Williams said, 'You won't go wrong, but get your own pack plant before you cross the border or you can be stuck in a bad place for months.'

He was right. Out on the Barkly Tableland, which takes in a good slice of the eastern Northern Territory and western Queensland beyond Mt Isa, where the skies are big, the horizons far and the rolling plains of grassland stretch across some of Australia's premier cattle stations, you have to be prepared.

Alwyn appreciated the older man's advice. Apart from putting him off crossing the Barkly, that conversation was the start of a friendship that lasted until R.M.'s death in 2003. Thinking about his mate in later years, Alwyn remembered Williams as having a business mind and working hands: 'While having a conversation with you he would be plaiting a belt or building a bridle, anything to do with bushman requirements.'

Back in 1956, though, with R.M. Williams' words still resonating in his mind, Alwyn moved on through the outback rodeo circuit. It wasn't always easy going for the 19-year-old and his mate Bob Kelly, travelling from one show to the next.

Less than 200 miles west of Rockhampton, Alwyn and Bob left the Taroom Rodeo just before the Dawson River flooded across the only road east to the town of Theodore, around 50 miles downstream. They were lucky, considering that several competitors hoping to make it to Theodore found the brown, fetid floodwaters of the Dawson River blocking their way.

On through Central Queensland the two young men travelled from Theodore to Springsure, where a wild horse called Crazy Jane wounded Lindsay Black's pride as she threw him into the dirt in seconds, and their mate Shotgun Cannon rode to victory after his leg was hurt, crushed by a buckjumper while still in the chute.

On to Monto, Eidsvold, Chinchilla they travelled, along the fine powdery roads of bulldust to the New South Wales outback town of Bourke on the Darling River, then east to the small town of Kempsey, only 9 miles from the Pacific coastline on the Macleay River.

The birthplace of country music star Slim Dusty and rodeo champion Dally Holden, Kempsey was an important stopover for Alwyn on the way to establishing himself as a significant rodeo champion. The simple timber town in the beautiful Macleay Valley put on a hard-hitting rodeo for the New South Wales championships.

Alwyn stuck to his routine, resting out the back of the chutes between rides, talking carefully to each buckjumper and bullock before he rode, steadying himself in the chute and then riding hard with all the skill he possessed. And it paid off. After several hard rounds on the backs of some cantankerous stock, Alwyn strode out into the centre of the Kempsey rodeo ring to claim the title of New South Wales state champion bullock rider.

Chapter Six
DOING THE CROSS: 1957

Alwyn remembers – an invitation in the mail

By the end of 1956, I had ended up with my first state championship, which meant there would be better rides lined up for me in the future, as rodeo committees usually liked to line up the best horses with champion riders.

After winning the New South Wales title at Kempsey it seemed like a good time to head home to Myella. I wanted to help Dad tend my horses. Also, I might have been craving a bit of my mother's cooking and loving care.

Heading back home always helped to replenish the bank account. With lower dairy prices we turned to supplementing our income by harvesting grass seed. That's a real hard and itchy job.

One day while I was working harvesting and bagging the seed, Dad came out to the paddock carrying a letter from the president of the ARRA, R.M. Williams, inviting me to ride bullocks, saddle horses and barebacks at the Sydney Royal Show. The show also hosted the Australasian Rodeo Championships.

I accepted R.M.'s invitation along with Lindsay Black and 23 other roughriders to make a team of 25 boys selected from the ARRA (Australian Rough Riders Association) to take on

25 NBCA (Northern Bushman Carnival Association) boys put up to ride against us. We'd go ride for ride.

The only trouble was, not having rodeoed for a few months, I was lacking practice. I needed to get a few shows under my belt as soon as possible. To do that, I needed travelling money. So, I took a droving job with Bob Kelly's brother Brian.

Brian Kelly was as hard-nosed as they came, and a better cattleman than he was a horseman. He'd swear and curse regularly and, if given a chance, drink just as much. Yet, he could work cattle like a master, knowing exactly where to place his horse to coax the beasts this way or that. He understood their movements and their temper better than he understood those of his two-legged mates. He was far less confident when it came to fast riding, however. Accordingly, he was at his best with a handy horseman riding by his side.

Brian had asked all over Baralaba and Kokotunga, looking for good stockmen to ride with him on a droving trip from Baralaba to Calliope up the Boyne Valley to the tiny town of Dalga. Getting stockmen to take on droving a small mob during the wet season, when all it could mean was days in the saddle below an inky black sky, rain, mud, heat and flies, and for little return, was near impossible.

I was the only taker and joined Brian for three weeks of pushing 200 snorting, roaring, bellowing bullocks southeast along a hot, humid stock route to Dalga with just 14 horses.

There is a law by which outback drovers abide – the law of the overland. 'This is the law of the overland, we in the west obey. A man must move with travelling stock, a 10-mile stage a day.'

We'd stick to that adage for fear of things going to custard and do no more than 50 miles a week, with two days being slower than the others.

During that trip, every now and then, I'd let out a curse as I'd have to ride hard to chase off a stranger bullock that had wandered into the mob, or Brian would tuck in behind another that was lagging and give it a hurry up. 'Come on,' he'd bellow, 'Come on. Get on up.'

Then, at night-time, we'd be waiting and watching for the inevitable cattle rush. The night is the most dangerous time on a droving run, even when there's a full complement of stockmen. Cattle will rush at the smallest sound, a possum scurrying up a gum tree, or a spark from a fire; almost anything is likely to start the mob stampeding into the bush. And when they rush, it's hell with hooves and horns, especially at night when the chance of being trampled is very real.

As it turned out, on that trip with Brian Kelly – beyond the relentless wet, the days of trudging along muddy tracks, the harsh tropical heat and the fear that the whole trip would turn into the stuff of a drover's nightmare, with cattle rushing night after night – we delivered the stock safe and sound.

On our way back, perhaps by way of relieving the tensions of the trip or perhaps just out of sheer bloody-minded habit, Brian let loose.

At the end of most droving trips, when the drovers were heading home, it would often happen that the boss drover would know the publican at a township hotel somewhere along the route. As on this occasion, when we rode into a tiny settlement on the Biloela Road south east of Kokotunga, called Goovigen.

We rode up towards the hotel and let our horses loose in the neighbouring paddock to spell for the day. Then we strode onto the timber veranda that stretched around the lower storey and walked into the cool shade of the hotel through the front door, above which a sign read 'R. Peters, Licensed Hotelier'.

Brian obviously knew the publican at Goovigen very well,

for as we entered Peters gave a loud cheer and immediately poured Brian a schooner of beer, saying, 'Get that into yer, Kelly.'

That evening no one else came by the hotel, leaving Brian and the publican to do their best to keep the night interesting – and they excelled themselves. Once they'd suitably cleared their throats with beer, Bundaberg rum was the drink of choice and they went glass for glass. With each measure of rum the stories of how we mustered the cattle to Dalga or of other great adventures and droving expeditions just got louder and longer.

When the night was a little older, I remember helping Brian to his swag. It was a slow trip of two steps forward and one step back. But that's what a drover does for his boss. That's what a bloke does for his mate, when he's been caught under a cloud of thirst and gone all-out to overcome it.

It was that trip that helped me on my way to discover Kings Cross in Sydney. I recall that was an adventure.

* * *

With money in his wallet from going droving, Alwyn could afford to join the Australian Rough Riders Association team in Sydney taking on the Bushman Carnival boys.

For the most part, the rivalry between the two rodeo associations was friendly, albeit highly competitive. The ARRA had developed from the Bushman Carnival Association, which in turn had grown out of the Bushman Carnivals that had developed in northern New South Wales in the 1920s and were well established by the 1930s.

The Royal Easter Show in Sydney in 1957 would be the first and only chance that Alwyn and the other ARRA riders would get to take on the Bushman Carnival Association. The two teams would never clash again at any rodeo, least of all one with a full program of campdrafting, buckjumping, bullock riding and bulldogging.

What's more, Alwyn had heard that the Royal Show in Sydney had an arena that was so large it needed two teams of pick-up riders strategically placed around the ring to have any hope of keeping riders safe and clearing away stock. This, to Alwyn, seemed too much of a drawcard to ignore. After all, when it came to buckjumping he preferred the challenge of a large rodeo ring.

In the run-up to the Sydney Royal Show rodeo, Alwyn flew to Melbourne and took on a rapid run of rodeos starting in Kyabram and on through Deniliquin and Hay then up to Boggabilla near the Queensland border.

Boggabilla, up the road from the Toomelah Aboriginal Mission, normally has little to offer except the last hotel before crossing the New South Wales border and a rodeo once a year. Here, Alwyn met up with his mate Snowy Lamb, whom he hadn't seen since winning the New South Wales championship in Kempsey the previous year. On that occasion Snowy had also made his dream of becoming a rodeo champion come true, taking out the New South Wales saddle bronc riding championship.

In Boggabilla, Alwyn and Snowy helped Kevin McTaggart muster 45 buckjumpers for the rodeo then drove them on horseback into town. That gave them the opportunity to practise on many of the buckjumpers that were set for the Boggabilla Rodeo, and it was a valuable boost to Alwyn's Sydney rodeo preparation.

With Boggabilla under their belts, Snowy headed to the New South Wales championships at Tumbarumba, while Alwyn joined the ARRA team in Sydney.

A cool, blustery wind swept across Sydney as the gates opened at the Royal Easter Show. Camped inside were two teams with 25 roughriders in each.

There wasn't a single rider in either team who wouldn't give their back teeth and all those in between for a chance to draw one of the three featured broncs – the meanest rides anyone would find anywhere.

Called Boomerang, Badger and Black Widow, they had reputations for providing unnerving, bone-shaking rides that'd send a rider into the dirt or kick them skyward so high they would have no idea what time they might return to the ground.

These fearsome beasts stood out among a field of strong stock as the real barriers between the roughriders and the show's £600 prize money in a buckjump contest hailed as 'bigger than ever'.

Then there was the bullock ride, with £200 on offer. Here, the riders had to stay atop strong, fast-bucking Zebu bulls for eight seconds each round. The Zebu, once riled, had a certain mean-spirited cussedness about them and they made sure that the riders knew it.

Sid Long, the 1954 bulldogging champion, reckoned that the Zebu were formidable beasts. 'If you fall off a buckjumper,' Sid said, 'you lie still for safety. If you fall off a bull you get up and run.'

The ARRA roughriders had made their camp in the dairy pavilion above the stalls that kept the lowing dairy cattle safe, not far from the roar and bluster of sideshow alley. The riders lumbered up substantial timber ladders and into wooden stalls. The cramped, fusty spaces would be home for the duration of the rodeo. Considering the usual lodgings that roughriders endured, these were first class. After all, they had gas stoves and hot showers.

Heading out to explore Moore Park showground, the roughriders made their way beyond the high clock tower, past the imposing outer wall of the double-storey grandstand with its candy-striped awnings, out of view of the grand art deco architecture of the Radio and Electrical Industries Hall and beyond the swirling crowd of show-goers – the men in their white cotton shirts and gabardine trousers or dark brown suits, the women in ankle-length billowing blue skirts and pink short-sleeved tops, and an apparently endless array of children all dressed to the nines and tens.

Night fell and Sydney's Kings Cross beckoned. Here, in a neon-lit flash of restaurants and nightclubs, in an ever-churning haze of cigarette smoke and the odour of stale beer and spirits, young men and women from town and country gathered, usually somewhere along the notorious Darlinghurst Road.

Kings Cross of the 1950s was like nowhere else in Australia. In the gaudy glare of a large neon clock that announced to the world that it was 'Time for a Capstan', down among the many clubs, pubs and bars that were, more often than not, under the patronage of Sydney underworld boss Abe Saffron, an endless party blazed. And the party called to anyone willing to indulge, put aside their inhibitions and take the Cross and all it had to offer.

As Alwyn settled back in camp with a hot mug of black tea and read a letter from Marion that told him that she'd picked up work as a domestic at the Brisbane Chest Hospital and was disliking being away from the bush, his teammates, those rowdy boys from the Queensland outback, some who had never before crossed the Queensland–NSW border, decided to visit Kings Cross's nightclub strip.

The consequences of a night on the Cross were plain to see the next day in the rodeo arena. The unrelenting pace of the city nightlife had drained the roughriders' enthusiasm – although their recollections of exactly what they got up to while 'hitting the Cross' were, to say the least, just a little hazy.

Many years later, when thinking back on their Sydney adventure, Lindsay Black recalled that the red glow and pulsing neon green of the Kings Cross nightlife had presented a more formidable challenge than any outlaw bucking bronc for young lads who knew only the thrills and spills of the rodeo ring and the simple life of the Queensland outback.

Rather than being seductive, Kings Cross was challenging to the point of intimidating for many of the team who left the safe confines of Moore Park showgrounds, Black said. 'We never went very far. We went in a taxi down Kings Cross and nearly got cleaned up by a bloody car. Our driver was going through this narrow street and this bloody car nearly cleaned us up. Kings Cross was pretty bloody rough. My bloody oath, it was an eye-opener. The taxi drove us round and showed us everything.'

Whatever their experience in Kings Cross, the one thing that is certain is that few of the 25 ARRA riders found success. In the harsh light of day, the only members of the team who did any good were Alwyn (thanks to a bone-shaking ride on a tough horse called Badger), Chilla Seeney, Dally Holden, Gordon Black, and Kevin and Colin MacTaggart.

After a dazzling display of bullock riding, Alwyn had landed a first on the bullock ride. Then came the saddle bronc first round and another top score. It's hard to know what happened after that, but it was as if a little muddle-headedness had taken hold of him and he bucked off in the final too easily. Thankfully, Alwyn's combined scores were high enough to land him the highest score for the Australasian championship rodeo, which meant he walked off with a little spending money and the confirmation that he was a champion rodeo rider and not just a journeyman riding the circuit.

Chapter Seven
A NEW AUSSIE CHAMP: 1957–1958

Alwyn remembers – losing Lamb

A roughrider mate called Snowy Lamb had just won the Queensland saddle championship, riding really well, but the tut-tars were setting in. The tut-tars happen when your nerves are shot, when your hands tremble and shake as if you're waving good-bye all the time. Yet, Snowy was still riding.

To help him face each ride we would keep him active about the camp, which was what we were doing on this particular morning at the Richmond Rodeo. Snowy had dressed, puts on his spurs and polished his boots three times. He had never polished them so much at other rodeos.

Then he drew a big brown thoroughbred. I saddled him up. As Snowy climbed on the thoroughbred, some of the older boys like Lindsay Black and Chilla Seeney gave him a bit of sledging, all in good fun. They were probably wishing they were riding that thoroughbred instead of Snowy.

Anyway, Snowy bucked out clean, almost riding to time. Then, just before the bell rang, the thoroughbred gave an almighty buck, turned over, lay out flat in midair and then came down on his side with Snowy still in the saddle. Snowy and the thoroughbred hit the ground and the impact crushed Snowy's skull.

The roads to Townsville were all dirt and terribly rough so taking him to hospital by road or plane, we thought, was going to be very chancy. The ambulance crew organised to have him flown to hospital.

Although it was probably the best choice, given the state of the roads, it seemed to us that flying had its own risks. Several of us worried about how his fractured head could possibly withstand the changing air pressure of the flight.

We went on to the next rodeo with heavy hearts, not knowing how he fared. We heard later through the rodeo 'bush telegraph' that Snowy's injuries were so bad that he died on the way to hospital. It sent a wave of sadness through all those who knew him.

I was bequeathed Snowy's bareback rigging. It wasn't very stylish, but I top scored in the Australian finals with it the next week, only to buck off my horse in the 1957 championship finals.

Not to let Snowy down, I used it the following year at the Australian championships at Longreach and rode it into second place. It now sits proudly in the Warwick Rodeo Hall of Fame. Snowy is among the many mates I remember from rodeo – wonderful men and women.

* * *

Clayfield Station manager Bill Ferguson loved rodeo, yet he was no horseman. A thin, wiry, one-eyed cattleman, Bill was known for three things: his ability to grow sturdy cattle, his love of riding his bicycle and his interest in breeding pretty horses.

There was no question that Bill's cattle were among the best in the district. There was also little doubting his love of riding his pushbike. He had legs like tree trunks and would hop on board his bike, focus his good eye in the direction he wanted to ride and start pedalling.

Getting him to start riding his bike was far easier than stopping him. With his glass eye fixed straight ahead, his good eye following the twists and turns of the road, Bill was known to keep riding until he reached Yeppoon, a coastal village near Rockhampton, before he would turn for home – a pedal of around 140 miles, which he would do over the course of a weekend.

Unable to keep a rough horse under him, Bill would tag along from rodeo to rodeo, but never had the riding skill with which to compete. He'd followed the ARRA troupe down to Sydney and then enthusiastically offered his Holden panel van to take some riders, including Alwyn, to rodeo in Victoria's Gippsland at Lang Lang and Meeniyan.

The trip was unsuccessful. So, carrying a total of ten roughriders between three cars, they rodeoed their way north until the band arrived in Warwick in Queensland's Southern Darling Downs, where most of the roughriders chose to head to a rodeo at Mitchell, further west.

Mitchell is the sort of place in which any outback bushman is sure to feel at home, located as it is 365 miles west of Brisbane - marking the gateway to Queensland's outback on the banks of the Maranoa River. Nonetheless, Alwyn was hankering for familiar stamping grounds and he and Bill decided to head home.

Although he was still single and didn't feel the same pressures the married riders felt, even the Kokotunga Kid needed to head home once in a while – to catch his breath, as it were.

Bill offered his mate a lift as he was ready to return to Clayfield Station and Alwyn accepted, eager for a break from the whirlwind of the rodeo circuit before taking on the Dingo rodeo and starting all over again.

The long, often single-lane journey north led Bill and Alwyn into the beef cattle and dairy country of Queensland's South Burnett. One day, just outside the small town of Goomeri, Bill was steering his car along a road weaving through a valley. The sun glinted through the trees as the Holden roared along, bouncing from melon-hole to melon-hole, skidding through the loamy sand, sending a plume of powder wafting through a stand of eucalypt scrub beside the road. Bill was a reliable driver, but on this particular day he had been driving for some time. With every sliver of sunlight that speared between the trees, his eyes grew steadily heavier until they closed.

Bill blinked, straightened up, steadied himself on the wheel and was just getting his bearings when he realised that in his short slumber he'd picked up speed and was now careering through a rather windy part of the trek. Before his weary mind could react, he hurtled into a sharp bend. Instinctively he plunged his foot onto the brake pedal. The brakes screamed; the car fishtailed and skidded towards the rough verge. Still braking, Bill turned hard away from the verge, yet his van kept sliding. There was no slowing it. His right leg was locked straight; he had the pedal firm to the floor before the van started to respond.

Alwyn pushed himself hard into the bench seat, and gripped on for dear life. The rampaging Holden clipped the verge and rolled once, twice and then came to rest on its hood.

For several long moments, there was no sound save the constant drum of two wheels freely rotating in the air. Then, breaking the almost perfect silence, Alwyn and Bill scrambled out of the car and away from the wreck. As the shock subsided, each checked the wellbeing of the other – no injuries. Beside them lay the broken body of Bill's panel van.

The two men brushed the dust and broken glass from their

clothes and sat for a little while in the shade of a tired eucalypt. Feeling worse for wear, Bill opted to stay behind while Alwyn walked to a nearby farmhouse to call the Goomeri police and then his father.

Bill Torenbeek answered, the sound of his son's voice over the phone turning his initial joy at hearing him into worry. Hearing what Alwyn had to say only cemented that worry like chewing gum on a boot sole.

'We've rolled Bill's panel van, Dad,' Alwyn explained. 'No, we're both okay,' he said, in answer to his father's questions.

Bill Torenbeek was never one to dawdle when someone was in need, especially when it was a member of his own family. He flew out of the house and jumped straight into his Vauxhall Velox to drive almost 6 hours south, drawing every ounce of 6-cylinder horsepower, to collect his hapless son and his mate.

He was relieved to find his son and Bill Ferguson reasonably unscathed, and the three headed back towards Kokotunga. Bill and Alwyn saw Ferguson safely home and got back to Myella in just enough time for Alwyn to team up with his old travelling buddy Bob Kelly and head off to the Dingo Rodeo.

The Dingo Rodeo wasn't the only thing on Alwyn's mind. He needed to see Marion Sainsbury, and caught a flight to Brisbane to catch up with her for a few days. The chance to catch up with his girl was a welcome break, but before long his hankering for the outback in general, and rodeo in particular, tempted him away and he didn't tarry.

It was July and time to take on the rodeo at Mareeba, on the edge of the rich green Atherton Tableland in Far North Queensland, then travel to Queensland's central-western cattle country and the Richmond Rodeo.

Travelling with Alwyn was an assortment of roughriders and campdraft riders including former stock and station agent, bomber pilot and Queensland Country Party politician and government minister Walter Rae.

While Wally Rae would eventually put his riding days behind him and go on to become Queensland's agent-general in London, not all of the roughriders travelling with Alwyn had such a rosy future. One would remain a roughrider forever. He was Charles 'Snowy' Lamb and he'd hooked up with Alwyn, Bob Kelly and their mate Bluey Ensby to take on the Queensland western circuit. Snowy was a great friend to Alwyn and to most blokes who crossed his path. He rode his last ride ever at the Richmond Rodeo.

The *Sydney Morning Herald* reported that the 20-year-old Lamb had died in hospital on 25 August as the result of 'head injuries he received in a buckjumping contest at Richmond, 1115 miles northwest of Brisbane', before he was even old enough to legally drink or vote.

Lamb's death sparked a furious debate about the safety of the sport and encouraged the Queensland rodeo committee to suggest riders wear helmets. The idea was perhaps more of a reflection of the esteem in which Snowy Lamb was held and the impact his loss had on the rodeo community than of any real desire on the part of organisers to change rodeo rules. The push for change failed.

It was a hard lesson for Alwyn about the toughest side of rodeo: losing a mate.

Later in August, Alwyn rode in the Cloncurry Rodeo. The Curry was right in the heart of Bob Katter Senior's country. Katter, who at various times was a member of almost every major Australian political party, had wanted to put his district on the map, so he and his brother came up with the idea of a rodeo at the weary cattle town 480 miles west of Townsville. They called it the Merry Muster and it was in its third year by the time Alwyn came by in 1957.

By September the Kokotunga Kid had moved on from The Curry and was riding in the outback village of Hughenden, 230 miles west of Townsville by the brown clay banks of the Flinders River.

He had a hard time getting there, rattling along in an old Austin A40 on some of the worst roads in Queensland. The Austin didn't make the going any easier, given it took the best part of 30 seconds to get to 60 mph and within that time the road would have thrown up some sort of lump or bump. Moving at speed was near impossible.

Sometimes on the circuit moving on seemed like a bad idea. At least, that's the way it seemed to fellow roughrider Jack Sullivan when he picked up first prize on the bronc ride at Hughenden. He asked his mates to drive his Morris Z to the next rodeo while he made use of his winnings in Hughenden.

The Morris Z was a small, if not altogether reliable, unit that boasted a four-speed gearbox with synchromesh on second, third and top. In its way it was as good as any of the roughriders' cars, but Jack couldn't bear the thought of rumbling his Morris along those dusty, dirty byways, at least not while he had his Hughenden winnings. He just didn't want to 'kill himself on a rotten bush track while he still had all that money in his pocket'.

Eventually Sullivan's money ran out and he met up with the roughriders on their return trip through the west.

Alwyn's northern rodeo run extended from Blackall to Rockhampton, through Central Queensland and then finally down to the Warwick Rodeo. Always keen to show off to the crowd, at Warwick he planned a dramatic dismount from his bullock by stepping off the beast in the centre of the arena.

Alwyn was lithe enough to pull off the dismount right on the timekeeper's bell. He'd ridden it to time. Now was his moment and he couldn't resist. He stepped off. The beast moved away from under him perfectly. He smiled and looked around at the crowd as the bullock tore off, running a fair way away from him. But then it turned back.

Its eyes glistened and it charged straight for him, determined to plough him into the ground. Alwyn caught sight of the beast and every fibre in his body knew what was likely to be in store for him. He reckoned he had no way to avoid it. All he could do was stare it down and face the attack. With a noise like rolling thunder the great beast stormed towards him and, with a crunch that echoed around the arena, it broke his riding arm in one pass.

Bracing himself for the animal to turn swiftly and take another swipe at him, Alwyn waited – trapped. Yet all fell silent. The bullock had decided it had made its point. It seemed it thought that one pass was enough. Relief flooded through Alwyn. Every experienced roughrider knew that if the beast stayed with you for another pass or two, things could get really bad, to say the least.

Nonetheless, that single pass from the bull saw Alwyn spend a few days in hospital. After that, the sad and sorry roughrider hightailed it to Brisbane to see his beloved Marion.

After a few days with Marion, he formed the opinion that a bush lad can't live on sympathy, or for that matter in town, for long. So he headed for home. He never did get the knack of sustaining his good humour for more than three days in town – especially with no way of going for a ride.

Back at Myella, while waiting for his arm to come good, he was on the lookout for work to top up his funds. The drought of 1957 meant there was plenty of work droving cattle along the long paddock, or travelling stock routes.

Such was the severity of the 1957 drought that the Comet River near Rolleston was just a series of muddy waterholes threaded together like pearls on a string of cracked and baked clay.

That winter, large numbers of wild cattle wandered across the landscape, searching out any ground water with which to quench their thirst.

There was a stint of droving with Bob and Brian Kelly and Henry Adams on offer, and Alwyn took it happily. That way he could keep fit away from the rodeo arena while his broken arm fully recovered, as well as putting some money in his bank. The first of their droving jobs started at Moura.

Moura in the late 1950s was like many other towns up and down the Dawson River: struggling. The tiny town had little of which to boast except for the fact that it is just over half a mile from the 150th Meridian on which Queensland Eastern Standard time is based.

Near this ordinary town, one station was swapping from cattle to sheep. Its 1000 head of cattle had to be moved off the property in two trips, 500 head on each trip from Moura to Taroom, 90 miles to the south. Each trip took them along the Dawson River.

There are many memorable episodes from Alwyn's time droving with the Kelly brothers and Henry Adams, but few are lodged in his mind more strongly than what happened on their second trek to Taroom.

Alwyn was taking his turn to look after the horses as the 'horse boy' or 'horse tailer', whose job it was to make sure the horses were fed, watered, hobbled or unhobbled and so on, ready for the other drovers to put them to work.

In Alwyn's words, 'Old Man Drought was right with us and water was scarce.' Shortly after 3 a.m., Alwyn rode out on the night horse Couch to unhobble the team of horses. The morning birdsong mingled with the random melody of the packhorse bells and jangle of hobble chains as the mist gave way, allowing Alwyn to see around 13 horses, including the three packhorses, where there should have been 35.

This was unusual. Hobbled horses would normally stay close by the droving camp, grazing and waiting to be released in the early hours of each morning. Without looking for the rest of the mob, Alwyn quickly caught up to the 13 he'd already found and got to work freeing them. He'd just finished releasing the last of them when it dawned on him that 'Old Man Drought' had, in fact, tempted the entire horse plant away from the camp and back towards the Dawson River.

The baker's dozen he'd just released were the tail end of the mob that were still busy shuffling away from camp as fast as they could go, having yielded to the seductive idea of a cooling drink. Trouble was, the closest bank of the river was in entirely the opposite direction to where the drovers wanted to go.

Before Alwyn could put too much time into tracking the remainder of the droving plant, the freed horses, realising they could get a move on, lifted to a canter and rushed away towards the river.

Whinnying and neighing excitedly, the baker's dozen quickly trotted through the bulk of the mob that were still walking towards the Dawson. Taking inspiration from the smaller herd, the remainder of the plant tried to keep pace. The longer they ran, the more the firm leather hobbles would rub and chafe, barking the horses' fetlocks, yet still they hurried on.

Alwyn couldn't risk the plant running too far. In his mind's eye he could imagine the hard sweat-stained hobbles turning red as blistered legs became bloodied. Alwyn gave Couch some rein and the horse responded enthusiastically, throwing his ears back, leaning into his lengthening stride as he galloped out after the mob.

As he'd not saddled Couch, Alwyn rode almost silently, save for the percussive beat of the horse's stride. The two moved quickly from horse to horse, frantically riding up beside each one and steadying it. Alwyn would dismount even before Couch had come to a stop and would scramble and scurry to release each restraint. Then, with the same athleticism that folk around rodeo arenas throughout western Queensland had come to expect, he'd leap back onto his ride and race off after the next wayward horse.

The morning passed in a welter of pounding hooves, neighing and braying horses, and the almost imperceptible thud of leather pounding flesh as Alwyn worked to free the entire mob.

In the time that it took the young drover to rescue his horses, the mob had run the full 12 miles to the river. Then, tired and tormented by an error that could have sent any of the plant horses lame, Alwyn exhaled slowly, leant forward and thanked Couch. He allowed the mob to quench their thirst, then gently and with little fuss guided them back to the drovers' camp.

Six hours had passed since he'd mounted Couch before the break of dawn. Without a saddle or a blanket for protection the loyal horse had worked hard all morning, and the effort had left him with a case of gripe – a nasty condition that can cause sorts of pain.

Working to overcome his gripe, a somewhat sore and probably indignant Couch, who'd been allowed to join the other plant horses, rolled in every patch of warm sand that he came across as they moved along the route, until he eventually relieved the pain.

Alwyn would never again take a horse out at that time of day without saddling it, because 'riding bareback for hours of work is not particularly good for horse or rider'. He'd also learnt not to unhobble horses in a droving plant without first making sure that all the horses were in one mob.

By the time they lifted that morning, the four drovers were facing many miles of riding to the next water with the sun already high and savage in the sky. It was a long, hot day, and it seared itself into Alwyn's memory.

The trips to Taroom were only the beginning of their droving stint. A grazier called Colin Cornford was in need of some drovers at about the time that the heat of summer and the drought were both in full swing.

He had a property down by the Dawson River just above Baralaba that had water and feed in abundance, so he'd decided to invest in a mob of recently trapped renegade cattle in the hope of making a profit as times improved.

Cornford had ventured out to the Rolleston saleyards and purchased 800 bullocks and dry cows and weaners. They were quite a mixed mob in all sorts of condition – some were still fit while others were starting to show early signs of dehydration.

As the saleyards had no water or feed, Cornford knew that he'd have to inoculate the cattle against the feared bovine pleuropneumonia – a lung disease that could incapacitate a herd, even killing some of its members within weeks if they contracted it – as well as dipping them for cattle tick, and move them as quickly as possible to his greener pastures by the banks of the Dawson.

Cornford put the word around that he needed the mob moved from Rolleston as soon as possible. The Kelly brothers, Henry Adams and Alwyn were up for the task.

It was now mid-December, and the days were too hot for riding hard. The men organised 18 horses and all the gear they needed for a 10-day trip and travelled to the Rolleston saleyards down by the Comet River on a semi-trailer.

By the time the cattle were inoculated, they had been penned up without water for 48 hours and were quite restless. Nonetheless, the drovers threw open the stockyard gates and moved the mob quickly down towards the Comet for a drink.

The cattle's thirst was voracious. The mob roared and bellowed and something akin to rolling thunder rose up as if from the belly of the earth as they rushed towards the river. Bob and Alwyn gave their mounts plenty of rein and took off at a gallop to head them off.

Their horses' hooves pounded on the broken, parched ground as they raced through a cloud of billowing sand, running with the front of the herd. The drovers bellowed like bulls as they rode fast before the mob; the mob bellowed in reply and started to settle.

Then, as if in one last act of defiance, 50 desperate bullocks took one look at the river and bolted. Not content to stop by its muddy banks and drink, they swam the river and fled into the nearby scrub.

As they fled, Bob let out a yell that got Alwyn's attention. They each gave their rides their heads and raced away to herd the bullocks back to the riverbank. The two riders charged along the bank for a while and then thundered into the river, sending shards of water skyward as they chased the breakaway mob, frantically trying to swing the 50 back.

Bob and Alwyn rode hard, with all the skill and balance of capable horsemen, each of them knowing full well what they had to do, their hearts and minds racing. Ducking and weaving through the bush, they ran with the bulls, tearing through the Brigalow until the great beasts were browbeaten and quietened.

For a brief moment they stood still, their horses' sides white with sweat. Then the men wiped the loamy dust from their eyes and herded the renegade bulls back to the river.

Unfortunately, they didn't realise that they were short four head until later, when they had an opportunity to take a count of the mob. By the time Bob and Alwyn had returned their rebel bullocks to the main mob, the day was old and the last rays of light were draining from the landscape.

The next morning they started driving the mob east as they pushed on to Racecourse Creek, 12 miles away.

In good weather, Racecourse would offer a mob a worthwhile drink. But the drought had a firm grip on the land and the only water the mob could find was the few pitiful puddles that their hooves squeezed up out of the sandy creek bed as they walked. Eventually they made camp by some old cattle yards that were still in good order despite a good many years having weathered them.

The next morning, just getting through the routine of breakfast, breaking camp, packing, unhobbling horses and so on demanded all hands on deck. That was the trouble with being so short-handed; there was always a tremendous amount of work to do, even before they got the herd moving.

The drovers were almost ready to move the mob. They did a head count and discovered they were short four head. As the youngest rider with the best horse, and given that Aboriginal stockmen had taught him how to track when he was about 14, it fell on Alwyn to ride back to collect the missing cattle.

Alwyn left Racecourse Creek and made good time getting back to the runaway cattle, which had settled into the saleyard reserve by the Comet River.

As the drovers had already lifted camp that morning, Alwyn hadn't had the chance to take any food or tea-leaves, so finding the cattle was only part of the battle; he had virtually no tucker and a long way to ride as the bulk of the mob were already moving on to Planet Downs.

The sun was low on the horizon by the time he had moved the wayward cattle back to Racecourse Creek. Getting that far still left him with another 13 miles to go before catching the others at Planet Downs. Aware that he shouldn't walk a mob much more than 10 miles without resting them, he pulled them up for perhaps 15 or 20 minutes at Racecourse Creek, then headed them out on the route again to catch the rest of the mob. At the very least, the brief stop meant they had a break and browse, even if Alwyn couldn't.

Luckily, most lost cattle will pick up the scent of their mates as they move along the trail, and then they'll usually travel along well. Alwyn's wayward four did just that. They followed the scent of the others quite nicely and made good time.

It was close to midnight when the wayward cattle and the weary drover followed the jingle of the packhorse bells into the Planet Downs horse paddock. The yards in which the main cattle mob were camped were a welcome sight, even if only just visible in the light of the waning moon. Once again they had somewhere safe in which to camp the mob. They had still drunk scarcely any water all day, however.

The next day the early-morning bird sounds called the drovers to work. They now faced the rugged Expedition Range – a daunting proposition, with 300-feet-deep gorges cutting through the sandstone. But Alwyn, Bob, Brian and Henry trekked the cattle from the west along the southern boundary of the ranges and escaped much of the harsh, almost impassable country lying to the north. Hot and weary, they walked the slow-moving mob through the day. The cattle marched like soldiers over the range, as if hoping for something better ahead.

Once over the top of the range and deep down into narrow, dry Conciliation Creek, the cattle strung out along the creek bed. Some, whose eyes were starting to sink away from their eyelids, stomped along the creek bed in the hope of walking the water out of the sand, forcing up only small amounts of 'slurping' water. Just enough to make the sand wet, but not enough to provide a soothing drink. The men urged the cattle on, hoping to rest them at Molar Box.

By the time they arrived at the Molar Box yards after trekking over 15 miles along the stock route, the mob were reasonably settled but still mighty thirsty. It was 20 December.

After camping the night at Molar Box, early the next morning they lifted the cattle and trudged on to set up camp for the night at Bauhinia Downs, still having found very little water for the mob. They hadn't been long in camp when the cattle decided to try on a little run, but they pulled up quickly without too much trouble. And more importantly, they pulled up without any injuries to men or beasts.

Bauhinia Downs was a well-known drovers' camp. It had been so since grazier, politician and squatter Charles Boydell Dutton settled there in 1857. The four drovers knew that even in drought times brigalow, wilga, lancewood, bottlebrush and native bauhinia trees all grew abundantly in the area thanks to a usually reliable supply of water.

On this trip, however, the eucalypts were as split and brown as old fence posts, although still frantically clinging on to every ounce of life that the remaining moisture in the salty soil could offer.

That evening a new moon made distinguishing bush from beast, horse from rider all but impossible. Only the light of the stars, and that cast by the drovers' campfire, fell across the central highlands.

A dew-laden night yielded way to a morning that was already hot and weary as the drovers hurried to break camp, eager to start out before the sun lifted above the horizon.

They followed the parched stock route and found no water, except for the smallest splashes within the almost desiccated sand at the lowest points of the riverbed, until they reached a watering spot called Dick's Dam, further onto Bauhinia Downs. There the cattle got a good fill of water.

With their bellies full of water, they moved on to Beranga, an outstation of Redcliffe Station and their night camp. The next day they travelled on over Mimosa Creek, which had little water, and the drovers walked their stock into the dense eucalypt and wattle forest of Redcliffe camping reserve.

By Christmas Eve, the drovers were looking forward to getting the stock to Lemon Tree Waterhole. It was safe there, with good-quality stockyards and potentially plenty of water.

The Lemon Tree waterhole was a little off the track near Perch Creek on Coclabinda Station. Not wanting to take the mob too far off the track on what seemed like a gamble given the drought conditions, Alwyn did a quick scout ahead, taking only the horses with him, to see if the waterhole had any water. To his disappointment he found barely enough water for their horses, let alone enough to sustain 800 head. That meant heading to Nullalbin Station.

Christmas Eve started early for the drovers. The summer sizzle settled across the land as the clanging of quart pots and the ringing of the packhorse bells sounded in time to the clip clop of their mob.

The group were hoping for a good night camp at Nullalbin Station. Perch Creek usually flows strong and wide from the Expedition Range beyond Coclabinda Station through Nullalbin to eventually join a confluence of streams that run into the Dawson River. But Nullalbin provided no comfort. There were stockyards for them to use, but absolutely no water. The station cattle were already walking the water out of the sand. They were in for another dry camp, with a 10-mile dry walk to the Dawson River come daylight.

On Christmas Day 1957, the youthful Queen Elizabeth II made her first televised Christmas broadcast to the Commonwealth. For Alwyn, the Kelly brothers and Henry Adams, the message went unseen and unheard. It was just three hours after midnight when the stockmen mustered up their breakfast, put a quart pot on to make a cup of tea, shook out their swags and made themselves ready for another day. One of them dowsed their fire, as each in turn offered the others a resounding 'Merry Christmas'. That would have to do.

Not a sound echoed through the bush; no impatient hollering of bulls and bullocks; no incessant mewling of hollow-sided calves; no plaintive mooing of thirsty cows. Despite their thirst, the cattle were asleep. However, the four men had an uneasy feeling. They felt sure the cattle would rush.

Soon one or two cattle woke, and then came an unmistakable sound – a rumbling bovine hullabaloo that was every bit as foreboding as it was breathtakingly noisy.

The stockyards had been built strong and firm many years before the four drovers and their 800 head arrived. They were built of the strongest stringybark, with each post rammed 3 feet into the soil. The years had taken their toll, however. The timber had long since turned a soft silver-grey. The sun had dried and cracked the framework. All together, the old yards were looking somewhat disinterested in doing their job.

At three o'clock on that summer morning, hours before the tropical heat had seeped across the landscape, there was a ferocious crash as all the cattle hit the stockyard's fence at once and turned the inner yard into matchsticks.

It wasn't surprising; overtired cattle are likely to rush. Luckily the perimeter of the yards held and they still had their mob. When the dust finally cleared, out of the 800 they found only 12 dead and another 14 that were just too weak to carry on.

Wally McCaul, the owner of Nullalbin, had a strong feel for the Christmas season. Instead of expecting them to rebuild the centre yards and bury the dead cattle, he knocked the remains of the yards down and volunteered to dispose of the bodies. 'Don't worry about the yards, they needed replacing anyway. Merry Christmas!' he said to the grateful drovers.

That day the dehydrated mob struggled on – strung out over about 3 miles, staggering rather than walking. Hoping to save as many as possible, Alwyn cut off 50 to 60 of the tail-enders, walked them through a fence and stole a drink for them at a small dam without checking with the landowner. Had he not done so, there was a chance all of the tail-end mob would have perished. That drink gave them the strength they needed to soldier on and catch up with the main mob that night, and to reach the Dawson River the next day.

Looking at the mob as they quenched their thirst, Alwyn reckoned those beat and bedraggled beasts looked for all the world as if they had reached the promised land.

Finally, on Boxing Day, Colin Cornford received a handy mob of cattle that were much more manageable than they had been 10 days earlier. Although it wasn't a long trip by outback droving standards, it was the toughest Alwyn had ever been on. Each day temperatures had ranged between 95 and 102 degrees Fahrenheit, and along the entire trip there had been only three decent spots at which the drovers could provide the stock with water: the Comet

River at the outset, later at Dick's Dam and finally on arrival at the Dawson River. Not one of them had expected they'd get so many cattle through.

Throughout those weeks, Alwyn had been working with a broken arm. After collecting his pay from droving he returned to Myella to practise in his rodeo arena, determined to change his riding style so that he could continue rodeoing, despite his still very weak and painful arm. That meant changing his riding style from left hand down to right hand down.

He got to work on the problem. Practically every day, after helping around the property, he'd head down to his practice chute, organise two or three of his buckjumpers and put in a solid workout.

Day after day for about a month he worked. Time after time, his balance would be off and he'd find himself having to scramble out of the dust and try again. Between each attempt he'd take a break and think about what each ride had taught him, desperate to find the right way to work his ride off the opposite arm. It was about this time that he was asked to ride at the Baralaba Rodeo.

Although the Baralaba Rodeo was not ARRA sanctioned, the organising committee thought having the rising star ride would boost their chances of raising funds for the local ambulance service. Alwyn couldn't turn them down. He never did when the local community needed help to raise money. Besides, the show offered some fine stock and the chance to get back into the ring and see if his modified technique would work in competition.

The somersault routine he'd started when he was about 11 years old had become part of his pre-ride preparation. He flipped three somersaults – out of sight of the other competitors, so as to not give away his 'secret' – and then rested in the shade of the chutes for a little while immediately before his ride.

The announcer's voice crackled across the arena, telling all about that their local hero, the Kokotunga Kid, was readying himself for his ride. Alwyn lowered himself into the chute and onto a piebald outlaw. He bent over and told the horse that it had to give the audience a good show – they were fundraising, after all. The mount chewed on his bit and snorted indifferently.

The chute gate burst open. A storm of dust swirled around the roughrider as the piebald bandit ripped from the chutes, detonating into the arena.

Riding that roller-coaster of snorting, grunting horseflesh, the Kokotunga Kid's saddle position was good and his balance felt fine; he was riding well. But perhaps the horse sensed that he was still a little tentative – or perhaps it was just a mean, bad-tempered cur of a horse out to cause some mayhem. Whatever the case, after about five seconds it had his measure and gave one almighty buck, as if from a tightly wound steel spring. The kick sent Alwyn skyward.

It wasn't the flight through the air that caused him any trouble. It was landing on ground as hard as marble that broke four ribs. As they broke, pain shot around and through his body with a cruelty he'd never known before and with it, air hissed from his lungs. It felt as though the night train from Rockhampton had trampled over his body without offering up so much as a how-do-you-do.

That evening, resting back on the Myella veranda, every breath, indeed every movement, was absolute agony. If anything hurts worse than injured pride, Alwyn now knew it was certainly the pain of four broken ribs. He also knew not to mess with trying to change his balance – ever. For the next week or ten days, the most Alwyn could do around the homestead was crawl a little. He couldn't even support his own weight to stand, let alone walk.

With his younger sons heading to school each day and his wife away working at the Banana Post Office, Bill Torenbeek was left to nurse his son – in the hope that when he was better, he'd be able to help out around the dairy.

Eventually the day came when, without too much groaning, Alwyn was able to get up out of bed or off the veranda and move about the house. Before too long, although hit by an occasional twinge of pain, he was ready to ride. So just as Bill Torenbeek was thinking that his son would be fit enough to take up work on the dairy, the young lad was saying goodbye and heading out to do the western rodeos of 1958.

As usual, Alwyn started his western run at Dingo, which that year provided its customary rough-and-tumble in the rodeo arena. He rode well at Dingo, turning and twisting through every ride, taking each as if he were joined to the bucking bronc or pugnacious bull beneath him.

After Dingo, he took on a droving job from Baralaba to Thangool, just a small mob of 200 bullocks. He also broke in six young horses to add to the well-broken half-dozen he already had. With all that out of the way, he was ready – or at least as ready as any lad can be – to turn 21, which in Australia in 1958 meant the simultaneous pleasures of being allowed to vote and purchase alcohol.

Alwyn was always keen to help around Myella, and his coming-of-age celebrations were no exception. He was more than happy to muck in putting on a party that offered an open invitation to Kokotunga and Baralaba locals – come one, come all for a bush shindig out at Myella.

Bill Torenbeek killed and butchered the fattest bullock while Alwyn took possession of three five-gallon wooden kegs of beer, despite his father insisting one keg would be plenty. Alwyn knew that outback folk were enthusiastic drinkers and they'd need every drop.

Marion, keen to see Alwyn, flew up from Brisbane. Alwyn's brothers Lester and Ralph, with the help of their father, dug a 20-foot by 2-foot, 6-inches fire pit, then hauled in two long ironbark

Early Days at Myella

The Torenbeek family ready to go to a picnic at Double Gully circa 1939.

Sixteen-year-old Alwyn breaking horses in the rodeo yard he built.

Alwyn and younger brother Lester share a moment on Myella, 1958.

The Kokotunga Kid in Action in the 1950s

Alwyn rides to take the money on Nobb's Bed of Roses, Theodore, 1958.
This was the only time she was ever ridden.

The Kokotunga Kid rides Crazy Kate
in Blackall, 1959.

Alwyn tangles with Off Spinner at Warwick, 1956. The horse always twisted out of her gear and was never ridden.

Alwyn doing a clean buck off from New Zealand's King of the Ring feature ride at Opotiki, 1960.

The Roughriding Circuit

L to R: Kokotunga boys and good mates, Peter Eather,
Bob Kelly, Collin Hutchinson, Brian Kelly, Vern Hetherington.

Noel Toomey riding hard
at Blackall, 1958.

Wally Mailman and Alwyn deciding how to tackle
New Zealand while in Blackall, 1958.

L to R: Alan Hicks, John Duncombe, Blue Ensby,
Buddy Grovnor and Tom Cannon relaxing before a rodeo.

Alwyn's Bachelor Days

Best friends in camp, Alwyn and June Mossiter
at the Longreach rodeo, 1958.

Marion Sainsbury and her friend Doreen Rider sharing time, 1955.

Torrie taking a break before a Te Puke bronc ride, 1959.

Wedding Bells and Family Ties

L to R: Alwyn, Marion, Noel Toomey, Wilma Torenbeek and Sharon Sainsbury.

Right: A beautiful bride: Marion Torenbeek nee Sainsbury, 1959.

Groomsmen Doug Flanagan (left) and Noel Toomey flank Alwyn on his wedding day.

L to R: Four Generations: Charlie, Alwyn, Bill and Michael Torenbeek, 1964.

L to R: Aldo, Shayne and Vonda Torenbeek with Mary and Anne Birchley heading off on a droving trip from Woolton to Theodore, 1978.

New Pastures: 1967–87

Alwyn on Steelo 5th in the
Quilty Gold Cup Endurance ride, 1967.

Alwyn rides the Australian bucking horse of the year, Spring Hill, 1968.

Jeff Torenbeek (left) teaches saddle technique to Dean Bayles at Woolton Station, 1983.

Alwyn in Shotover hut 100 km along the valley from Planet Downs homestead.

Family and Friends

A top group of trainees at Planet Downs Stockmanship school with Michael and Alwyn Torenbeek (left), 1987.

Great friend R.M. Williams started ARRA in 1945 and Endurance Riding in 1966.

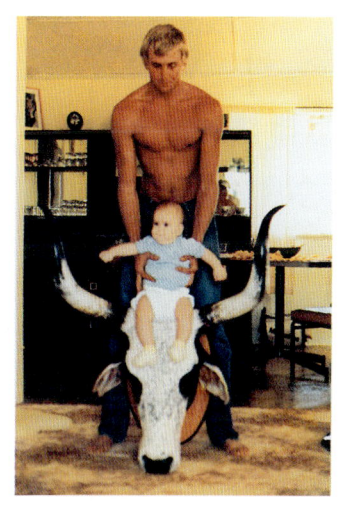

Aldo plays with niece Emma on the biggest bullock caught on Planet Downs between 1985 and 1989.

Bull catcher Aldo at Planet Downs, 1987.

Grandkids at Hobartville, 1999.

Endurance Riding: 1998–2010

Vicki Hogan and Alwyn sharing Endurance riding State Championship success at Kilarney, 1998.

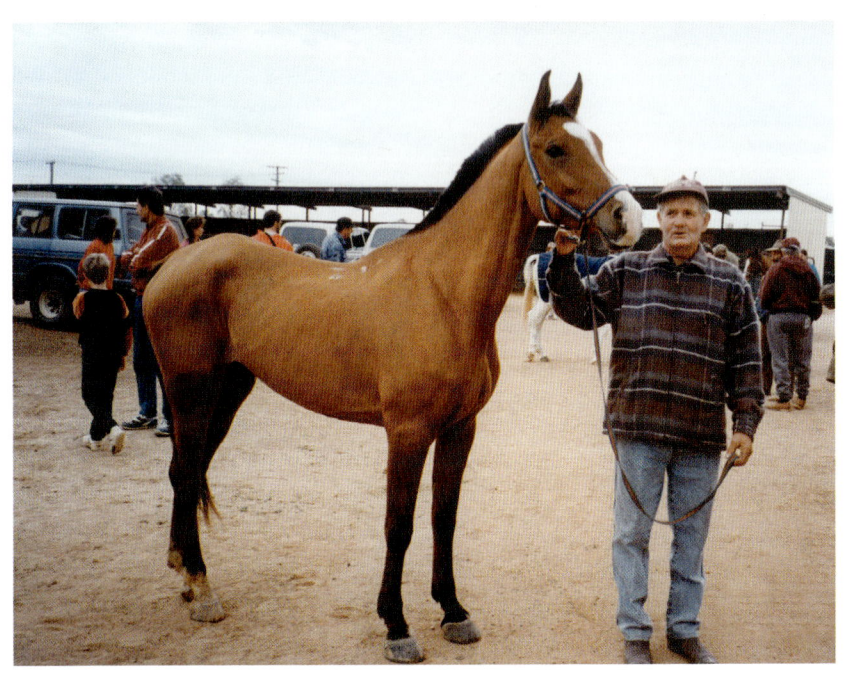

Alwyn with Once Only, winner of Lightweight division ridden by Gwen Caves at Longreach to Winton Endurance Ride, 1995.

Alwyn riding in the President's Cup
in Canberra, 2003.

Bringing in the fittest horse and Queensland Heavyweight winner,
Dalgangle, at Dennison Creek Endurance Ride, 2010.

The Adventure Continues

Alwyn wins first heavyweight division
at Dennison Creek on Anvil, 2012.

logs to line each side and built the pyre in between with split billets. They had it lit by mid-morning and covered the lot with wire mesh. By 7 p.m., when the guests arrived, it was one big, glowing ember.

The fourteenth of July 1958 was a very cold night, but what a party night. Phil Roth, Alf Ohl and Reg Hutchinson, all local Kokotunga lads, brought their piano accordions and got the party dancing out on the lawn and up and down the homestead veranda. The grog flowed and steaks sizzled on the fire pit as a chorus of tall tales and wonderful bush yarns mingled with the cadence of accordions playing bush ballads and folk songs.

The ladies of the Kokotunga School of Arts had donated the crockery and cutlery plus the long tables and stools, while the Kokotunga tennis and Baralaba football teams, as well as the Kokotunga CWA ladies acted as function coordinators extraordinaire.

Sometime quite early in the evening Bill Torenbeek looked over his round-rimmed glasses at his son and said despondently, 'I think we need some more beer – the keg is near empty.' Alwyn smiled and rolled out the second keg, and his old man positively glowed with relief. He did the same much later in the night when Alwyn rolled out the third keg.

Meanwhile, Alwyn and Marion were growing all the more deep in love. Marion stayed with the Torenbeeks that night and Alwyn drove her to the airport the next morning to catch a plane back to Brisbane by 9 a.m. The drive home was particularly lonely. Alwyn knew that his rodeo plans would mean long spells away from the woman who was obviously the love of his life.

Eventually, that busy circuit led Alwyn out to Longreach, where the proverbial breezes murmur of a 'vision splendid of the sunlit plains extended,' to quote the great Banjo Paterson.

Stay long enough in Longreach, and you will encounter every aspect of outback life – sheep and cattle properties that stretch to the horizon, laconic bushmen, weatherboard pubs, red and blue dogs. Any bushman who loves the bush loves Longreach, and the town was about to play an important part in this young bushman's life, as that year it was the host for the Australian Rodeo Championship.

The Australian Rodeo Championship was the pinnacle event of a sport that was still among the most popular entertainment options across the country. Folk flooded to rodeos despite having to navigate in rough-and-ready vehicles across equally rough roads. Perhaps some of rodeo's appeal was due to the fact that few Australians had television by 1958. So they'd leave their lounge rooms, hop in unreliable cars or fill country-bound trains like the Sunlander, Midlander or Westlander, and head to a rodeo – especially the Australian championship.

After all, a ticket to the rodeo often meant three or four days of excitement. Some fans would even take their holidays and travel the rodeo circuit barracking for their favourite rodeo stars.

By Longreach, Alwyn was travelling with two more champion riders, Noel Toomey and Doug Flanagan, who were among the up-and-coming roughriders who would take the sport into the 1960s. And while camping at Longreach with his mates, he had the opportunity to make another friend.

Alwyn had noticed that a young journeyman roughrider camped nearby wasn't joining in with the throng of happy horse folk, enjoying the rodeo. Instead, he was sleeping in late, keeping to himself and walking with a somewhat downhearted trudge.

The Kokotunga Kid strode away from his camp and approached the despondent roughrider. Sitting himself down by the young rider's camp, Alwyn offered his hand, saying with a smile, 'Alwyn Torenbeek, pleased to meet you, mate.'

'Bluey Drayton,' the rider replied.

Feeling that Drayton hadn't won enough prize money to afford to feed himself, but was too proud to ask for help, Alwyn explained that he'd noticed Bluey looking a bit 'down at the mouth'. He looked squarely into Bluey's eyes and asked, 'Are you okay, mate?'

Bluey's eyes reflected a sense of relief. 'I'm okay,' he answered. Then added, 'The police took my motorbike. They nabbed it when they noticed it was unregistered. That was back at Blackall.'

Alwyn smiled in sympathy. 'Oh, I suppose it's fair enough,' Bluey said, 'I'm too young for a licence yet.'

That wasn't the worst of it. The young rider had ridden around 1200 miles without a licence on an unregistered motorbike all the way from Victoria.

'Do you have any money?' Alwyn asked.

'Yes' Bluey replied, 'I still have a shilling and six pence.' That was the equivalent of around 40 cents. Without further ado, Alwyn pulled out his wallet and slipped Bluey £10.

The young rider's eyes lit up. Ten pounds wouldn't get his motorbike back, but it did mean he could get something to eat. He was up and out of that swag and down town for steak and eggs in a flash.

Alwyn now had quite an array of inspiring roughriders providing support and companionship on the rodeo circuit. Meanwhile, his other friends and family had to be content with hearing about his exploits courtesy of the national broadcaster, the ABC. Four hundred miles east of Longreach, they waited by the radio at Myella, listening carefully through the crackling signal to the dulcet and perfectly clipped voice of the ABC announcer, imagining every high-kicking outlaw that Alwyn battled.

In their mind's eye, they'd see him rest before heading to the chutes. They'd imagine how he climbed into the chutes ride after ride – talking to the saddle bronc, bareback bronc or bullock before the gates were flung open.

They knew that two pick-up men would be waiting in the wings, ready, keen and able to help the Kokotunga Kid in the event he got into trouble. They knew the typical grin he would be carrying with each lap of honour. They knew that despite that grin, he'd be underplaying his win so as to not seem too boastful among the other, older, more experienced riders.

At Myella Alwyn's family waited on every word as they followed his progress through the finals, as he took on the best of the roughriders of the 1950s and the roughest stock that any rodeo could throw at him and came out on top. For several minutes, speech evaded them as they took in the news that Alwyn 'The Kokotunga Kid' Torenbeek was the 1958 Australian Rodeo Champion.

As the perfectly enunciated, hollow vowels of the ABC announcer read out the result, the news of the homegrown roughrider taking out the Australian title ricocheted around town. In some of the more exuberant households, folk celebrated the Kokotunga Kid's win by clambering up onto their kitchen tables and dancing a jig. All over town, people were recounting Alwyn's wins, reliving his success blow by blow.

Alwyn had stormed into the week-long Longreach rodeo and picked nine good rides in two days across the three main events – saddle, bareback and bullock – which set him up for an active afternoon in the ring on the Saturday.

He went on to complete six more solid rides by the Friday, putting him in an enviable position, with one-third of a point separating him from Alan Bennett in the saddle bronc and the same margin splitting the two in the bareback.

On Saturday Alwyn picked up some handy points from a clean ride on a saddle bronc, which put him in first place ahead of Alan, and two points ahead of John Hughie, who was also known as 'The Kynuna Kid'. The atmosphere was buzzing and the crowd was roaring.

A front-end rider with a similar style to Alwyn's, John Hughie was a tough and capable roughrider – a drover from the west who knew how to handle rough stock. What's more, he was the 1957

Australian champion – that spoke for itself. The Kokotunga Kid versus the Kynuna Kid was going to be no easy contest.

Next came the bareback final, and score-wise there wasn't the width of a horsehair between Alan Bennett and Alwyn. In the end, Alan rode past Alwyn, winning by just one point.

Despite Alan's win, Alwyn had collected one win and one second and had enjoyed taking two laps of honour in front of around 8000 absolutely screaming rodeo fans.

The bullocks were tough stock at Longreach, and Alwyn was reluctant to take on a bullock ride. Nevertheless, he got to work trying to better the bovine beasties. By the bullock final he'd placed second behind Wally Woods and was enjoying yet another trip around the arena. Collectively, his grab bag of successful rides meant that the rider from Kokotunga was the 1958 Australian Rodeo Champion. Alwyn had realised his dream.

Helping Alwyn celebrate his championship win was a who's who of 1950s rodeo champions, many of whom were his best mates. Their presence made the win all the sweeter. However, a small postage-stamp-sized photograph in Alwyn's wallet reminded him that his success meant much more than just a chance to gather accolades from friends and fans. In quiet moments, the new champion would open his wallet and drew out Marion's photograph. He looked at her soft eyes and knew that this win, this championship, as well as being the realisation of his hopes, meant he was free to dare to dream of a life with Marion.

Just the same, he wasn't quite ready to return to Kokotunga. Yet Marion was ready to marry him.

Chapter Eight
A PHOTOGRAPH: 1958–1959

Alwyn remembers – walking off

With my success at Longreach, my main ambition had been fulfilled. Now, it was time to get on with the rest of the season.

I headed off to Hughenden Rodeo in the far northwest of Queensland. With the Longreach excitement still in my blood, I drew a big tough bronc and instead of riding him out, I decided to play with him – to put on a bit of a show.

While he was still bucking, I just walked off him – straight over his neck. It was a game that I loved to play. I always left on a high buck, which let me land on my feet. Do it after the bell and it's known as walking off, but get too excited and walk off early and to the judge it's a buck-off.

Fellow roughrider Lindsay Black and I could walk off to perfection – timing it just right and landing on our feet. Anyhow, on this Hughenden buckjumper I was a little too cocky and hopped off just before time.

That hurt my pride a bit. But not for too long. I looked around at the crowd, shrugged my shoulders and walked back to the chutes. Some of the riders gathered by the chutes realised what happened and said, 'Lucky you didn't get him last week.'

I replied, 'Last week I wouldn't have played so hard.'

A week earlier I'd been riding for the championship – concentrating hard, unwilling to let the chance to take the title pass me by. The week after the championship ride, I was taking it a little easier, relaxing and to eager to show off.

Among the many roughriders and rodeo fans who helped me celebrate my championship win was a young woman called Vera. She'd been travelling with us for some time.

Vera and I had maybe been having too much of our own company at Cloncurry Rodeo when Richie Fraser brought out everybody's mail, which had come to the secretary of the rodeo.

There among the bundle of letters was a letter for me from Marion congratulating me on my success of the last month. At the end she had added, 'Please don't get yourself badly hurt, I want you for my husband next year, our children are waiting to be born and they don't want a cripple for a dad. P.S. Now you have been proposed to, what do you think about that?' Marion went on to suggest we marry in 1959. She had given me a full year to get rodeo out of my system.

I was struck speechless for a time while I read and re-read the letter. Neither Marion nor I, in our three years of courtship, had ever made a commitment of any sort, or even asked for a commitment – although I had always hoped against hope that one day we would come together.

My good friend June saw my tension and came to my side. 'You've had bad news?' she asked.

'No way,' I answered, offering the biggest smile, and then adding, 'But Vera has.'

Thankfully Vera took the news well. We finished our Cloncurry rodeo and I took Vera to the railway station. She was bound for Townsville, and although we went our separate ways on good terms, we both vowed not to make contact ever again.

I remember sending Marion a return letter to tell her she had made me the happiest roughrider on the circuit. It's one of my most treasured memories.

* * *

The Flinders River snakes its way 620 miles from its headwaters in the Burra Range, part of the Great Dividing Range, through Hughenden and Julia Creek to the Gulf of Carpentaria. It was through this prehistoric country that Alwyn and his mates travelled to take in the Hughenden Rodeo.

They were now a substantial group and sometimes fans rather than riders would join the merry band. Vera was a rodeo obsessive. She loved everything about the sport and had decided to spoil herself with a good dose of excitement by following the western circuit.

Vera had come across Alwyn and his mates at the Hughenden Rodeo ball, which was everything a rodeo star like Alwyn loved – fine music, good company and plenty of young ladies with whom to dance.

Margaret Nowack was one of those young ladies. She and Alwyn looked so good together on the dance floor that the master of ceremonies asked the two of them to do the championship waltz – quite appropriate considering that both were champion riders.

Alwyn and Margaret burnt up the floor, dancing beautifully, holding the attention of everyone present. The floor was theirs alone for several minutes until, inspired by the champions' lead, the rest of those present joined them.

Many people thought he and Margaret looked so good together that they would say things like, 'When are you two going to start breeding bronc riders?' However, he and Margaret only ever thought of each other as good friends.

On the same evening, rodeo groupie Vera also scored a couple of dances with the Kokotunga Kid. She took the opportunity to ask if she could stay with the group and travel with them as they made their way around the circuit.

Alwyn, who had laid his swag by June and Margaret's, asked them if they minded if Vera joined them. Neither objected and Vera joined the group. The only trouble was, they had no spare swag, so Alwyn cheerfully offered half of his swag to the enthusiastic Vera.

However, the young man from Kokotunga still carried Marion's photograph in his wallet; it was his most treasured possession. That meant that no matter how close Vera might have wanted to get to Alwyn, he was always ready to draw the line. Going dancing or enjoying a laugh was okay, but when Vera or any other young woman hoped for a little closer attention, Alwyn was ready to pull out Marion's photo and let the lady in question know that his hopes for the future lay with Marion. It was a line he held fast. He couldn't expect Marion to wait for him to return home to Kokotunga and to her, but he could hope that she might wait. And that hope was as much as he needed to turn down any other woman who might be drawn to him – sharing a swag or not.

When the group moved to the Cloncurry Rodeo that May, the good times in their camp by Coppermine Creek continued. Musician-roughriders Richie Fraser, Hedley Parker and Mick Thomas played their guitars and had the camp jumping, singing and dancing to Top 40 hits for hours every night.

One of those nights by Coppermine Creek, Alwyn received a letter from Marion congratulating him on his success. In it, she proposed that they marry in a year's time, in 1959. She was giving Alwyn that year to get rodeo out of his system.

For Alwyn, there couldn't have been a better place to receive a proposal from the woman he loved – at a rodeo, surrounded by friends that he thought of as family. Although it did mean bad news for one young lady called Vera who'd taken quite a shine to Alwyn.

Everything was falling into place for the newly crowned champion – life was exciting, he was riding well, winning and feeling great, travelling with friends who were as close as family. Having found great success, Alwyn completed his triangular trek and returned to the southwest, to Winton.

Once known as Pelican Waterhole for reasons lost in the historical ether, Winton lies in an expansive red landscape where three artesian bores bubble to the surface from a vast natural water reservoir deep underground.

At Winton, Alwyn went 'train' droving with Bob Kelly. That meant loading the bullocks onto the train at Winton, then riding the rattling cattle cars with them until the train reached Duaringa. They'd then work the cattle through the Duaringa railway cattle yards, past the small timber and corrugated iron station house, the solid post-and-rail fence at the back of the station, the weeping bracts of white-flowing bougainvillea, down the main street of the aged cattle town and then along by the Dawson River to Baralaba.

Alwyn had agreed to help Bob until he got the cattle to the Dawson River; after that he had to get along to the 1958 Rocky Round-Up, where his father had agreed to join him. It'd be the first and last time Bill Torenbeek would see his son compete at a full-scale rodeo. Too worried for her son's safety, Alwyn's mother never saw him ride.

With an Australian championship title to his name, rodeo fans, roughriders and committeemen alike were keen to see Alwyn ride the roughest, toughest horses. For Alwyn, that meant rising to the challenge of taking on the wildest broncs and getting them ridden.

The bigger the record a bronc had, the more Alwyn wanted to get on him. Of course, the rodeo committees would make sure the better riders got the most fearsome rides to boost their top horses' names.

Although Alwyn loved the challenge of blotting the escutcheon of a fierce bronc by riding it to time, the victory often left him feeling a little sad at having beaten the beast. It was a sadness that'd last until he met the next horse and then he'd throw himself into the job again. His attitude was simple: there is a crowd to please and a title to uphold.

Not only did Alwyn find that he was getting the tougher rides and the attention of thousands of adoring fans, but he started to see his name – The Kokotunga Kid – featured on rodeo promotional posters. And he loved it – as did his father.

The local newspapers got in on the act, reporting his daring rodeo exploits, telling readers how he'd battle against his 'famous rival' Lindsay Black. Of course, out of view of the rodeo audiences Alwyn helped Lindsay saddle his mounts and even washed Blackie's shirts, while the veteran rider offered Torrie riding tips and advice, looked out for him and kept him safe. And so they made their way through the circuit.

In November 1958 Alwyn was in Monto for their rodeo. He drew Duck-in, a real devil of a bronc with an impressive record. She was a big tough brown mare and when the chute opened and she burst into the arena she seemed to be doing double twists like an acrobat. It was quite a ride. But Alwyn got the job done.

The following week his travelling group moved on to the town of Eidsvold. Out there they had two unridden horses, Desert Gold and Blue Spec, and it seemed the committee was determined to see one or both of them put the Kokotunga Kid in the dirt.

On the opening morning when the group were still in camp, a committeeman came by. Alwyn was sitting a little out of sight getting the boys' breakfast ready – even champions get cooking duty – when the man stepped into the camp and said, with a hint of concern on his face, 'I believe the kid is riding pretty good.' Noel Toomey smiled and with all the guile he could muster on short notice said, 'Nah, he's just a flash in the pan.' Doug Flanagan chimed in, adding, 'Day of reckoning's close at hand.'

The committeeman left feeling secure that by putting their two roughest mares up against the Kokotunga Kid, the spectators would be sure to see the young upstart thrown to the ground.

The rodeo kicked off and predictably Alwyn drew Desert Gold. She was a beautiful thing and she put everything into Alwyn's ride, bucking over about nine seconds. Just before the timekeeper struck his bell, she bucked high and fell over. That meant a re-ride.

This time Alwyn was called to chute three. There below him, standing proudly, was the clean-built Anglo, Blue Spec. Wally Woods had him saddled for Alwyn and watched as he slid onto the horse's back. The two roughriders shared a knowing look, acknowledging the strength of the brute.

Not far away, the one-time welterweight boxer Bluey Bostock and rodeo clown Noel Toomey were in a huddle, taking bets as to whether Alwyn had a chance of riding Blue Spec.

Alwyn leant over and whispered to the horse, then nodded at the chute boss – the battle was on. As Blue Spec exploded out from the chute, Wally ran his thumb along her jugular to get her jumping. That suited the Kokotunga Kid perfectly. After Blue Spec sent him skyward and then sucked back to land behind the spot from which she'd taken off, the champion rider's confidence grew. The harder the horse jumped and bucked, the more Alwyn took control.

At eight seconds, Alwyn looked at one of the judges and smiled because Blue Spec had never passed five seconds in her career before. And when the timer struck 10 seconds and pick-up rider Stan Beazley rode over to collect Alwyn from his mount, a wide beaming smile greeted him. The Kokotunga Kid had ridden Blue Spec.

Across two weekends, Alwyn had become the first to ride three of Australia's best bucking horses: first Duck-in at Monto, and then Blue Spec and Desert Gold at Eidsvold.

Next, Alwyn and his posse of roughriders moved on to the Western Downs town of Chinchilla, 111 miles west of Brisbane.

Chinchilla was tough on and off the rodeo arena, as Lindsay Black and Wally Mailman discovered. Like most roughriders, Lindsay and Wally enjoyed the opportunity to cool their heels in the shady bar of a country pub. Naturally, they were eager to make the most of that opportunity in Chinchilla.

The two riders were a picture of sartorial elegance as they strode into the red-roofed Chinchilla Hotel – a two-storey hotel standing on a main street corner. Lindsay looked particularly stylish, as befitted a well-known rodeo icon, wearing a tailor-made cowboy shirt that Alwyn had dutifully washed. Lindsay was the highest earning Aboriginal rider on the circuit, and among the highest earners black or white. Wally was respected for his gentle ways and useful horsemanship. But none of that seemed to matter in Chinchilla.

The publican looked decidedly uneasy to see Lindsay and Wally standing at the bar and quickly scrambled over to them. Disregarding their celebrity status, he told them to keep their money – it wasn't wanted in that pub, not money from Aboriginal men – they'd best leave.

Years later, Lindsay would say that he'd shrugged off that episode of racism, adding that it was by no means the first or last time it occurred. However, it shook Wally Mailman, who'd always made an effort to treat all folk respectfully.

Trouble found Alwyn in Chinchilla too. It started when he woke from his habitual pre-ride nap and moseyed over to the chutes.

Like most grounds, the Chinchilla rodeo ring was a large, solid structure made of the very best ironbark. The chutes were well kept and the whole effect was that of a highly professional establishment.

As Alwyn approached his chute, he noticed there seemed to be an inordinate amount of attention being given to the gelding residing there.

If evil could be embodied in a horse, then this chute contained pure evil – a saddle bronc known as The Condamine Widow Maker. This bronc's name was no idle boast. The Widow Maker was large by anyone's standards. The great colossus of a horse had to be housed in two chutes.

Around the back of the chute a gaggle of roughriders had gathered, taking bets on the beast which the Kokotunga Kid was about to battle.

Keeping calm, Alwyn took a long look at The Condamine Widow Maker and sat quietly on his back. The bronc refused to acknowledge he was even there. Alwyn went about securing himself in his saddle and then gave a nod to the chute boss.

The forward chute gate burst open and the crowd roared, the cheer echoing across the Western Downs.

The beast swung away from Alwyn's riding arm and burst into the arena like a whirling dervish. However, a bucking bronc like the Widow Maker doesn't put too much energy into twirling – that's the stuff bullocks prefer, not wily broncs. No, the Widow Maker had a far better strategy.

With the horse swinging away from his riding arm, the ride instantly became more difficult for the young roughrider, but that wasn't by any means the last of The Condamine Widow Maker's tricks. That was only the entree.

The huge animal then played his trump card, jump-kicking like he was possessed, and then hitting the ground like a pile-driver. The offensive continued for the better part of ten seconds, bending and twisting Alwyn's backbone with every great kick-jump followed by the unavoidable crushing landing. Thud, thud, thud went the Widow Maker; thud, thud, thud went Alwyn's spine. Yet, the Kokotunga Kid weathered the equine storm and landed a win over the gigantic bronc.

Back at the camp, when the day had already faded into early

evening, a committeeman told Alwyn to get ready for a bareback ride. Still recovering from his ride on the Widow Maker, Alwyn was in no mood for a bareback ride, particularly one so late in the day when there were only about four spectators left.

Nonetheless, the committee insisted he ride the last bareback bronc, a creamy mongrel of a horse. Despite the fading light and the lack of an appreciative crowd, Alwyn reluctantly agreed.

Once he was readied on the beast's back, the chute was opened and the horse put on the sort of performance that no rodeo crowd ever enjoyed – it bolted around the arena. Well, the pick-up men took off after it, one going flat out behind the runaway as if he were chasing it down in the final leg of the Melbourne Cup. The second pick-up rider made a bee-line across the arena, cutting Alwyn off on the far side. Alwyn hauled himself across the pick-up rider's saddle and eased himself down onto the ground.

The Kokotunga Kid hadn't survived another 10-second bareback ride – he'd managed a full-blooded, flat-out gallop that lasted 35 seconds, on a wild-eyed runaway.

Alwyn's success wasn't all in the rodeo ring that year; he had also become engaged to marry Marion. He finished off the season in Warwick, where he caught up with his fiancée. It was one of the few times she'd watch him rodeo. Alwyn wasn't about to stay put, however, despite the two talking about getting married almost immediately.

Thanks to a great rodeo year Alwyn had a solid bankroll, so it seemed as if the time couldn't be better to get married. With that in mind, he asked Marion to follow him on the New Zealand rodeo circuit. It was a plan he, Doug Flanagan and Noel Toomey had hatched as part of Alwyn's final year of rodeo before marriage stole him away.

However, before their romantic notions ran away with them, Alwyn's unreliable financial situation firmed in their minds and the two lovers realised that marriage was out of the question for the time being. They didn't even put the idea to their parents. Although Alwyn got on well with Marion's parents, he was sure that 'they would rather their special daughter do better than a vagabond roughrider'. So, for the moment, making their engagement formal – let alone marriage – had to wait. Marion would stay behind in Queensland while Alwyn took the next chapter of his roughriding adventure to New Zealand.

After the Warwick Rodeo, Alwyn returned to Myella to do a spot of horse-breaking with fellow roughriders Doug Flanagan and Noel Toomey while Marion returned to her life in Brisbane.

During their time at Myella, Alwyn, Doug and Noel began fine-tuning their plans for their New Zealand campaign. That meant sorting out the required tax department clearance and organising travel times and tickets. The trip started to take shape as Alwyn travelled to and fro between Brisbane and Rockhampton to get his tax clearance to travel. Then he chose his travel dates and bought his trans-Tasman airfare.

That done, he found that he had about two weeks to fill in before embarking on his Kiwi adventure. Sticking to his policy of never missing a rodeo whenever humanly possible, Alwyn realised that he could hop on the train from Rockhampton to Sydney and then make his way to the Myrtleford Rodeo before returning to Sydney to skip across 'the ditch' to the land of the long white cloud. From his point of view, things were looking up. He had a girl he loved, even though she wasn't joining him in New Zealand; he had a ticket to Auckland; he had mates who wanted to travel with him. A win in Myrtleford would be an absolute bonus and boost his coffers.

With his horse-breaking out of the way, Alwyn went to meet his travelling companions at Rockhampton Train Station. Doug and Noel had been working on properties further west and had caught the train to join Alwyn in Rockhampton. From there they'd travel to

Sydney, then head on to the Myrtleford Rodeo, back to Sydney and off to New Zealand.

It was morning, yet the heat of the day was already forcing a steamy miasma to rise off the bitumen as the young man from Kokotunga strode confidently into the train station, through the central foyer and out onto the platform.

Before him lay a long train trip of about 12 hours, through the Brigalow Belt, on to South Brisbane and through the lush green of the Southern Downs and the Granite Belt, then onwards through the mosaic of New South Wales towns and country to Sydney. All of that travel would be on a new stainless steel diesel-electric air-conditioned train, which had only been in service since 1955.

As planned, Doug and Noel were already on the platform, but without any goods and chattels. At the same time the great diesel-electric engine hauled the Sydney train along the length of the platform. As it came to a stop, the boys shook hands and Alwyn looked them over. 'No luggage, no swags?'

'We're not going. We've changed our minds,' Doug said, mustering a smile.

'What's more,' Noel insisted, 'you're not going either.' They explained that they were all earning good money lugging wheat bags at the local merchants and keeping fit doing it, so why leave? It seemed that lack of confidence had eroded their enthusiasm. Not surprising really, considering that Alwyn was a champion rider whereas the others were still working at making their marks in rodeo.

Alwyn wasn't one to miss an opportunity. He had decided on New Zealand, despite having to leave Marion behind and despite never having travelled beyond Australian borders.

The conductor blew his whistle, signalling all those who were travelling to board the train. Noel and Doug didn't move, perhaps thinking that their companion would get the jitters and stay. But Alwyn opened the stainless steel door and stepped up and into the train carriage, expecting that the boys would stop mucking around and join him.

Alwyn stayed in the doorway as the train started down the platform. The long growl of the engines took the strain of the numerous carriages. Alwyn still didn't move from the carriage step. It was then that Doug and Noel made their move.

Together they bolted for the train. Alwyn laughed, thinking his mates had come to their senses. Instead, as the two caught up with the slow-moving train, always one with slick reflexes Doug grabbed and snatched at Alwyn's swag and got it.

'Get off now,' Noel demanded breathlessly. But Alwyn wouldn't get off. The train gathered pace and drew ever closer to the end of the platform.

Noel and Doug called out for Alwyn to leave the train. But he stood firmly on the carriage step even though they had his swag, believing that at any moment his foolhardy mates would give up and get in the train.

The two roughriders were by now sprinting along the platform carrying his swag. They gave one last shout that echoed along the platform, imploring Alwyn to 'hop off', telling him in clear terms 'we're not coming'.

But their chance of changing Alwyn's mind ran out at exactly the same time as they reached the end of the platform. It was clear that he was determined to leave, with or without them.

'Oh bugger,' Doug growled. The two men gave an almighty heave-ho and hurled the swag into the train, just in time to watch it rumble beyond the end of the platform, down the track that bisects Dennison Street, past the newsagent and the railway café on the corner, and out of sight. Their Kokotunga mate was New Zealand bound.

Chapter Nine
CROSSING THE DITCH: 1959

Alwyn remembers – a new year dawns

Just as I got unpacked in my Auckland hotel room, twelve o'clock midnight erupted. Kiwis sure know how to bring in a new year. I went down to watch an entire city dancing, singing, loving life. The night sky was alive with fireworks.

In their enthusiasm people were picking up cars and turning them around and things like that. While I was down in the street, I got invited to a party. I happily went and drank a fair bit of beer, which made things a bit rough the next morning.

I had a quick, early breakfast. I was short of time, but had paid for my breakfast so I had to be fast. The travel terminal was only a few yards away from my hotel room, so I was able to walk to meet my bus.

I arrived at the bus terminal, only to be told that my bus had already left. The driver had arrived and, on seeing that nobody was at the terminal, collected the few packages that were stacked and waiting to be loaded and left ahead of schedule. This meant that I would have to catch a taxi to make it to my first New Zealand rodeo. The catch was, the airport was 20 miles away. That ride took most of my remaining money, leaving me with one Australian shilling on which to survive in Wanganui. All I had to do was make it through my flight – given I was still a little seedy from my New Year celebrations, that was easier said than done. I can report that my hangover took its toll on the flight.

My memories of my trip to New Zealand are strong. The people I worked with, my experiences with the Maori boys, deer and pig hunting, remain up front in my memory to this day.

Until I went to New Zealand I had felt like I had a monkey on my back. New Zealand removed that monkey.

* * *

The shrewd Kokotunga Kid had realised that fitting in one more Australian rodeo before his flight to Auckland would give him the best chance at winning in New Zealand. It would settle his nerves, get him some last-minute practice and, if successful, pick him up a nice winner's purse that would help him on his travels.

That rodeo was at Myrtleford, in the Victorian Alpine region. Beautiful country. The trouble was, Myrtleford is around 400 miles southwest of Sydney and Alwyn was in Sydney.

Without any travelling mates, Alwyn had no one with whom he could catch a lift. To get to Myrtleford, he'd have to travel by train. And there was the rub: the little town wasn't on the train line. The closest train station was more than 50 miles away, on the NSW–Victorian border at Albury.

Undeterred, Alwyn rode the rattler from Sydney to Albury then hailed a taxi. 'Myrtleford please, mate,' he said to the astonished driver, whose longest trips were usually to local picnic spots like the picturesque swimming hole near town known as Munga Bareena Reserve or perhaps to the Bonegilla migrant centre. This fare was quite a treat.

Alwyn's taxi meandered through the Chiltern Valley's magnificently tall stands of box-ironbark forest, along the Hume Highway, across the windy farming country of Dockers Plains and through the lavishly timbered braes and glens of the Victorian high country where Ned Kelly once roved.

Finally they turned off the Hume and towards the southeast to follow the Ovens River, whose flow is a brilliant crystal blue rather than the coffee brown of the tired rivers Alwyn knew. The Ovens mirrored the last leg of their journey as it zigzagged through vibrant red gum forests, rushing down from the Alps to Myrtleford and Wangaratta for a never-ending rendezvous with the King River.

Alwyn arrived in Myrtleford as keen for rodeo action as ever. The long drive hadn't rattled his enthusiasm loose. Nor had the amazing scenery distracted him. He was ready to rodeo.

He quickly organised somewhere to camp and took himself off to the Myrtleford showground to try to get some practice before the rodeo started.

Alwyn organised a horse on which to practise. Saddled it. Then he climbed into the chute and a helper swung the gate open. The horse blasted from the gate, which swung vibrating into Alwyn's jaw – well and truly dislocating it. It was 10 days before Christmas; the rodeo was Boxing Day, and Alwyn's dislocated jaw threatened to spell the end of his Myrtleford campaign, before it even started.

So instead of flying high on buckjumpers, Alwyn built his bank account digging a well for local farmer Dan Mitson, who invited the unfortunate roughrider over for Christmas dinner. Trouble was, Alwyn's jaw pain meant settling for a festive dinner of soup and ice cream while the Mitson family enjoyed a traditional dinner with all the trimmings.

Never one to let the chance to rodeo get away, come Boxing Day, Alwyn gritted his teeth and rode into competition. It would be wonderful to say that he scored with ease, but it wasn't so. He was a fearsome rider, but no matter how hard he tried he couldn't score a decent ride on any of the stock he drew.

It wasn't all bad news though. While Alwyn was at Myrtleford a young red-headed roughrider had spied him. The rider quick-stepped to catch up to him, holding something in his hand. It was Bluey Drayton and he had remembered the Queenslander's generosity. Good fortune had smiled on Bluey and somewhere along the rodeo track he'd earned enough to repay Alwyn the £10 that he'd borrowed. It seemed that things might be turning in the Kokotunga Kid's favour.

Meanwhile, ARRA representative and fellow roughrider Peter Poole was doing the rounds out the back of the chutes. Peter was searching for four particular riders, one at a time, to offer each a potentially life-changing invitation.

Chilla Seeney caught sight of him and stayed in earshot every time Peter stopped to talk to one of the champion riders.

Eventually Poole strode over to Alwyn, the youngest of the riders for whom he'd searched. He told him that the ARRA had invited him and three other champion riders to compete in the USA, the home of rodeo, and by inference become part of rodeo history.

Alwyn was the youngest Australian to be called to ride in the USA. The problem was, well before he arrived in Myrtleford, even before the Longreach Rodeo, he'd already decided to travel to New Zealand and the USA proposal clashed with his plans.

But there was something else on Alwyn's mind too. Although he was a mate of the other invited riders, he wasn't sure that he could drink as much or play as hard on an extended US tour. It took him just a few minutes to consider the invitation and turn Peter down. Within minutes of that, Chilla Seeney, who was still skulking in the background, pounced on the offer – putting himself forward as Alwyn's replacement.

Not long afterwards Alwyn was back in a taxi to catch the Sydney train at Albury and then fly on to New Zealand. He farewelled Australia on New Year's Eve, winging across the Tasman.

Behind him was his wide brown land; before him lay a land with a somewhat different style.

After one night in Auckland and an expensive taxi ride to the airport bright and early the next morning, Alwyn's funds were further drained by an excess baggage charge on his flight to Wanganui. Then the luckless roughrider had to watch as New Zealand Customs officials confiscated his riding gear for fumigation. He wasn't going to be reunited with his riding gear until he reached Gisborne Rodeo further down the track.

Despite these setbacks, Alwyn landed in Wanganui brimful of optimism, sure that he could turn his fortunes around. He'd arrived in time for the New Year's Day New Zealand Rodeo Championships.

He strode into the airport terminal and over to a porter, asking, 'Can you tell me where and how far away the rodeo grounds are?'

The porter smiled and, pointing out of town, said, 'Three miles up that way.'

Alwyn left desperate to make the rodeo in time to register. He hadn't gone too far when a car pulled up beside him carrying two young men – rodeo fans out to catch the championship action. One of the lads leant out the car window and asked Alwyn if he knew how to get to the rodeo. Recognising his opportunity, Alwyn grinned and answered, 'I'll hop in and show you!'

Thanks to the ride, Alwyn made it in time. Better still, the two grateful lads paid his way into the rodeo, which, he reflected, saved him from 'a lot of sweet-talking' at the gate.

Alwyn was not yet at the chutes when he heard a deep voice chime in from nearby, asking, 'Young fella, what are you doing here?'

The voice came from a familiar face – a solid bloke called Max Taylor. For Alwyn it was an absolute delight to bump into someone he knew from the Australian rodeo circuit. What's more, his finances were getting very low, almost to the point where he'd have to give a shout for help to his parents. But he avoided that embarrassment when Max lent him the nomination money.

That was all the help Alwyn needed. Although he'd arrived too late to enter the saddle bronc competition, he was able to nominate for the bareback. By that evening he'd won a third-place bareback ribbon and prize money – enough to take care of Max's loan as well as make his way to the next rodeo. Things were lookin' up.

Apart from coming away with prize money, Alwyn's first taste of New Zealand rodeoing showed him that New Zealand crowds very quickly accepted new competitors into their rodeo fraternity. Plus, as he was about to discover, the local rodeos drew large crowds, had softer and smaller arenas, and provided tough broncs; and in between you travelled on good roads over short distances – it was a slice of heaven.

Next in Alwyn's sights was Gisborne, just short of 200 miles northeast of Wanganui, on the easternmost tip of the North Island.

Gisborne was a good rodeo town with a nice-sized arena and big, appreciative crowds. More importantly, it offered reasonable stock that gave Alwyn the chance to add to his bankroll with another third in the bareback. While there, he met Rod Campbell, a matter-of-fact rodeo judge.

Rod was the manager of a large property on the Waihaha River, part of a big government program that was bringing virgin country bordering Lake Taupo into production, and he needed a horse-breaker. Alwyn, the Aussie blow-in, needed a job. So, after only 24 hours in Gisborne, Alwyn found himself moving to the tiny backwater village of Waihaha, in New Zealand's Northland, with Rod as his new boss.

Rod Campbell's horses were big strong four- and five-year-olds living on clover and had never had a human hand on them. Alwyn rolled up his sleeves and got to work. This was his first New Zealand job and he was determined to make an impression.

At home he'd broken horses and been riding them within four days. However, the strong-willed, muscular New Zealand-bred horses took two or three weeks to get to the same point.

Alwyn's technique involved using a breaking-in horse. He'd start off on the ground and secure a short rope from his horse's bridle to the bridle of the unbroken horse and walk the two together for a little while. Then he'd mount his horse and, with the two still tethered together, he'd ride both horses around the yard. Then he could get his breaking-in horse to lean over on the unbroken horse while he put some hobbles on him. Alwyn always worked on the principle that if you can hop on a horse without hurting him, you're halfway there.

On day one he went down to Rod's yards to have a look at his break-in stock and a little chill ran up and down his spine. Rod's wild horses were whopping muscular creatures with a nice bit of colour in them. That should have been okay, except Alwyn didn't have much in the way of breaking-in gear, and nothing like what Australian horse-breakers would call a breaker's saddle.

Alwyn lassoed the first colt. The horse took that as an insult and dragged him all around the yard. Tired of being dragged around, Alwyn put a half-hitch around a post. Belligerent and stubborn, the great brute pulled back on the rope; then, before Alwyn could do anything else, it shuddered and dropped dead.

Alwyn looked the horse over and in his usual laconic fashion asked himself, 'What will I do about that?'

With horses to break and nobody to help him, there was nothing Alwyn could do about the dead animal. All he could do was let it lie in the yard while he got on with the job. His next horse did everything he asked of it and by the end of the week was his breaking-in partner. Thankfully, that first horse was his only catastrophe. Still, Alwyn was in a cheerless mood when the Stratford Rodeo came around.

Winning the saddle bronc and bullock rides at Stratford improved

Alwyn's financial position, and his mood. From then on, at rodeo after rodeo, he drew up well in the saddle bronc events, winning five bronc rides out of six and some bareback and bullock-riding prize money to boot. Collectively, those wins made him the All Round Champion of New Zealand for 1959.

There was just one dark cloud hanging over Alwyn's success. During the season he noticed that when it came to bareback riding, he was starting to feel uneasy, a sort of nervousness beyond butterflies in the stomach. In fact, Alwyn thought it was essential to have the butterflies, but this was a different thing altogether; it seemed to him for all the world like the onset of the tut-tars.

The tut-tars were intense nerves that would start a rider's hands shaking, overcoming him or her with fear or dread. They potentially spelled the end of a rodeo career.

Alwyn had seen it in other riders. He'd seen them ignore the symptoms and he'd witnessed the dreadful consequences. Too many men who ignored the tut-tars had been sent to early graves, pushed to drink or left permanently stupefied. He wasn't about to let that happen to him.

Alwyn gave some thought to what might be the cause of his bareback tut-tars. Then in a sudden moment of clarity he looked at his rigging and said, 'It's you, and I don't want you.'

The rigging was fine quality and had been made by fellow champion rider Wally Woods. Despite that, and the fact that it had helped him gain several victories, Alwyn sold it to Mason Waipaki and never contested another bareback event. That put an end to his bareback tut-tars forever.

In giving up bareback riding he was leaving behind an event that had, of recent times, seen him put up with having to ride out on 'bolters' that just wouldn't buck. The bareback event almost always ran last, leaving the rider tearing around the ring in the semi-dark – as arenas then were not under lights – performing before the few stragglers left. He wouldn't miss it.

Having stymied the onset of the tut-tars and found great success, Alwyn was ready to head home. He was still carrying Marion's photograph in his wallet and he was more sure than ever before that he wanted to marry her.

It was time to travel home to Myella, to become 'formally' engaged to Marion, then to work his horse plant and get ready for the western rodeo run.

As the second half of the final year of the 1950s drew to a close, Alwyn was on his way back to Australia. Around him, the world had started to change. *Six O'Clock Rock* and *Bandstand* were sharing rock'n'roll with Australian youth. Not long before, the New South Wales premier Joe Cahill had declared the Opera House project underway, and a horse named MacDougal had won the Melbourne Cup. (For the record, 31 years later Alwyn helped his son Jeff break in the progeny of MacDougal on Silver Hills Station near Richmond.)

But on that day in 1959 when he arrived back in Sydney, Alwyn was in for his own very special surprise. While he'd been travelling through New Zealand's North Island, Marion had given up her job at Brisbane's Chest Hospital and had accompanied her girlfriend Fay to Melbourne, where she'd picked up work as a domestic at a boys' college. She and Fay had plans to travel around Australia.

Those plans fell apart when Fay decided to return to Brisbane. Marion decided that it was no good travelling around Australia on her own and packed in her job in Melbourne to head home. Her new scheme involved returning to Kokotunga after a surprise reunion with Alwyn in Sydney.

Marion set out on the interstate bus from Melbourne, thinking of little or nothing else than the great surprise Alwyn would get at Sydney Airport. For mile after mile she sat in the bus, travelling through much of the night, watching the silhouettes of silver and grey bush flicker past her window. For mile after mile she imagined how they'd meet, how romantic it would be.

She arrived as daylight lit up the bus terminus and went straight to the airport. Such was her eagerness to surprise Alwyn, she arrived some hours before his plane landed. With time to spare, she curled into a chair in the arrivals lounge and fell asleep.

The searing blur of white light from a large flashgun shattered Marion's sleep. A journalist from the local Sydney newspaper the *Daily Telegraph* had crept up and taken her photograph. He was there to cover the inaugural Qantas 707 trans-Tasman flight – Alwyn's flight.

To his delight, Marion explained that she was waiting for the man she loved, the newly crowned rodeo champion of Australia and New Zealand. This was a story the reporter couldn't ignore – a young woman waiting patiently for her dashing cowboy hero, the Kokotunga Kid. His readers would gobble it up.

Finding Marion meant the reporter had scored a double hit. Not only would he file a story about the new plane, but he would also be returning to the office with a nice piece about the rodeo champion's New Zealand success, with a beaut photo of the love of the roughrider's life.

Alwyn's plane had taken off at 8.45 a.m. New Zealand time and arrived in Sydney at 9.15 a.m. Sydney time, a fact that boggled the roughrider's mind – two hours' travel reduced to virtually no time at all thanks to the speed of jet flight and the peculiarities of crossing time zones from east to west. The Boeing landed smoothly on the tarmac at Mascot. Glad to be home, Alwyn walked down the passenger steps accompanied by two hairy-armed Kiwi mates.

Marion stood behind a glass window overlooking the tarmac. Behind her, the *Daily Telegraph* reporter was committing the scene to film.

Her heart lifted as she saw the man she loved walking towards the terminal. He strolled through the exterior doorway and momentarily out of her sight again. Then, after a few minutes that seemed to flow by far too slowly, he emerged into the arrivals lounge. She watched his every move. She admired, as if it were the first time she'd noticed it, his confidence, the glint in his eye, his bushman style.

During the hours that she'd waited for him to arrive she'd let the idea that they could marry in Sydney and then go home as a married couple fill her mind. She'd thought how she'd greet him with a kiss and perhaps put the idea to him straight away. She felt sure he'd go for it; they'd talked and written to each other about the idea. It was, she thought, only a matter of doing it and she didn't want to wait a moment longer than she needed. She was ready to marry.

Alwyn strode over to Marion, looking amazed to see her there, and just as he said hello, the realisation that he'd arrived with two others sank in. It wasn't a complete surprise that he had a couple of Kiwi roughriders with him. She'd half expected it anyway.

She kissed him and greeted his mates warmly as he introduced them, waiting for her moment to suggest marrying before they left Sydney.

Alwyn smiled and held her tight. He looked into her eyes and told her how he had longed to see her again and how being home meant he could head straight back to Kokotunga with his mates and hit the rodeo circuit straight away.

Before she could say another word, he explained that he and his mates had pre-nominated for three Queensland rodeos and had already made travel arrangements to go straight on to Rockhampton and then out to the rodeos.

Marion's heart sank just a little as her hope of marrying her beloved roughrider in Sydney collapsed. 'The rides came first,' she recalled. 'I was a little disappointed, but we got engaged and I was happy with that.'

The other problem was Marion didn't have a flight booked to

travel back to Rockhampton; she'd expected to sort out travel when her man arrived in Sydney. Luckily, Alwyn and Marion had a Good Samaritan with them.

The *Daily Telegraph* reporter went in to bat for the love-struck duo and talked to someone at the airline booking office. He strode back to them with a broad grin on his face. He'd wangled Marion a seat on the flight north.

Ecstatic, Alwyn telephoned his father and told him that they'd need enough transport at Rockhampton Airport to get him, Marion and a couple of keen Kiwi riders back to Myella.

The remainder of 1959 was a busy time, to put it mildly. The day after they arrived back at Myella, the Kiwi riders and Alwyn took to the rodeo circuit. Marion stayed on at Myella and waited patiently.

Chapter Ten
MARRIED COUPLE'S PROBLEM: 1960–1964

Alwyn remembers – honeymooning

Marion and I spent our first night of married life sleeping by the road to Mt Morgan. We were heading to the mining town for the night but had to have a sleep on the way down, as we were just so tired. That was because I hadn't packed my port and had to get that done before we left Myella.

My sister Wilma and her husband Tiger Slater had made their house vacant for us in Mt Morgan, so we stayed there the first night. The next morning we left the car for Dad to pick up later, and caught a bus to Rockhampton and then a plane through to Sydney.

Kings Cross had changed since my first visit; it was nowhere near as good as it had been when I was single. When we arrived as man and wife it was just a bit tamer. There wasn't much going on for us.

There was something else that had changed too, although we didn't really notice it until we were on our return trip at the end of our holiday. We saw cross-dressing in the street. I was absolutely amazed.

After Sydney we moved on to New Zealand, where I was determined to show Marion all the wonderful places that I'd seen the year before.

I took her out to places like Waihaha – right on Lake Taupo. I'd loved it when I worked there on my first New Zealand stint. The visit brought back so many memories. I remembered how I'd get on a horse and go riding out with the Maoris and have deer nearly bloody jump over me. It was fantastic.

When I had been there on my first visit, I had consolidated my reputation as a horseman through my rodeoing and horsework. That reputation persisted, so while Marion, Wally Mailman (who had joined us for a stint in New Zealand) and I were living on Roydon Downs, folk would bring horses to us to break in.

One morning, there was something on Wally's mind other than the next rodeo. Wally was sitting at the Roydon Downs kitchen table with me as Marion surfaced for breakfast. She'd not been feeling too well in the mornings for some time, and Wally looked her over this particular morning and said, with a grin, 'Marion, I think you must have the young married couple's problem.' He was right; our first son Michael was making his existence felt.

That very welcome news turned my world upside down. As the ramifications of the news filtered into my mind, I gradually began to feel exactly the same morning-sickness symptoms that Marion was experiencing. Our lives were about to change forever.

* * *

Hot, humid air lay heavy on the tropics as Alwyn and Marion planned their December wedding. The rodeo season was well finished for the year and the couple went to see their local priest. That, of course, was their first problem. Marion's parents' priest was Catholic and Alwyn's creed was Church of England. However, neither Marion nor Alwyn were particularly vigilant on the subject of religion.

It was a time when religion and going to church was all about being Roman Catholic or Protestant, where Protestant meant Church of England or any other Christian belief that was not Catholic. Your religion influenced which football team you barracked for, if you ate fish on a Friday and much more.

It was a fierce contest and its origins went back 500 years. At stake was eternal salvation or eternal damnation. That meant any couple hailing from different religions yet wanting to marry appeared to be doomed.

Although he may not have thought that they'd be doomed for all eternity, Marion's Catholic priest's theological opinion was certainly in line with the idea. The only way to avoid such an outcome was for the groom to accept the sacred and unerring Roman Catholic tradition, see the right path to salvation and convert.

That wasn't a solution that appealed to either Marion or Alwyn. Instead, after some negotiation, the priest compromised, accepting the eminently sensible idea that Alwyn would promise to take heed of Catholic teaching while continuing to make his own decisions, and to let his children 'make their choice of religion when they became old enough to find their way in life'.

Next came the trauma of negotiating the guest list. As Alwyn put it, 'Shock horror, we were having Aboriginals at our wedding.'

That idea caused outrage and not just with the local priest. Marion's mother was horrified at the thought of her daughter being married in a ceremony at which Aboriginal guests would be looking on. That was despite Marion having befriended an Aboriginal girl when at school. It was as though it were a completely different proposition to invite a black friend to something as important as their wedding.

'You have just got to get over that, Mum,' Marion said to her mother. 'If Alwyn can't invite some of his best mates who happen to be Aboriginal, then there will be no church wedding,' she explained.

The couple had decided that if they couldn't have their way, they'd abandon the idea of a church wedding and settle for a civil ceremony at the nearest registry office. What mattered most was that they get married and no obstacle, big or small, was about to stop them.

Their determination paid off. On 12 December 1959, the hottest day for around 30 years, Marion walked down the aisle of the little Catholic church in Baralaba to marry Alwyn. He reckoned theirs was not just a mixed marriage in terms of religion, but a 'multicultural wedding' where Aboriginal guests like Shane Goddard, Richie Fraser and Wally Mailman enjoyed the celebration together with their white guests.

Later, in the church hall, Richie Fraser picked up his guitar and started singing Top 40 hits like Johnny Horton's 'North to Alaska' and Sammy Davis Jr's 'Candy Man' for the 70 wedding guests and the newly wedded Mr and Mrs Alwyn Torenbeek. According to Alwyn, 'he stole the show'.

Somehow his singing broke whatever tension remained. Not long afterwards, the echoing crash of thunder announced the arrival of a tropical storm, which quenched the heat. In the end, it was a perfect day that bound Alwyn and Marion together completely, for every day that followed. And still does, more than 50 years later.

The young couple's honeymoon was another matter. They started it in Sydney's Kings Cross, after a long journey from Central Queensland. The Cross seemed very different from the amusing nightspot that Alwyn remembered from his first visit in 1956. The young Torenbeeks were largely uninterested at the start of their honeymoon, but found it alarmingly devious and breathtakingly dodgy on their return trip. Kings Cross was not for them, on either leg of their journey.

Auckland, on the other hand, was exactly as Alwyn remembered it, albeit without the New Year's Eve atmosphere. Just as on Alwyn's first visit, however, the couple spent little time in the city of sails.

Before they could even set foot in Auckland, a gregarious Kiwi mate of Alwyn's called Keith Green met the couple at the airport and told them he had a place for them to stay, a job for Alwyn and a car waiting to take them there. With that, Keith herded them into his car and whisked them off to Te Puke, 100 miles southwest of Auckland, where he managed a property called Roydon Downs.

Keith, Alwyn and Marion drove on through the Papamoa Hills until they came to the rolling, jade-green hills of Roydon Downs, where Alwyn and Marion made their home in one of the married couples' quarters – although initially they stayed in the homestead with Keith and his wife Patricia between Christmas and New Year's Day.

The idea was that Alwyn would work as a truck driver and horse-breaker on Roydon Downs for the New Zealand Department of Lands and Survey, with Keith as his boss. The opportunity provided the newlyweds with a beautiful home in a landscape of striking natural beauty, and turned out to be an excellent arrangement in other respects as well.

Te Puke was handy to an assortment of towns including Tauranga, Waitangi and Rotorua. So, for three months, the young Torenbeeks were able to travel to a new rodeo every weekend and mix and mingle with the young set of rodeo couples and families.

One morning, Wally Mailman, who had joined the couple on Roydon Downs, was having breakfast with Alwyn when Marion wandered into the kitchen. Wally took one look at Marion, who was mysteriously sick that morning, and promptly told her that she had 'the young married couple's problem'. He was right. Marion was pregnant.

With that news ringing in their ears, Alwyn, Marion and Wally finished their three-month stint at Roydon Downs and moved on to another property near Te Pahu.

Fellow roughrider Jim Olsen had invited the Torenbeeks to spend some time with him and his family there. It was hard for Alwyn and Marion to believe that anything could match the magnificence of the Roydon Downs countryside – but Te Pahu did. Plus it was just far enough away from the nearby metropolis of Napier to feel like a rural slice of heaven, yet close enough to benefit from being near an important New Zealand city.

This corner of the North Island of New Zealand was just right for the Queensland roughrider. Here Alwyn could head off stalking deer or go mountain climbing and take in breathtaking vistas of rich green farmlands spread out like a chequered quilt, distant snow-capped mountains to the south. Before he could take on any adventures, however, he found he had to get past breakfast each morning.

Although Marion had overcome her morning sickness, Alwyn, who was adjusting to the responsibility and reality of becoming a father, found he felt quite queasy each morning – in that sort of unnerving way when your stomach feels like it's upside down and is unwilling or unable to hold any food.

Although the symptoms would never last too long into the day, seeing her husband's discomfort morning after morning encouraged Marion to say to him gently on one especially bad morning, 'Let's go back to Aussie.'

Still grey from his flip-flopping nausea, Alwyn gave her a thankful smile and agreed. It was five months since they'd left Myella. With Marion pregnant, Alwyn experiencing her morning sickness and their funds running low, it was time to go home. By this stage their intrepid companion Wally had already left for home, about a week earlier.

The couple farewelled Te Pahu and headed to Auckland to catch the trans-Tasman ferry, the *Wanganella*. The sturdy 9360-ton steamship had done war service as a hospital ship and had all the right credentials to get them back to Sydney safely.

The only trouble was, the already unsteady bushman and his pregnant wife had no experience with the sea. What's more, many an experienced sailor will tell you that the passage 'across the ditch' is renowned for being rough. The four-day trip heaving and rolling on the open sea, watching the horizon rise and fall, would be a challenge even for the most seasoned sea dog; it was unbearable for the new-chum seafarers.

Over those four days their skin colour – and, for that matter, their disposition – changed from the lightest shade of porcelain to a colic green and back again countless times. There was no relief until the ship was well within the confines of the tall sandstone cliffs at the mouth of Sydney Harbour.

So traumatic was their passage on the *Wanganella* that neither Marion nor Alwyn could ever entertain even the idea of another sea voyage.

It was May 1960 and the cool of winter was setting in when the couple arrived back at Myella considerably short of funds. Alwyn solved the problem by putting his horse plant together again to go droving. In between droving jobs he went contract mustering.

And if there was a handy rodeo nearby, he'd give it a go. Despite having agreed to retire from the circuit after his marriage, Alwyn's rationale for taking on the occasional roughride was simple: 'The extra money was good, plus after eight years of enjoying the adrenalin rush from the thrills and spills of practically full-time rodeo it's very hard to stop cold turkey.' Nonetheless, retirement from the rodeo circuit grew closer with the birth of their first child.

Alwyn and Marion's son Michael was born in Biloela on 5 September 1960. He was the light of their life, a strong and happy baby. By the time he was three weeks old he had joined his parents droving. Marion would drive their Holden utility with all the gear and Michael lying beside her in a bassinet.

Very soon after Michael turned three or four weeks old, they drove 400 bullocks from Baralaba to Chinchilla, a distance of around 250 miles. By the time they got home Michael had spent three months of his first four months of life on the road. He had also had two brushes with danger.

First, a big storm hit them at Knock Break, in the Burnett region between Eidsvold, 250 miles northwest of Brisbane, and Cracow, a town said to be named after the sound a whip makes.

The storm blew fierce as they hunkered down under a swirling tarp that they strung between two trees. Thunder crashed. The wind howled and whipped up a furious maelstrom. When it had passed the only thing they'd lost was Alwyn's hat – never to be found.

A few weeks later, at a property called the Auburn Six Mile, about 80 miles north of Chinchilla, mosquitoes attacked them in hordes. They placed netting around Michael's bassinet and huddled beside it, hiding from the miserable biting insects in the smoke from their campfire.

When seasons are bad, watering spots for travelling stock get further and further apart, and so do the droving camps. Days grow longer and nights shorter. Horses and humans need water sooner than cattle, so a drover sneaks or cadges a drink for their horses or themselves here or there as they travel along the stock route.

On this trip they covered aome 250 miles with the stock and, as felt usual, it was dry. Needing clean water for Michael, Marion asked a station manager if she could have six gallons of fresh water. His curt reply was, 'No. Harden up, get your water from the billabong.'

Marion answered courteously, 'Yes, we do that for ourselves, but this is for my baby and also to keep him in clean clothes.' Then the old cocky softened and the fresh water was forthcoming.

By contrast, a grazier called Billy Bell near Taroom saw the Torenbeeks coming and met them with corned beef and whatever supplies he thought they might need.

Getting water for themselves was one thing. When you are out droving, you also have to have water for your horse – it can't go much beyond two days without a drink before you risk losing it. Sometimes they had to steal it.

Generally, stealing a reasonable amount of water wasn't a problem. Alwyn reckoned, 'If your horses needed a drink and you were johnny-on-the-spot, you'd just go and get it. You may tell the cocky later, but you wouldn't cause any trouble and the cocky wouldn't cause any trouble.' Nobody would begrudge a horse a drink of water – otherwise Alwyn would 'give him a thumpin''.

There were other droving trips for the young family. Alwyn walked one mob of bullocks from an old abandoned town called Piggott, around 40 miles south of Mundubbera in the Burnett, south to Chinchilla, through some of the most interesting country in that part of Queensland.

The route followed the Auburn River for much of the way. Light pink, coarse-grained boulders framed the banks, and the shallow boulder-strewn riverbed was flanked by forest. Along the southern bank of the river grew silver and black ironbark forest and brilliantly hued red gums. Along the steep northern bank Alwyn would cast his eye over softwood scrub punctuated by grey-green Queensland bottle trees. The bottle trees were worth noting, as in times of drought graziers could use the leaves and soft, fibrous tissue of the trunk for cattle fodder.

As Alwyn walked the bullocks ever closer to Chinchilla, Marion took all the packs, hobbles and so on in the ute. That meant that Marion could rattle and bump along the dirty, dusty bush byways and find the campsite well before Alwyn arrived. She could usually get ready in plenty of time to make her droving husband a hot cup of tea when he arrived.

Once in camp, Alwyn would saddle his night horse for the evening. Then early the next morning they'd go through the entire process again.

After they reached Chinchilla, Alwyn paid off the stockmen and was faced with a solo ride home while Marion drove back in the ute. He rode from three in the morning till ten at night to cover 50 miles per day and knock over the trip in five days. It was his longest ride after a droving trip, and he did it in very short time.

The couple worked the stock routes for the remainder of 1960, with baby Michael along for the trip each and every time. That changed in 1961.

That year, Alwyn spent as much time on Myella as possible, helping with maintenance around the property. Bill Torenbeek needed more help as Alwyn's brothers were away at boarding school and the drought still persisted.

However, there were still times when Alwyn would take droving work to help fill the coffers a little. One such job took him away from Myella in early 1962. By that time Alwyn was the father of two sons, Michael and Jeff. Two babies on a droving trip was too hard, so Marion increasingly stayed at home when Alwyn took droving work.

Along with fellow drovers Bill Beazley, Terry Munns and Russell Priestly, Alwyn took delivery of 785 steers, in store condition, at the Baralaba saleyards. Goldsbrough Mort & Co had commissioned them to walk the steers along the stock route to Rosehall on the Auburn River. As the season had been kind and their first seven days of travel were in a fenced lane, mostly 10 chain wide and reasonably grassed, Alwyn felt that four hands would be sufficient.

The first day was an easy crossing of the eastern side of the Dawson River behind Baralaba township. On the second day the team crossed the Dawson River to the south then followed the river up past Gibi Gunah Crossing to camp at Bindaree. The stock was traveling well; there was plenty of feed and water for the cattle, and for the 21 horses.

The third day was rather different. It had been a fairly long day, but they were able to get the stock to creek water before sundown, and then make camp at Kianga Station laneway.

As darkness settled over the landscape, a rhythmic hum of electricity from a new power line asserted itself over the usual symphony of night noises. The constant hum made the drovers feel uneasy, because cattle will rush at even the slightest unusual noise. With the light fading fast they had no chance to find another camp for the night. Instead, they worked hard to settle the steers on the open ground that had been bulldozed for the new power line, but not one beast would lay to rest.

So, to be safe in the event of a cattle rush, they took the horses a full mile up ahead in the three-chain-wide lane and made a camp with the horses hobbled between them and the cattle.

Bill and Alwyn were still worried and decided to each keep a night horse. Every half an hour they'd ride back to the stock to find the mob still restless. They knew this was a tight situation – they could feel the danger.

At half-past ten that evening Bill and Alwyn went back to camp to have a pint of tea and to tell the boys to be ready to move and move quickly. They scarcely had time to drink their tea or secure their tuckerbags when out of the pitch black beyond the fringe of light from their campfire they heard the thunder of 785 cattle rushing – a nightmare noise that grew as if from the bowels of the earth, shaking the ground.

Alwyn had hold of his horse and was just starting to swing onto his saddle when Russell started up out of his swag – but Terry, using Russell as a starting block, pushed him back down and ran. Russell jumped up and started running before his eyes could adjust to the darkness. Smack – the panicked drover ran fair up Alwyn's horse's bum. The impact sent the horse cantering into the darkness and left Bill as the only one riding.

With Russell still staggering about, the whole horse plant thundered through the drovers' camp in a mishmash of galloping horses, bells and hobbles, pounding straight over the fire and tucker gear. One of the packhorses put the most beautiful horseshoe print in an aluminium beef tray just before the panic-stricken steers careered through the camp like a steam train with a swollen pressure valve.

Fortunately the fire split the mob, with about 100 steers following the horses and the main mob swinging right, taking the fence as they hurtled into a paddock.

Bill rode hard to keep up with them as Alwyn raced away after the horses that were in front of the mob going straight ahead. Russell and Terry went over the fence to the left and disappeared into a patch of scrub.

Alwyn's cattle mob pulled up at the same time the horses did – some two miles down the line – but refused to move a step back towards the power lines until well after sunrise.

Bill's mob wouldn't budge until Alwyn had got his mob beyond the camp, which, considering the rampage, wasn't in too bad a shape. They had four dead steers up against logs and two with broken shoulders that couldn't travel any further. It could have been much worse.

Still the stock would not go near the power poles. That meant the drovers had to push the mob out away from the hum of the power lines to be able to move on to Moura. Moura was then only a township wrapped around a railway – little more than the station, butcher shop, general store, post office and a few houses. The travelling stock camp was on the town common, not far out at all.

Alwyn and the drovers knew that the mob, having rushed once, was likely to go again. A rush while they were on the common could be disastrous if hundreds of rampaging cattle ploughed through town.

The railway yards were large and sturdy, so Alwyn went, cap in hand, to the stationmaster to ask permission to use his yards. The stationmaster glowered at the drover and offered a resounding 'No', adding, 'It's a big mob and they'll put dust all over the township area.'

Alwyn smiled and started to leave the station house, then turned slowly and, with as earnest a look as he could manage, explained that the mob had jumped the night before. 'If they go again tonight they may end up in your front lawn or garage,' he said. Then he spun around and made for the door. The stationmaster coughed out, 'Okay, but put them in late and get them out early.'

True to their word, the drovers headed the mob out early and were at the Nipan trucking yards by nightfall. Lonesome Creek saleyards was their next night camp, and the last yard camp for a while, with the lane fencing finishing after the Castle Creek reserve on the Woolton Station boundary.

From that point on the mob travelled as if they'd never rushed, and they marched through Woolton and Camboon stations and on to Moocoorooba, where all the stock had to be dipped and cleared for going into tick-free country. Then on they went through Knock Break, Calrossie, Redbank, Watchbox, Sujeewong, Mt Auburn and finally over to Rosehall, to be delivered to the New South Wales drovers who would carry on over the downs with what was, by then, a beautiful mob of road-broken cattle.

With plenty of work around, by 1962 Alwyn was able to replace the Holden ute he used for droving with a much larger truck. That truck was a godsend. It was a Thames Trader, a slow but fearsome thing whose V8 engine could haul him anywhere. Importantly, it could carry feed and six horses. It also had a 'dog box' above the cabin, in which he'd carry tucker.

On one occasion they were heading home after delivering some droving stock to Taroom. Marion was driving the truck, and Michael and Jeff were beside Alwyn. The two stockmen who had accompanied them were up in the dog box and there were six horses in the back.

They drove out of the Dawson River crossing, but Marion hadn't got the truck down into its low gear, leaving it running too fast. She hit the brakes, the truck jack-knifed and the momentum destroyed the brakes.

After taking a moment to check on everyone, Alwyn took over the driving to get the truck moving again. On the road again, they were climbing over the range – working the gears so as not to tax the truck too much. The thought of pushing too hard and putting a piston through the motor was never far from their minds. As they crested the range, the truck picked up more speed than Alwyn liked and they were fairly floating. The cooees were tumbling out of the poor blokes on top as the truck careered down the range. One of those stockmen was Terry Munns, who went on to become the Aboriginal Council Chairman of Woorabinda – a largely Aboriginal settlement in Central Queensland.

By the waning days of 1962 Bill and Agnes Torenbeek were ready to move off the land. With none of their children either ready or able to take on the property and poor market conditions, Myella was now too small to be a viable proposition, so they sold up. The property passed through two owners in a short period of time before the Eather family bought it and turned it into a successful farmstay attracting many international visitors. Meanwhile, Alwyn bought a humble weatherboard house on the edge of Baralaba.

The dry weather had continued throughout 1961 and 1962, which meant that there had been very little opportunity for much cropping to be done throughout their district. The dry also meant that keeping stock healthy became a major problem as food became scarce and grain silos stood empty or near empty and farm sheds were filled with high-priced hay.

Alwyn kept busy by making sure that his droving plant was ready to go to help graziers move stock along the long paddock to find water and feed. He, and sometimes Marion, moved cattle in all directions right across the vast Brigalow Belt, as mobs of thirsty and hungry cattle were moved for agistment on other properties.

One time Alwyn was droving near Eidsvold, on a station called Calrossie. He was driving 400 bullocks, thinking about his pregnant wife and his sons, when a cocky caught up to him with a telegram.

The message was simple. The drover from Kokotunga was now the father of a baby girl – Shayne Margaret – a pink, 7-pound 3-ounce bundle of joy born on 19 March 1963.

There was no chance of leaving the cattle so Alwyn didn't get to see his baby girl until 10 days later. This was a major disappointment for a young man who had realised right from the announcement of Marion's first pregnancy that being married and raising a family was a serious responsibility. It meant trying to earn a reasonable living to support his young family. After all, maried for all of four years, he now had three children under five years old.

Over the course of 1963, Alwyn moved more than 10 000 head of cattle through the outback and, with the drought far from over, 1964 was even busier. Besides droving work, he and a crew of capable young stockmen kept busy contract mustering in the sandstone country east of Rolleston and throughout the Central Queensland Brigalow Belt.

As the drought tightened its grip, the stock routes became not much more than dusty tracks through the outback with little water to sustain a sizeable mob. That led Alwyn to move his horse plant up to Shoalwater Bay.

The army were taking over the whole area, so the previous owners wanted as many as possible of the wild cattle taken out before settlement. On the coastal country, grass and water were plentiful so Alwyn's team stayed there for the long haul, only leaving to bring the Goomally bullocks home from Maryborough.

Goomally is on the eastern side of the Expedition Range near Repulse Creek. The bullocks were returning because, although the weather hadn't improved greatly, there was enough feed and water to bring back agistment cattle.

By this stage, Brigalow development was in full swing and larger properties were being reduced in size all round the Moura, Bauhinia and Rolleston area. The need to take fresh cattle to new pastures and move other mobs to market kept Alwyn's plant flat strap. They did some very long, dry stretches with big mobs. The longest was a 75-mile ride with 1000 head. By the time that mob got a drink they emptied a 10,000-gallon tank in two hours, with a pump delivering 2000 gallons per hour as well.

Droving in 1964 meant working without Marion following along in the truck. It had become too difficult to manage a mob of unpredictable cattle while they had two toddlers with them and needed to look after baby Shayne as well. So after Shayne was born, Marion gave up droving.

Living on the edge of Baralaba, Alwayn had access to the nearby church paddock, in which he could spell a mob of around four 'travel' horses ready for short droving or mustering work. Each job that came his way would take him away from their tiny home for weeks at a time. Then in the middle of 1964, things changed again. Vonda was born on 21 July 1964. Her arrival made Alwyn re-evaluate his lifestyle and he took his first full-time job contract mustering at Darling Plain, Rannes, with the children going to Banana State School.

Chapter Eleven
ENDURANCE: 1965–1967

Alwyn remembers – a champion con

Working cattle was my life and it changed the life of others. It was the making of my nephew Ted.

In 1966, I took on a job contract mustering cattle on Brackenleigh Station, a rather wild, rough place that backs onto the Expedition Range.

One day my sister-in-law Barbara dropped by our home at Baralaba. Looking somewhat down in the mouth, Barbara explained that she was worried about her eldest son, 14-year-old Ted. Ted was a champion in the boxing ring, having taken out the Queensland schoolboy title, but outside the ring had proved to be a little troublesome. His mother was worried that he'd find himself in trouble if he didn't learn to curb his wilful and potentially wayward ways.

The fact that Ted's father was the Mundubbera baker and worked all night then slept all day compounded the problem. Barb was sure that if I could employ her son, he'd soon learn a little responsibility and settle down.

Now I quite liked the lad, so I said, 'Okay, four dollars a day starting today and oh, by the way, can he ride?'

'Yes,' said Barb, 'he's ridden a fair bit lately.'

For Teddy's first job I asked him to bring a mare called Lindy May up to the saleyards, with me following in the truck so we could then load her. Michael, then six years old, Teddy and I caught and saddled the mare. Teddy mounted up while Michael and I walked off to get the truck. Lindy May was my top bull-catching mare; 16 hands, quiet as long as she wasn't set alight.

I happened to look back, and saw Ted and Lindy May flying! The words 'big trouble now, Michael' just came out of me as I ran to the truck to follow Ted and Lindy May. Michael ran straight into the house to the women, yelling, 'Big trouble now, Mum.' They raced to the veranda to see Teddy disappearing past the saleyards, which were almost a mile away.

I took the old truck as fast as possible past the saleyards up the road towards Moura. Something made me look to a paddock to my right and there sat Teddy, cool and calm on the mare. She had jumped the fence and, realising she had no cattle to muster, stopped running. That was a good introduction for our Ted to what type of horses he would be expected to ride.

Quite a bit later, I was short of fresh horses to take a mob of bullocks from Baralaba to Goomally, so on my way through Mimosa Park I picked up a couple of my spell horses. I told Ted to ride Pee Wee. He replied indignantly, 'I'm not taking him, he's a packhorse!'

'Oh, yes you are,' I said in a commanding voice.

While Ted was begrudgingly saddling Pee Wee, the horse, probably taking his revenge, bit him on the butt. Ted complained, 'This horse is dangerous, he bit me on the arse!'

'Bit you be buggered,' I said. 'He's old and has no teeth.'

Not game enough to contradict me, Ted said, 'Well, he pinches with his lips!'

In time, riding wild horses and mustering cattle were the

making of young Ted. While he was growing into a very reliable young man, canny bushman R.M. Williams was about to make me an endurance rider.

R.M. asked me to ride with his team at the first Quilty Cup endurance ride in 1966. Although I was looking for something sporty to take my mind off roughriding, I was still doing some good rides on tough horses. There didn't seem to be much of a thrill in riding a quiet horse 100 miles. So I passed up on the offer. It was a decision I'm still sorry I made. But R.M. didn't give up on me.

R.M. was judging at the Moura Rodeo in 1967. He made a special effort to catch up to me around the back of the Moura chutes and he said, 'Now, I have the horse for you to ride at the Quilty.' That got my interest and I suspect he knew it. He continued, 'I'm lead-training him because none of us can get him rode. He's beautiful; if you can get him rode he's yours for the Quilty.' He went on to say, 'Torrie, you're the only man in Australia who could ride him when he's bucking and go on to ride him 100 miles.'

I didn't come down in the last shower and knew he was baiting me. I thought, 'now here's a con, but okay, I'll accept it'. So I went to Rockybar to ride and train a horse named Steelo.

He had been hard-fed oats, lead-trained well over 100 miles a week, shod all round, brushed and rugged. I sized him up. It felt as if we were boxers and, having met, shook hands and returned to our neutral corners to think a wee while, we were now both ready to come out blasting. By the end of our tussle, I guess I won on points but we sure had a lot of respect for each other.

The next day he gave me a good battle but was nowhere near as tough. On the third day he was showing only little reminders of his previous aggression. He was my horse for the second Quilty in 1967.

* * *

Alwyn 'The Kokotunga Kid' Torenbeek was a household name around the Central Queensland rodeo circuit. That adulation meant that the 12 months Marion had given him to get rodeo out of his blood was at best a tall order; at worst – near impossible. After all, he'd been riding rough horses since he was a schoolboy racing the train down by Ghost Gully.

What did slow him down, rodeo-wise, was his need to earn a living to keep his family fed, clothed and, eventually, schooled. Over the course of the first half of the 1960s he restricted the few rodeo events he entered to saddle broncs and bulldogging, with a little bit of pick-up work.

It was around this time, in 1965, that the sport of endurance riding took hold in the imaginations of legendary bushman's outfitter Reginald Williams and his wife Erica. R.M., as most Australians remember him, and Erica were living and working on their well-timbered cattle property Rockybar, 50 miles west of Eidsvold.

As well as managing the R.M. Williams business and running cattle on their property, the Williamses were keen horse-breeders busy crossing Arabian stallions with stockhorse-type mares to produce quality workhorses. As if that wasn't enough, R.M. also edited the magazine he had founded, *Hoofs and Horns*.

Hoofs and Horns had grown over the years from a rodeo magazine into a purveyor of many good yarns covering just about anything related to horses, barring thoroughbred racing, and was considered the voice of the equine enthusiast. The readers of *Hoofs and Horns* keenly followed the latest national and international news on dressage, jumping, American Western-style riding and much more. That meant that Erica and R.M. had to keep up with the latest horse news.

One day Erica was scouring the weekly mailbag of overseas publications – magazines like *Horse & Hound*, *Western Horseman* and *The Chronicle of the Horse* – when she came across an article that would change the course of her and R.M.'s life, as well as the lives of many others including that of Alwyn Torenbeek.

The article talked about the Western States 100-Miles-One-Day Ride, commonly called the Tevis. The seed of the idea of an Australian endurance ride was planted and it started to germinate when Erica read another article, on conditioning endurance horses, in the March edition of *Hoofs and Horns*.

Erica was convinced that Australia had the horses and the horsemen and women capable of on taking the challenge, and her enthusiasm for the idea was infectious. R.M. was immediately behind it. He took up the cudgels in the July 1965 edition of their magazine, writing, '*Hoofs and Horns* would be happy to provide a modest purse for something like the 100-mile endurance ride that makes annual news in America. If there are others who would care to contribute in that way, perhaps we could collect £1000 for Australians to match and sort out their champions.'

In October, the ever-determined R.M. devoted his entire editorial to the idea, writing so enthusiastically that anyone coming across the idea for the first time would be sure to be convinced that it was worth backing.

Hoofs and Horns continued firing salvos in the form of articles supporting the merits of endurance riding. By the first sultry days of January 1966, the avid readers of the magazine were learning how to manage a 100-mile one-day ride, and Erica Williams was receiving many letters from keen riders wanting to be involved in endurance riding.

One month later, R.M. wrote in his editorial, 'It is proposed to hold a meeting during the Sydney Royal Show for the purpose of organising the 100-mile endurance ride.'

The same issue ran an advertisement for a 50-mile endurance ride at Dowling Forest Racecourse, Ballarat, on 8 May. That ride was the first Australian endurance ride. Unfortunately, the ride was not well-attended and the committee that established it never staged another ride at Dowling Forest Racecourse.

Looking to learn from the committee's mistakes, R.M. Williams realised that the sport would need a patron or sponsor to provide the essential impetus to make sure that there would be a 'next ride'. The answer came in the form of a rugged bushman 2500 miles away.

The Kimberley is one of the most isolated regions of Australia, and its rugged landscape of ochre-red gorges and mighty waterfalls is unlike any other in the continent. This was the home of respected cattleman Tom Quilty, who owned more than five million acres of cattle country north of the Tropic of Capricorn.

R.M. asked Quilty if he'd like to help out with the purchase of a Gold Cup for the first Australian 100-mile one-day endurance ride. Quilty wrote back saying, 'I am enclosing a cheque for $1000 to purchase a Gold Cup. I will leave everything in your hands. As you suggested, the Cup has to be run for each year, the winner hands it back to be run for the following year . . .' Then, with the business of his letter out of the way, the cattleman added, 'I am 79 today, too bloody old, but I cannot make myself believe it, neither can anybody else.' He signed off with, 'I am in a hurry. All the best to all at Rockybar. May you all enjoy life's pleasures for many years to come. Cheerio old stallion, mine's a rum. Sincerely, Tom Quilty and Olive.' With that letter the prestige Australian endurance-riding event, the Tom Quilty Gold Cup, was born.

R.M. and Erica had their Gold Cup sponsor; now they needed to sort out rules and regulations. They would also need some high-profile riders if the sport were to catch any national attention. A meeting at the Australia Hotel in Sydney sorted out many of the initial rules and regulations, and the committee decided to hold the inaugural event in the ranges of Colo Heights, near Richmond in the Blue Mountains outside Sydney.

Attracting celebrity riders was a less formal process; R.M. clearly knew his fair share and among them was his mate Alwyn Torenbeek – the Kokotunga Kid.

Alwyn had turned down the chance to join the first Quilty Gold Cup ride, but a few well-chosen words from the shrewd bushman had him hooked for the second Quilty in 1967 – especially after his win over the roughest horse R.M. and his Rockybar crew had failed to ride.

It was mid-spring. Twenty-four riders had gathered for the 1967 Tom Quilty 100-Mile Endurance Ride at the Hawkesbury Racecourse in the foothills of the Great Dividing Range.

RSPCA and Animal Welfare League representatives were at each of the checkpoints along the track together with the official timekeepers, who had synchronised their clocks with the Wilberforce Council clock. All was ready.

It was barely past midnight and each rider, including Alwyn, started at one-minute intervals. Not even the light of the moon and the stars lit the nearby crepe myrtles, jacaranda and waratahs, let alone the trail, as they rode away.

Val and Ron Males from New South Wales led off the ride, followed by riders from New South Wales, Tasmania and then another from the host state. Alwyn rode out second-to-last with Erica Williams on the tail end.

As the dawn chorus echoed across the Hawkesbury, the women riders were showing their mettle. Rhonda Ryland on a feisty 11-year-old gelding and Rhoda Sayer on Black Watch arrived at the end of the first leg after just short of five hours in the saddle.

Alwyn, on Steelo, the roughie nobody else had ridden, had started 20 minutes after the first riders and by the end of the first long leg, he and Erica Williams on Stormy landed in equal sixth place.

By the end of the second leg, as the heat of the day was rising, a strategic ride saw Rhonda Ryland still out in the lead, with six out of the first seven riders across the line hailing from Queensland. Among them, Alwyn and Erica were still battling things out in fifth place.

The third leg really started to sort out the riders. As they wound their way through the hilly country, the first rider withdrew after completing a total of 56 miles.

When they were within a half-mile of the end of the leg, two more riders called it a day, exhausted by 9 a.m. Four other riders didn't see the stage finish line until around four-thirty that afternoon, almost five hours after the stage winner, Victorian rider Pam Austin-Carroll.

Meanwhile, Erica was battling for fourth place up against the champion roughrider, both of them coming in 40 minutes behind the Victorian.

The final stage was a fast-paced 16.5 miles, with accomplished riders Rhonda Ryland and Les Bailey powering in off the mountains and sweeping into the valley for equal line honours in just one hour and 17 minutes. Not far behind them was the overall winner for the Gold Cup, Sam Timms on his spritely six-year-old ZigZag.

As for the rodeo champion who had initially scoffed at the idea of wanting to ride 100 miles in one day, he rode across the finish line in fifth place, just two minutes behind Erica Williams, whose canny husband had goaded him into competing. From that ride on, Alwyn was hooked on endurance riding.

Chapter Twelve
ALLAN 'ALDO' ARRIVES: 1968–1969

Alwyn remembers – a new endurance horse

Darling Plain owner Fred Nott and his brother Bill were survivors of the Great War. Both were top bushmen with large landholdings in the Callide Valley and Don River area.

At the age of 78 Fred was riding a beautiful black mare called Loch Linnie. She would and could buck. I was too reticent to suggest that he should let me ride the mare for a minute or two first for him, before the day's work, to give her a chance to settle down.

Early one morning in 1968, she unseated Fred in the horse yard with a king buck. Being a light and nimble 78-year-old he was able to roll down her neck and tumble onto the ground, unhurt. Fred picked himself up, gathered his reins and handed them to me, saying, 'Here you go, she's yours from now on.' Loch Linnie and I got on in fine style and training began for the 1968 Quilty Gold Cup.

Arriving at the Quilty, I found the course to be much the same as the 1967 track, so I was able to train without maps of the area. There was going to be a roughriding rodeo at Bowen

Mountain – the last checkpoint of the ride. So I asked R.M. if he could organise an exhibition bronc ride for me when I came through the checkpoint, while Bill Elwood took my mare to the vet check. After a thoughtful half-hour, R.M.'s answer was 'No, they may put you on something mad and get you hurt.' What a disappointment. I wanted to be the first and perhaps only person to complete a Quilty and a bronc ride on the same day.

But remember, although it doesn't have the same adrenalin rush, endurance riding does have its own demands. There was one point during the 1968 Quilty when a quiet ale was needed to get through the ride.

As I was taking my saddle off at Bowen Mountain they put a stethoscope on Loch Linnie and found she had a high heart rate. That wasn't surprising considering we'd just climbed a mountain.

Perhaps a little worried, R.M. told me to be careful over the last 17 miles and that I should make sure I got through. The sport of endurance riding was depending on this ride's successful completion, as the RSPCA were causing quite a fuss about the horses' safety. I had no trouble keeping Loch Linnie's heart rate low, however. The solution was simple.

I rode steady, easing her right down and singing as we went along. Now, when we were in the vicinity of the North Richmond pub I took time out for a beer. I found a keen lad who was happy to watch her graze along the grassy strip beside the road edge while I quenched my thirst.

That little break refreshed us both and we skipped along to the finish. It is Loch Linnie's buckle that is exhibited in the Longreach Stockman's Hall of Fame. That's even better than riding a bronc and an endurance horse on the same day.

But more importantly than any endurance ride, I remember how one young boy arrived late and surprised us all.

* * *

It was just one minute past midnight on a moonlit night when the first of the 1968 Quilty riders set off near Richmond in New South Wales. That year it was the first long leg that took the ride's first victim.

Frank Bright, the owner of a sheep station and not a strong endurance rider, was representing Western Australia. It seemed the distance of the leg got the better of Frank and made him think seriously about the quality of his saddle. Suddenly more intensely interested in saddles than perhaps he'd ever been before, Frank realised his wasn't quite doing the job and decided to dismount and walk his horse the last 9 miles to Mandalay.

Frank was heard making voluble comments on the various drawbacks of his borrowed saddle until he reached the end of the leg – and the end of his 1968 Quilty. The word was that the despondent shepherd was so sore he'd be having dinner off the mantelpiece for some time after he got home to Western Australia.

Frank's misadventures weren't the only troubles along the route. Shortly before Frank had arrived at Mandalay, a furious farmer had stood out on the track and refused to let a group of young Quilty riders pass any further.

The farmer, almost foaming at the mouth, was convinced that they were the cattle duffers who had been shooting his cows and stealing his bullocks. It took their combined powers of persuasion to convince the livid man that the riders were not thieving or killing his stock and were actually competing in a prestigious 100-mile ride.

Although perplexed as to why anyone would want to suffer 100 miles in the saddle and all in one day, the farmer left them to their ride and returned to his house – to either stand vigil looking out for his cattle duffers or to catch some more sleep, as it was still the very wee hours.

Once again, women led the early stages. At one point the lead women, Sue Scantlebury and Pam Austin-Carroll, were clear of their closest rivals Les Bailey, Erica Williams and Alwyn Torenbeek by a solid 50 minutes.

The riders struggled up a steep climb, then rode carefully down a potentially treacherous incline to Wheeny Creek Reserve. Here, whistling whipbirds and the sound of running water welcomed the riders to their 56-mile checkpoint.

Sue Scantlebury and Pam Austin-Carroll were still riding well in the second half of the ride and, believing they were well clear of their closest rivals, they eased off. Then someone in a supporter's car told them that while they were taking things easier, other riders were whittling away at their 45-minute lead.

Sue, riding Steelo – Alwyn's mount the year before – cracked along at a fair pace after hearing that news. Desperate to keep up, Pam cantered after her. Over the previous 97 miles, Pam had steadily gathered a three-minute advantage over Sue. All she had to do was keep up with Sue and the win was hers. But Pam's cranky and tired horse was having none of it. The mare threw her twice in a short distance, breaking her arm in the process, and ending her chances of taking out the race just 3 miles from the finish line.

That left Sue riding hard, realising that line honours and even the cup was hers if she finished in good time. It was not long after two in the afternoon and the sun was starting to draw long shadows across the valley as Sue rode into view of the cheering spectators waiting by the finishing line. She sat tall in her saddle; surely the win was hers. She was within the last few miles and riding well. The cheer grew louder and echoed out across the Hawkesbury as the determined and skilled endurance rider from Queensland cantered her horse towards the finish line.

Sue and Steelo had just crossed the line when a puff of dust betrayed the fact that another rider was closing in. From over the rise New South Wales rider Les Bailey on his mount Jackass was stretching out for the finish line. A quick time from Les and Sue knew her grip on the Gold Cup for the overall win would be lost.

Les asked everything of Jackass and the superbly fit eight-year-old gelding answered in kind, making remarkable time.

Sue had started as rider number six 100 miles earlier and crossed the line to take line honours. But, with better times across the board, the prized Gold Cup was Les Bailey's.

Les wasn't the only rider to make up time on Sue that afternoon. Erica Williams and her dashing Arab stallion Sheik had shortened her time by 20 minutes on the homeward leg and she crossed the finish line for third.

Having rested his mare while enjoying a beer at a local pub, Alwyn crossed the finish line about an hour after Erica for fourth place. Happy to finish and pleased at the result, Alwyn leant forward and wrapped his arms around Loch Linnie's neck, thanking her for her effort. It was an especially proud ride for Alwyn considering that his treasured friends and owners of Loch Linnie were there to see him ride her across the line.

That year, competitors really got a feel for the importance good strategy makes in winning a 100-mile one-day endurance ride – despite Les Bailey quipping that his secret to winning was 'luck'.

Luck or not, Alwyn's successes in endurance riding still didn't totally replace the thrill of rodeo. He remained part of the rodeo scene, albeit competing far less than he once did.

It so happened that one day while in Rockhampton Alwyn came across a Dingo Rodeo committee member called Arnie.

Arnie was please to see Alwyn. The Dingo Rodeo was the following weekend and, as he explained to Alwyn, they had no pick-up riders. He asked if Alwyn knew anyone who might be able to help – and if he would ride pick-up also.

Alwyn knew of an Aboriginal stockman called Herb Barwick who moved well on a horse, and asked Herb to join him as a pick-up rider at the Dingo Rodeo. To which Herb answered, 'Oh yes, that's my long suit.'

The weekend came and Alwyn and Herb were unloading the horses when Digger Potter and a couple of the roughriders moseyed over to Alwyn and told him they were sure the young bloke helping him had given Chilla Seeney a 'touch-up at Blackall a few weeks back'.

This was quite a piece of news, on two counts. First, Alwyn was never a great chum of Chilla's. Second, if it was true, it was remarkable considering that Chilla was no pushover pugilist. In fact, he was a Golden Gloves finalist and Queensland's 1948 Welterweight Amateur Champion. Alwyn thanked Digger for the tip and put Herb on Darling Plain's prize mare Loch Linnie.

Herb may well have been useful or perhaps lucky in a fistfight, but he seemed to struggle coming to grips with work as a pick-up rider. Each time the chute gates swung open, Herbie would bolt after the bronc right from the jump, as if he were competing in some sort of oversized bulldogging contest, and try to clear the rider from the horse well before the timekeeper could take a second glance at his timepiece.

After each ride, Alwyn would have a quiet word in Herbie's ear and explain that he had to wait until after the rider had secured a 10-second ride before speeding to his aid.

It seemed like Herb was being just a little too enthusiastic after he prematurely collected the first roughrider. It was unfortunate after the second, irresponsible after the third and beyond stupidity by the time he had interrupted a good rider in the middle of enjoying a high-kicking and potentially high-scoring ride.

No amount of explaining settled Herb, so before he could hurry out on Loch Linnie to the 'rescue' of a fifth rider, Alwyn found himself having to relieve the keen stockman of his pick-up rider status. As it turned out the Elwood twins, Bill and Jim, who were Darling Plain stockmen and were regular rodeo roughriders and pick-up men, happened to be at the rodeo that day. Alwyn seized the opportunity and replaced Herb with the twins, who promptly sorted things out for the rest of the day.

After the Dingo Rodeo, Alwyn's rodeo opportunities and endurance-riding chances were limited – to say the least. That year, he missed seeing feisty gelding Jackass carry 17-year-old John Coyle from North Eelah across the line at the Quilty Gold Cup. Nor did he see Marion Robie, the granddaughter of Wendell Robie, the founder of the Tevis Cup in the USA, ride across the line in third place on his old mount Steelo. That was because in 1969, a truly fearsome drought ravaged Central Queensland.

The family drew on every available resource at Darling Plain Station to combat the drought. Although they were still young boys, Michael and Jeff were already capable of helping Alwyn around the property each weekend.

As the wretched drought turned pasture into dust and hopes and dreams blew away on the scorching winds, Alwyn, Marion and their sons worked every waking hour just to keep their stock alive, carting water and hay and providing 'stock lick' to give the cattle the energy, protein and salts they needed to prevent a variety of disorders. Newborn calves were even taken from their mothers to be hand-fed. Rodeo and endurance riding were out of the question.

The last really useful rain fell in September 1968 and nothing of worth had fallen since. Although the family fed the calves by hand, still the weaker ones died. Getting to town meant travelling along corrugated, rocky tracks that had been desiccated by the hot dry winds. Around the property trees shed leaves like tears. Sometimes the dust-devil wind swirled up the remnant topsoil, sending great clouds of it onto everything – cars, machinery, sheds, homesteads and people.

Then, as if that wasn't enough, fate dealt the Torenbeeks a cruel hand.

It was early 1969 and Marion was pregnant, and sure that she was carrying a girl. Alwyn had just finished butchering their regular kill to provide the station with fresh beef and, still covered in blood from the butchery, had decided that he'd shoe Loch Linnie before returning to the house to wash up.

The family owned a docile horse called Red Robin. He was a beautiful gelding, handsome, the children's favourite and gentle to boot. Marion and Alwyn's youngest daughter Vonda, in particular, had taken a real shine to Red Robin. They were quite a pair – almost inseparable.

The kids were encouraged to do their fair share around Darling Plain, and three-year-old Vonda was no different. To encourage her enthusiasm for looking after Red Robin, Alwyn and Marion had bought their daughter a new brush with which to groom the horse.

While Alwyn's attention was focused on shoeing Loch Linnie, Vonda quietly collected her horse brush and toddled down to Red Robin, who was feeding. Vonda, keen to groom her horse, reached forward to start brushing the gelding's hind legs.

Nobody knew that Vonda had toddled down to the horse. No one had noticed her collect Red Robin's brush or walk up behind him – least of all Red Robin. He didn't notice her until she reached out and stroked his hind legs. Then one awful sound rose above all the others, including the sound of Alwyn shoeing Loch Linnie – the dull, bloodcurdling thud as Red Robin kicked, and made contact with the little girl's skull, fracturing it.

The startled horse had meant no harm. He had just lashed out, instinctively, at whatever had snuck up on him and touched his leg.

The kick made Vonda's head snap backwards violently and sent her flailing into the yard.

Alwyn heard the dreadful thud. He turned. Vonda lay motionless on the ground on the other side of the yard fence. Alwyn's heart sank. He sprinted to his unconscious daughter's side, collected her in his bloodstained arms and carried her swiftly into the house.

Marion pleaded with him to do something. Distraught and almost frozen with despair, Alwyn found himself saying, 'It's too late. She's going to die.' As he said it, he knew that if his daughter died he'd feel like dying also.

Alwyn laid Vonda gently on the lounge and raced outside to the car with another stockman. Even in the late 1960s communication in the bush was woefully inadequate. Darling Plain had no telephone. The closest phone was just over a mile away along a rutted bush road. The closest ambulance was around 50 miles away at Biloela.

After tearing away to the phone, calling the ambulance, then returning to collect Vonda, they hurried off to meet the ambulance somewhere along the godforsaken track to Biloela.

The stockman picked his way along the melon-holed road, balancing as best as he could their need to save Vonda's life and the maximum speed the road would allow. After about 25 miles they met the Biloela ambulance.

Surrounded by scrub, with another 25 miles left to go, they transferred Vonda into the ambulance. To Alwyn, each precious second seemed eternal.

Alwyn climbed into the ambulance with his daughter and they sped onwards to Biloela. Somewhere along the road the little girl rolled her face towards her father and puked – if nothing else, as far as Alwyn was concerned, this showed that she was prepared to fight to live. So he wasn't about to fret about now being covered in puke, as well as blood.

Biloela was just coming of age in 1969. It had its own water supply, a meatworks, an engineering works, bulk fuel depots, local manufacturing and a Penney's variety store, all serving a population of around 3000. It also had the small but important hospital in which Vonda had been born. Unfortunately, Vonda's fractured skull was too much for a basic country hospital – the ambulance was told to take her on to Rockhampton. That meant travelling as fast as possible along treacherous and windy roads for a further 100 miles through the Mount Morgan Range.

The day gave way to night. Alwyn had no money on him and was still covered in blood and vomit as they sped towards Rockhampton.

When the ambulance finally wheeled into the main entrance of the hospital, nurses, doctors and hospital porters, many of whom Alwyn knew because of his occasional visits with rodeo injuries, scurried to Vonda's aid.

Alwyn was beside his daughter all the way from ambulance trolley to hospital gurney and then rapidly into X-ray. After hours of torturous travel, confidence in Vonda's recovery slowly started to fill his mind.

It was an interminable wait before a doctor spoke to Alwyn, telling him the news he had been longing to hear: 'You're out of the woods. Vonda will be okay.'

Later, Alwyn was sitting beside his daughter's bed when two young doctors interested in her case approached. Without asking Alwyn if they could examine his daughter, they asked a nurse to sit the girl up. Nodding in Alwyn's direction, the nurse replied, 'She'll do anything that her father asks her to do.'

Riled by the young doctors' arrogance, Alwyn growled, 'I'm going to strangle someone if you don't get out of here.' The doctors took one look at the bloodstained parent and decided that discretion was indeed the better part of valour; they sped away without another word.

It was a few weeks before Vonda could return to Darling Plain, but she did so fit and well, as if nothing had ever happened.

Around six months later fate rolled the dice again and came up with a more pleasant surprise – Marion gave birth to a baby boy.

Alwyn was away working Darling Plain cattle on the long paddock when his third son, a golden-haired boy named Allan, was born. It was 11 June 1969. The couple gave their new baby the name his father had used in his early rodeo days.

It was 48 hours before Alwyn made it home to hold his baby boy and see Marion. Cradling her new baby in her arms, Marion joked that considering Alwyn'd been away droving while she raised the other children, 'This one's yours.'

From about the time he could walk, Aldo, as he became known, and Alwyn were close. The boy would go everywhere with his father when he was working in the paddock, and by the time he was four years old he could ride a hell of a long way on Red Robin. The young lad idolised the placid gelding.

The horse wasn't the only animal for which Aldo developed a remarkable affinity. The family had a cur of a dog called April. She had all the traits of a station dog – she was often tetchy, extremely loyal, hardworking and a prolific breeder as well. She'd snap at anyone given half a chance, and generally played no favourites. Aldo was her only exception.

Like all boys, Aldo was occasionally mischievous. Whenever Marion caught him committing some misdemeanour or other, he'd cop a reprimand from her, then hurry off to seek solace from April. Recognising that the boy was upset, the bitch would pick up one of her pups by the scruff of the neck and offer it to him as if it were a toy for him to play with.

One day Aldo decided that April's pups were looking a tad dirty and carted them to the washhouse tubs to give them a thorough scrub. He was going well, with a tubful of pups soaking in cold water, when Marion wandered into the washhouse.

Instead of joining in the Aldo's pride at keeping April's pups clean, Marion saw nothing but a large litter of pups all freezing cold and in various stages of drowning. Incensed, she scolded her son and got to work drying and warming each pup, then returned them to their mother. Soon afterwards she discovered Aldo with his head snuggled up against April's tummy, and the other pups nuzzled around him.

The hard times and their growing family had forced the Torenbeeks to consider leaving Darling Plain Station to move closer to schools and the sort of amenities that young families need.

But Fred and Nancy Nott had given Alwyn his first real job away from Myella and the roughrider had felt a great deal of respect and admiration for them ever since. He could also see that the drought of 1969 was taking its toll on the old war veteran.

Fred watched helplessly as once healthy cattle's bodies hollowed out, their skin stretched over bony frames. All the while he, Nancy, Alwyn and Marion worked day in and day out trying to save them.

Then one October morning the sun pushed its light through thick, inky clouds loaded with rain. The humidity rose, the wind grew and a thunderclap marked the breaking of the drought.

There was a clump of blue gums that stood not far from the homestead. The gums had died decades earlier during what was known as the Federation Drought. The Federation Drought had started in January 1898 and didn't let up until Christmas 1902, when violent storms sent life-giving rains across the eastern states. Now those same gums were riddled with witchetty-grub holes and as the wind rose, the trees started to whistle as if they were a stand of giant clarinets.

When the first drops of rain fell and moistened the ground below his feet, the old grazier strolled over to Alwyn, who was down by the stockyards.

The two men stood side by side for a moment, listening to the whistle of the wind through the blue gums and the patter of the rain on the hard, baked ground. Then the old man turned to Alwyn with a smile that had waited a year to form.

'Things are about to change. This is how the drought of 1902 broke,' Fred declared. He was right – things were about to change, for the better. In October 1969, as in December 1902, it was as if the heavens had seen the sorrow of the drought and wept for every life it'd taken. Its tears swept across Darling Plain.

Chapter Thirteen
DEATH BECOMES ME: 1970–1980

Alwyn remembers – leaving my foolhardy past

My last bronc ride was in 1970. I was able to get to Dingo where the great Spring Hill was lurking. Spring Hill was an impressive horse, worthy of being my last ride. A tall, handsome gelding of around 16 hands, he was a buckjumper that had only rarely been ridden. I went there thinking there was a chance I'd get a ride on him, and that chance came my way.

It was quite a thrill to be asked considering I was now 12 years off my best. I didn't expect to get an offer on him, but I got there and nobody wanted him. Three younger riders had passed him over on the day – higher credentialed riders than I was at the time. Did I knock it back? Like bloody hell.

Riding Spring Hill was more than a passing ambition; I'd certainly entertained the idea for a little while. Taking on Spring Hill, I'd decided, would be the marker that would end my time as a roughrider. If I succeeded in riding him, I'd put away my roughriding days once and for all. If I'd not ridden Spring Hill, I might have had to consider competing as a roughrider for a while longer, as we're only remembered for our last encounter. That's the case in any competition sport be it boxing, swimming, tennis, whatever. I would give the ride my all and ask Spring Hill to do the same.

Marion had wanted me to give up roughriding for some time, although she was never vindictive about it. But giving up something like rodeo cold turkey had proved to be very difficult. The coming of drought and flood had sometimes slowed me down; the arrival of my children had certainly made me consider my future – but rodeo was my life.

I remember I didn't tell Marion that I'd planned that Spring Hill would be my last ride, just in case I didn't succeed in riding him. But by luck he came my way, so when I got home I was able to tell Marion she had seen the last of my foolhardy past. That's the way it was.

* * *

It was hot, unbearably hot, in the first two weeks or so of January 1970, and nowhere more so than in the rodeo arena at Dingo. Alwyn had taken on Spring Hill, the horse that would be Australian champion twice in three years – first in 1968, then in 1970.

The Dingo rodeo chute opened and Spring Hill went out hard, bucking, twisting and kicking as if bouncing on steel springs. The rodeo crowd cheered, whooped and hollered with each bone-twisting jump or kick, with each jarring buck. In the middle of most high kicks, Spring Hill would flip at Alwyn's left boot with his head, trying to force him to give up some rein by unbalancing him, and then attack his right boot, hoping to unseat him. Yet, the Kokotunga Kid held on.

So impressive was his balance, his dexterity as he rode forward in the saddle, weaving and moving to the chaotic rhythm of the great beast, that even the timekeeper temporarily forgot to watch the clock. The sheer athletic ability of both horse and rider had riders and spectators all around the arena mesmerised.

That day, the Kokotunga Kid – the boy who had dreamed of becoming a champion roughrider while racing the Rockhampton train through Ghost Gully, while working rough horses with names like Yellow Lad, while suffering beatings at school; whose riding had allowed him to explore more of this wide brown land than most folk of the era ever saw and who through it all had so doggedly followed his dream – walked away from the Dingo Rodeo a champion. He'd ridden the magnificent Spring Hill for 11 seconds, entertaining the crowd one last time and finishing his rodeo career in the ring in which he'd won his first significant rodeo ribbon.

Alwyn's life was about to change in several other ways too. It was in the air.

For seven years Australians had been shocked by the bloody conflict in Vietnam, as around 60,000 diggers battled in a war few understood. Hundreds of thousands of anti-war protesters were in full swing by 1970, taking part in the moratorium marches that were sweeping the globe. The largest Australian march saw 100,000 protesters take to the streets of Melbourne.

The chair of the Vietnam Moratorium, Jim Cairns, summed up the sentiment of the marchers, saying, 'Our spirit is opposed to violence, opposed to every motive that has produced this terrible war.' Men, women and children marched 60 abreast, singing 'we shall overcome'.

That charged social and political atmosphere persisted well into the seventies, permeating all areas of Australian life. By 1971, the Torenbeek family was also facing an upheaval of sorts.

The new year had started positively with the breaking of the drought. That meant Fred and Nancy Nott would recover on Darling Plain, and Alwyn and Marion could move closer to schools for their kids. So they moved to New Waloon Station, and then to

Woolton Station, only 18 miles from the Theodore school.

Woolton, a 30,000-acre property with approximately 4000 head of Hereford cattle, was one of the first settled properties in Banana Shire. It was a great place for a bush family like the Torenbeeks.

Sadly, Bill Torenbeek never set foot on Woolton. After selling Myella, Bill and Agnes had moved into Baralaba. Bill had taken up driving the local school bus and Agnes had bought a haberdashery. They'd been doing well and seemed hale and hearty.

One day, around a week after Alwyn, Marion and their family had moved to Woolton Station, Bill had just finished his route and stepped out of his bus when he collapsed. A blood clot had blocked the blood supply to a large part of his brain, causing a stroke. Later, in hospital, another stroke hit him. This time, he did not recover.

It was, Alwyn said, as if a lifetime of toil had worn him out.

Grief marked those first few weeks on Woolton for the entire family. Yet in the main they kept it to themselves; each shouldered their own burden of grief and in typical stoic fashion got on with making Woolton their home.

As their sadness subsided, the Torenbeeks began to realise how good life could be on Woolton. Beyond providing easier access to schools for the younger children, it provided horse and cattle work for the eldest boys. This was not without its dangers, though, as Jeff discovered in January 1972.

The 10-year-old was helping muster the Woolton cattle when his horse decided to drop its head and kick its hind legs into the air. Despite Jeff's skill as a rider, the mare threw him from his saddle – but he wasn't thrown free of the horse. One foot was caught in the stirrup and the mare continued to drag him for a short distance around the paddock as if he were a rag doll.

Alwyn raced over to his son, who was lying on the ground moaning in pain. He collected Jeff in his arms and carried him about a mile to the station's Land Rover, whispering to his son all the way, telling him that he'd have him to hospital as soon as he could and not to worry.

With the boy safely secured in the Land Rover, Alwyn drove fast through the back country to the Theodore hospital. He had had the presence of mind to phone ahead from a neighbouring homestead, so a doctor and a nurse were waiting for him to arrive. The Land Rover made good time and Alwyn stopped by the hospital entrance and carried his son inside.

The waiting doctor and nurse eased Jeff onto a hospital bed and got to work repairing his injuries – and they were many.

When the mare had dragged him across the paddock – for about 15 feet – rocks and stones had lacerated his face and one leg had been badly dislocated. By the time the mare had kicked Jeff free, she'd put a hoof through his ribs. So deep were the lacerations around one eye that the doctor had to use 15 stitches to suture his flesh back to where it belonged.

A few weeks later, Jeff had almost fully recovered, although the leg that'd been dislocated took the best part of two years to come completely good.

Despite Jeff's accident, mustering around Woolton Station remained a family affair, with all the Torenbeek kids involved, including Shayne and Vonda. Of course, mustering wasn't the only source of excitement for the kids. Even little Aldo readily found his own adventures.

All the other children were going to school by the time Aldo was two years old, so he was his father's shadow. Alwyn would take him out all day on water runs or to stock feed-outs, delivering hay and lick.

One day, after Aldo had turned three, Alwyn took him over to the two-mile windmill. The two-mile windmill was close to the main road, and at this time there were roadworks nearby.

Alwyn was up on the mill's fan head, oiling the bearings, when he saw two of the roadworkers staring oddly at him. Their faces registered pure horror. 'Surely,' Alwyn thought, 'they've seen a man up a windmill before?'

While he was mulling this over, he heard a little voice say, 'Me up here, Dad.' Alwyn was above the windmill platform on the cradle, around 35 feet off the ground. He gingerly looked down the ladder and there below him, at least 30 feet off the ground, was Aldo smiling up at him.

Alwyn caught his breath and reminded himself not to panic. After all, if he panicked, he reckoned, Aldo would panic too. Instead, he forced the closest thing to a smile he could manage across his face and said in a nice calm voice, 'Me best get down now, 'cause I'm getting down too!' Sometimes kids on a station learn lessons all by themselves, and not always when you expect it.

Michael, Jeff, Aldo, Shayne and Vonda all loved getting out into the bush to help around the property or just to enjoy the freedom. In fact, they loved being in the bush more than they enjoyed visiting town.

Regularly, the boys would jump on little 100cc motorbikes, the girls would hop into an old Holden panel van, and they'd head off to one of three bush camps they'd established around the station.

Each of the bush camps had its individual character. There was the Fairy Camp about 3 miles from the homestead, which was made out of cut bushes like an Aboriginal gunyah. Six miles from the homestead the Honeymoon Hut was set in a beautiful little glade. And just 2 miles from the homestead on a little rocky mound, in the middle of a rock wallaby habitat, was Wallaby Hut. Each camp was set up with enough rough gear for the kids to stay overnight, which they often did on weekends or whenever the fancy took them – so long as they'd done their work around the station.

The Torenbeeks' life on Woolton was in many ways the very epitome of the free and easy outback life. From time to time, however, they'd get a little bit of an unexpected shake-up. That happened one day in early 1974, when the family were pretty much still finding their way on Woolton.

The phone rang and it was Herb Barwick looking for work. Never one to stand by when someone was doing it tough, Alwyn agreed to put Herb on, saying, 'No worries, start as soon as you can get here.'

Herb arrived soon afterwards and got to work. Everything was going well until he collected his second pay cheque and teamed up with the head stockman. Both stockmen liked to drink.

By that Sunday afternoon, the two men had hunkered down in the shade by the engine room and got busy downing quite a few beers. When Alwyn found them, he frowned and reminded them that they needed to be bright and alert to muster 300 bulls at three the next morning.

Herb answered Alwyn by knocking the top off another tall bottle of beer and sucking down a long swig. Incensed, Alwyn glared at the stockmen, telling them they'd be no good for work.

Fearing the sack, the head stockman bounced up and took a wild swing at Alwyn, who promptly landed a one, two, three combination that put the stockman on his bum. Herbie rose to his feet and struck a proper boxing stance. Alwyn readied himself for a no-holds-barred bare-knuckle stoush. And it was on.

Fists and feet, blow for blow they went, tussling 60 feet. Herbie'd flow a combination; Alwyn'd counter with his own barrage. The champion would be struggling to stay on his feet, then his opponent would find himself staggering. And it wasn't all bare-knuckle boxing either.

Herb was as tough as they came and Alwyn had to throw everything at him, kicking at his knees, the full works – and Herb responded in kind. No wrestling; it was stand-up blow for blow. After what felt like ten rounds, Alwyn had Herb pinned to the wall and Herb went down – to Alwyn's great relief. Alwyn kept Herb down with a bare foot on his neck, then told both men to 'finish off things, and then pack ya gear'.

Michael and Jeff, who were expecting action, had planted themselves in the engine room to watch the fray and enjoyed the show. For a long while after they'd tell the story to anyone who'd listen.

When everyone had cooled down, Alwyn reinstated the two blokes. Herb's response to being reinstated was, 'Good, you're a fair and just man, just a man and a fair bastard.'

They were all too sore to work that Monday, but they got the bulls mustered on Tuesday, then both stockmen gave their notice, finishing up on the weekend.

About a year later, in April 1975, providence dealt the family a hard blow. Alwyn and Michael were preparing to load horses onto a truck to take to the Theodore country races. Alwyn bent down to pull the bottom pin on the truck gate to slide it open; at precisely the same time the truck driver, worried that the truck wasn't square onto the loading ramp, threw the truck into reverse. The gate pin pierced Alwyn's skull as his head was crushed between the truck on the right side and the ramp rail on the left.

His daughter Shayne's memories of that day are still vivid. 'First of all the ambulance had already rung that morning because they were the beneficiaries of the charity race. They were ringing asking where the horses were because we hadn't arrived – the truck was running late. Then the truck arrived. It seemed we'd not long hung up the phone when we heard Dad yelling to get the doctor.

'Mum then had to ring them back saying she didn't know what had happened, but it must be something bad because she could hear them calling for her to get the doctor. Then she went down to see.'

With Shayne trailing along behind her, Marion raced from the house. Michael caught sight of her and called out, 'Get the doctor.

Get the car and get the doctor.'

Marion called the ambulance back immediately and arranged to meet them en route to Theodore. Then she sprinted to fetch the car from the shed.

Michael noticed Shayne running towards the loading ramp. 'What's happened? What's wrong with Dad?' she asked.

Desperate to shield his sister from the horrible sight of her father's injuries, Michael hollered at Shayne, 'Get back in the house.'

By this time, Marion had brought the car as close as possible to her husband and was kneeling by his side, knowing that 18 miles separated her from the ambulance station at Theodore. If her husband was to live, there was no time to dawdle.

Frantic to get back to his parents, Michael had no time to explain, nor could he have found the words even if he'd felt able. So he started pegging stones at his sister.

Taken aback, Shayne stopped in her tracks and with her heart racing, unable to imagine what might have caused her brother to react so violently, asked again, 'What's happened? What's wrong with Dad?' This time her voice was shriller and more anxious. But Michael persisted with the barrage of rocks.

Shayne realised there was nothing to be gained from arguing with her brother and ran into the house, her face awash with tears.

Meanwhile, Vonda had heard someone yelling to 'get the doctor' and wandered towards the stockyard to see what all the fuss was about. When she saw her father with blood streaming from his head she took fright and ran and hid under the pakalaka trees, where she could see what was happening without risking being in the way.

Vonda watched as Marion and Michael eased Alwyn from the loading ramp into the back of the station wagon.

Marion steadied herself in the back of the car with her husband and readied herself for a long drive, holding his head still and together over every wretched bump, dip and pothole as Michael drove the station wagon to meet the ambulance somewhere along the track to Theodore.

Sometime after they left the stockyards, somewhere along the track, his voice barely audible above the din of the roaring engine, Alwyn told his wife, 'I'm not going to make it this time.' He was farewelling the woman he loved.

They were about halfway between Woolton Station and Theodore when Michael stopped the car, sending a swirl of dust wafting down the track. Then they had to wait for several unbearable minutes as the ambulance crew scrambled out of the converted Ford F-100 ambulance and swung open the truck's double back doors.

Looking down from somewhere above, Alwyn felt he was with his deceased father. For the few minutes that it took them to transfer him from the family station wagon to the ambulance, Alwyn was pain-free and enjoying his father's company once more. Then his father gestured to him to return to his body – death would have to wait. That was the start of Alwyn's battle to live.

Alwyn's near-death experience on the road to Theodore was not the only time he had the feeling of being away from his body. It happened again during the first few hours of his time in Rockhampton Hospital and also while the radiographer X-rayed his head.

During one of those episodes he watched as his doctor told Marion that Alwyn's chance of survival was 'fifty-fifty'. At which point he thought, 'Wow, that sounds all right to me. I thought it was about 10 per cent.'

The bush telegraph, that notorious purveyor of country gossip, news and half-truths, started broadcasting the story of Alwyn's accident, if not from the moment it happened, almost immediately after. The news had an unexpected effect on the business folk of Theodore.

Then, as now, it was customary for station families to take credit from the shopkeepers of their local town, paying their bills at regular intervals thereafter – usually monthly. From the moment the bush telegraph carried the news of Alwyn's injury around the Theodore community the affable temperament of the town traders changed.

With Alwyn recovering in hospital, it wasn't too long before Marion needed to collect her monthly supplies – all the usual things, groceries, bread, some fruit and vegetables. It was the first time she'd been to town since her husband's accident, and Marion walked into the bakery with the worry of Alwyn's uncertain recovery weighing heavy on her shoulders. The shopkeeper met her with a thin-lipped, insincere sort of smile and said, 'You will need to settle your account, please, Marion.'

It seemed the Torenbeeks were all out of credit in Theodore.

As Alwyn's convalescence continued, the bush telegraph sent whispers to Woolton Station that the community was fundraising to support the family. But when Alwyn recovered, the funds they had raised disappeared without the Torenbeeks seeing a single cent.

By the time Alwyn heard about the disappearing funds it didn't matter, because he still had his station job and could still provide for his family. The biggest concern was the fact that the station workmen wouldn't cooperate with Marion or the family. That was a matter he'd have to sort out when he returned to work.

Six weeks passed before Alwyn was allowed some respite from hospital. He went home for two days. In those six weeks, none of his children had seen him – Alwyn had asked Marion to keep them away for fear of distressing them. Except for Michael, his kids had no real idea of the danger he'd been in. After all, Michael had chased Shayne back into the house, Vonda had kept away hiding under the trees and Jeff and Aldo had been playing elsewhere.

After six weeks of fielding the caring questions of schoolmates or other Theodore locals who'd ask after Alwyn whenever they came across a family member, Shayne was keen to welcome her father home. Some of the questions she'd had to answer had puzzled her, as she had never seen her father's injuries and the accident had not been discussed among the family. So, expecting to see her father's familiar smiling face, Shayne ran out of the front door and over to the car, with her younger sister Vonda trailing along behind her – both girls excited to see their father.

Instead of their father, though, the girls saw only a hideous man in sunglasses leaning on the car to keep his balance. 'That's not my father,' they both thought. 'I want that man to get straight back in the car and go. That's not my father.'

The girls knew their father never wore sunglasses. And as for the face they saw behind the glasses, well, it was all dropped, sunken away like a sack of potatoes. They didn't know this stranger and they certainly didn't want to see him for one moment longer than necessary.

Tears welled up in Shayne's eyes. Up until that moment, she had been okay with Alwyn being in hospital. After all, he'd spent days or weeks away from home droving. He'd even been to hospital before.

The appearance of that disfigured man confirmed the one thing she hadn't had to face – her father was clearly seriously ill, injured beyond her imagination. And, for the moment, injured beyond the imagination of any of the children, except Michael.

The Torenbeek children now had to deal with the heart-wringing misery of watching their father, usually a fit, active man, fight the battle of his life to walk, talk, laugh, ride and live again.

Shayne didn't find out the details of the accident until years later when she was riding in the back of her uncle's car on the way to a local race meeting. Alwyn had gone ahead, and Shayne and Marion had caught a lift with Alwyn's sister Daphne and her husband. When the conversation turned to Alwyn's truck accident on a similar race day years ago, Marion opened up, letting out every detail as if relieved to have someone with whom she could talk about Alwyn's ordeal. She'd forgotten that there was someone else riding in the back of the car who knew little of her father's suffering. Someone who, like the rest of the family, loved him dearly.

As Marion told the story of the accident and Alwyn's recovery, Shayne wept in silence, turning her head to the window so that neither her mother nor her aunt and uncle would catch her crying. Until that moment she'd thought she had little or no reason to cry. 'Mum had never let on about all the worry,' she later recalled. 'She actually said then that she didn't know what she was going to do if Dad hadn't come back. And I had no idea until then.'

Shayne allowed the sadness she felt to subside, not speaking about it until the best part of three decades later. Her reaction was a powerful indicator of how long it took the family to really recover from the blow. They were used to the ups and downs of life in the bush. Accidents were part of that life. But this one had hit hard at the heart of the family.

After being discharged from hospital, Alwyn stayed with his mother in Rockhampton while he was in rehabilitation. Altogether, it was three months before he was given the all-clear to return home. He was told he'd never work again.

He'd been home about 18 months when he turned to Marion and said, pointing towards the cattle roaming in one of Woolton's paddocks, 'We've got to get this paddock mustered.'

Marion's response was swift. She frowned and said, hitting each word as if it were a gong, 'You've got to be joking.' Alwyn was serious.

He saddled a newly broken horse called Dargan, adjusted the eye patch he was wearing to protect his one particularly troubled eye and rode out to muster his cattle. Shayne saddled up and rode beside her father.

'He didn't stop coming off him all day,' Shayne said, years later. 'He'd come off. Then before I could ride over to him he'd say, "Just stay there." He was always being bucked off. But he knew Dargan wouldn't run away if I didn't let my horse get near him. It was the worst day.'

Shayne followed her father, working the cattle as they went, watching as time and again Dargan would throw him to the ground. Time and again he'd insist his daughter stay away while he caught the horse and got on again. As she followed she wept at the sight of this remarkable horseman struggling to keep his seat.

Of course, Shayne wasn't the only one of Alwyn's children to feel the impact of his accident. They all felt it, especially Michael, who had driven his dying father to hospital and looked after his sister by chasing her away from the scene of the accident. For years afterwards, even after the family had moved to Planet Downs Station, if Alwyn went missing for a while Mike would start to worry.

As time passed, however, worries and wounds healed. Two years went by, and Alwyn slowly recovered his strength and horsemanship. His love of riding – and of rodeo – was undimmed. He was working for the Theodore Rodeo committee when someone on the committee had the bright idea that they'd be able to raise more money if the former champion roughrider put in an exhibition ride at the rodeo.

The fact that he was just short of 40 years old didn't bother Alwyn. He still felt remarkably fit despite it being around eight years since his ride on Spring Hill. And he wasn't too worried about taking on the ride with his old head injuries. His attitude was that when you've had an injury 'you don't break at the weld'. So he accepted the ride.

It was June of 1977 and advertising banners all over the district announced that the Kokotunga Kid was once again the featured rider at a rodeo.

By this stage, Michael had already cornered Alwyn, saying, 'I want to ride a bronc at the next rodeo.' Not wanting to be seen to be encouraging the lad, Alwyn had said, 'No chance.' Then, after letting that sink in, he added, 'But if you feel that way, practice starts tomorrow.'

Mirroring his own preparation all those years earlier, he and his sons Jeff and Mike went about building a full-scale arena near the homestead, put 15 horses together, and selected their pick-up horses. Then, at every available moment, Alwyn took his boys through his own rodeo school.

The former champion was training hard to get into shape and keep up with his sons. They had turned the lounge room of a vacant house on Woolton into a gym, and Alwyn put in many hours there preparing for his feature ride.

When the rodeo rolled around, Alwyn thrilled the Theodore audience with the same athleticism he'd shown 20 years earlier. He rode for 10 seconds or so of thunderous high kicks and jarring bucks without a single thought for his fragile skull. He just enjoyed the moment, soaking up the cheers.

Chapter Fourteen
BUSH SCHOOLS: 1980–1990

Alwyn remembers – school starts

In 1980 the Department of Aboriginal and Islander Affairs approached me to run stockmanship training courses for underprivileged youngsters. Their plan was to have us teach 12 pupils for 12 weeks, 24 hours a day, seven days per week. Always up for a challenge, we took their proposal on.

The mob of four from the department had been looking for suitable families and properties for a year or so and numerous landowners had directed them to Woolton, telling them about my reputation as a horseman.

We soon worked up a plan. My two older boys were to help with outside training, Marion would coordinate the students and Vonda would be working in the shop to provide the students with any extra necessaries such as toothpaste and brushes, tobacco, lighters and soft drinks. Shayne, by this time, was boarding at St Ursula's College in Yeppoon.

Woolton was one of the early Cobb and Co horse-change stations for the carriages en route to Banana in the east and Taroom to the southwest. In those early days in the 1800s it had a shanty, or slab hut with shingle roof, that sold grog.

Although the grog had long gone, the old shanty was still on the station, now with galvanised-iron roofing. We could make use of it as a carport, but needed to build other facilities, so we built an ablution block with concrete floors, double showers, flush toilets, washing machines and a mess room under the big house.

The big house was once a girls' dormitory from the Mount Morgan hospital and had 25 small rooms, but we took a chainsaw to some of the walls and cut the number of rooms in about half.

The girls at Woolton were quartered in one large room upstairs that we reclaimed from three rooms in the station workers' quarters. Then we connected 240-volt power for lighting, and plumbed in hot and cold water.

We already had a well-equipped tack room with a plentiful supply of horses for the brave and not-so-brave kids we'd get. For those who were not cut out to be horse people there was always the chance to learn alternative skills like fence work, yard building and so on.

It only took about two weeks to put the idea into operation. Our first group of 12, 10 boys and two girls, came from all over Queensland. My first stockmanship school at Woolton was a great success.

It was as if the students realised that we were also finding our way, that the school to some extent was a trial-and-error experiment. They were good students and we had 100 per cent success placing them in jobs.

I particularly remember two students from the Woolton School, the third school, Raymond and Eileen. Raymond arrived from western Queensland along with 11 other boys and girls from all parts of the state. Eileen was a local girl from Theodore; she was afraid of large animals and had done secretarial work, but much preferred to be out on a station. It wasn't long before she became Marion's right-hand coordinator, while Raymond was fast becoming a useful station hand.

As graduation drew near I congratulated everyone on a 100 per cent successful attendance with a 100 per cent job placement. Raymond said, 'No, boss, I haven't got one.' I said, 'Raymond, I thought you would like to stay on with me.'

Then Eileen said, 'But what about me, I don't have a job yet.' 'Well, Eileen,' I said, 'I think Marion has plans for you, if you would like to stay on too.'

So that graduation day there were 12 happy students. Raymond and Eileen stayed with us for over four years; they became serious partners within a year and we were able to give them a good little station house to live in.

In time, they married and moved with us when we went to Planet Downs, southeast of Rolleston, where Raymond was horse boss and Eileen took care of cooking and coordinating food supplies for our outstation camp-outs. Eileen and Raymond didn't leave us until schooling became far too distant for their young kids to travel by bus.

Eventually, our stockmanship schools would become so popular that we attracted 77 pupils over two years and saw 66 benefit from our bush training and find employment. Some of the students were not up to living away from home and found that horseriding and bush work was not in their make-up. And we had a couple of bad kids too. I remember one called Hitchhiker.

Hitchhiker was a young chap who was put off the bus at Richmond in Central Queensland; he had no ticket, no money, no food and very little luggage. He was handed over to the police in the hope they could do something for him.

I usually didn't take on kids until they were 16, and he was still short of that mark. However, there was nothing the police could do with him and so I agreed to give him board and lodging as one of my students.

He got on well with Marion and would share his problems with her. We were able to get his parents' phone number in Canberra, so contact was made with them and they seemed pleased as punch to know he was safe. They agreed to pay for the things he needed – such as a new hat, boots, swag and toiletries – so I set him up with these requirements.

We liked to follow up on job placements and were proud of our success rate, which was 80 per cent over many years. However, regardless of the chance of getting work and despite our kitting him out, Hitchhiker sneaked off from the group one day while we were in the paddock with cattle. He was on horseback, so we all worried he may have had an accident, until I picked up his horse tracks going towards the homestead.

The road to town was about a mile from the homestead, so he had let the horse go to find its own way home, while he walked and hitched a ride 11 miles to town. Feeling sorry that he'd run away, he turned himself over to the police, who gave him an earnest talking-to and brought him back.

Hitchhiker was full of apologies and he hadn't hurt the horse, so all was well. He was working along compatibly with his peers when a man farming next door said he'd give him a paying job on the farm if he could still board and lodge with me. That was all fine, and Hitchhiker was given a decent Holden Rodeo ute to travel to and from his place of work.

On Anzac Day morning he asked Marion for extra lunch and a couple of packets of cigarettes (the extra lunch was forthcoming, but the cigarettes were not). I was doing book work in the office at eleven o'clock when the irate farmer from next door arrived to tell me Hitchhiker hadn't turned up for work and had obviously done a runner with his ute.

I immediately rang the Hughenden police, who were 80 miles east of Silver Hills, and then the Julia Creek police 120 miles west, asking both to be on the lookout for him.

I then thought perhaps I was being a bit hard on the lad, maybe he had got lost or bogged in one of the bore drains, so I took out the Toyota, which always had a shovel, axe, crowbar, wire rope and a few tools in the back ready for emergencies. As an extra precaution I threw in my swag, fuelled the Toyota and asked Fred, a young Aboriginal boy, to jump in with me.

Only 4 miles out from the homestead was the Willyarmor turnoff, with a sign pointing north to Croydon, but nowhere did the sign say that there were 250 miles of dirt and virtually no human contact likely along the track.

I stopped at the sign and picked up his tracks as plain as day – also his skid marks where he had planted the foot and taken off with glee. There had been a fair amount of rain and I knew the Yappar River was impassable for around 100 miles, so I radioed Marion to let her know what I was doing and where I was going, and headed north.

There were no other road intersections along the way, so I checked all the bush turnoffs that went into water points or outlying homesteads. We had got up over the Norman River near the Bellfield turnoff when I recognised the Rodeo ute coming back towards us. I told Fred to be ready for a wild ride, because Hitchhiker would never expect anyone to have tracked him up that far. I kept the Toyota in low gear while still travelling forward, as the road was only one-and-a-half vehicles wide.

Sure enough, when he realised who we were he drove straight at us at full revs. I swung the Toyota hard, and the Rodeo bounced off the bull bar and was sent off into the wattle scrub, knocking down small trees until it eventually ran out of puff.

Hitchhiker was lying unhurt on the front seat with the Rodeo still in movable condition. Fred and I shifted a few logs and got it back on the road. The Toyota's bull bar had been pushed back onto the front wheel, but with the wire rope and crowbar we were able to get her mobile again.

The Rodeo was almost out of fuel, so I mentioned that we would have to leave it there to be collected the next day. Then Hitchhiker piped up and said that he had two 20-litre drums of fuel in the back, but had had no means of transferring it into the tank and had been coming back looking for someone or something to help him do that. It didn't take us long to fuel the ute and shift all the gear from the Toyota to the Rodeo and send Fred off in it for home.

I made Hitchhiker strip to his shorts and ride in the back until we got home. Stripped to his shorts he was less likely to want to run off. Even Hitchhiker understood an unforgiving sun and hard hot earth could take their toll on a bloke scampering through the bush with no more for protection than his shorts.

Sitting him in the tray meant he couldn't take a crack at me if he decided to have a go while we were driving.

He had eaten all of his food and was out of smokes.

I'd radioed the police to meet us at the homestead. We drove in at about half-past eight that night to do the handover and farewell our Hitchhiker. I don't think he would ever try to put it over a bushman in his own country again.

I remember contacting his family to say sorry that we couldn't contain his wayward spirit and to remind them that he still had an outstanding bill for apparel and swag. They informed me that I'd have to make him pay, as he had to learn to pay his own way. I guess that helps us understand why some youngsters are sent that way.

* * *

The early 1980s was an eventful time in Australia. Baby Azaria Chamberlain disappeared at Uluru, the Commonwealth Games came to Brisbane and *Australia II* won the America's Cup. And, in Central Queensland, Michael Torenbeek came of age. He had grown into an independent young man with his own car and farm machinery, which allowed him to share-farm 500 acres at Woolton. He was ready to tackle the world head on.

In the opening months of 1982, the 21-year-old sold his farm machinery and followed the songline into the northwestern wilderness of the Kimberley. In the early 1980s there were still immense areas of the region that were unknown to European Australians and the wider world. Michael had become interested in the northwest when he'd travelled up that way rodeoing, and when he returned he found work as head stockman on some of the largest cattle stations in the eastern Kimberley: Springvale, Lansdowne and Bedford.

This was Tom Quilty's country. Quilty owned Springvale, Lansdowne and Bedford stations, just north of Halls Creek, until his death at 92 years of age in 1979. In 1981 Bruce Crowson bought the three properties and Mike Torenbeek became his first head stockman.

Soon after Mike left, his younger brother Jeff got a hankering for making his own mark on the world. Rather than take on the wild northwest, Jeff reckoned running bulls north near Weipa on Cape York was more his style. He loved the idea of chasing down wild scrub bulls, in the same way that Alwyn had enjoyed chasing tough horses almost three decades earlier. Jeff left Woolton when he was 20 years old.

Both boys were very capable horse and cattlemen, and even if Alwyn had wished to hold them back, he couldn't and wouldn't. Jeff and Mike had already travelled a lot while rodeoing in the Northern Territory, Queensland and New South Wales, so they knew how to be self-sufficient.

Meanwhile, Alwyn and Marion toiled to keep things going at Woolton. When all their kids except Aldo took up work elsewhere, things started looking rather bleak – help-wise. Then two English backpackers turned up unexpectedly. In their mid-twenties, fit and keen, the two girls had been working their way around the globe and had heard that Alwyn was on the lookout for help for his stockmanship schools.

Unlike others who might have had more stock experience but who didn't offer to work, they had the sort of have-a-go attitude that Alwyn liked and so were welcomed to Woolton Station on a brief trial basis. They ended up staying for the remainder of the season. For Alwyn, the unexpected arrival of two English girls with no experience was an absolute boon.

In the tropics most of the cattle work is done when the autumn days start to cool and shorten, across the relatively cooler months of winter and through spring, before the days get too long and too hot to do too much of anything.

By the end of spring, Marion, Aldo and Alwyn were well and truly ready for a break away, so they employed a sturdy cattleman called Winston Cox to look after the property for them and headed off to see Michael in the Kimberley at Springvale Station.

The Kimberley, Alwyn and Aldo both agreed, was just the sort of place they could imagine the whole family would eventually want to visit, with its carefree lifestyle and wild mix of jagged mountains, deep rich gorges and remote waterfalls. It was rugged country, yet beautiful beyond description. The light painted the landscape with a full palette of colours – from crimson red and burnt umber in the deep gorges, to all shades of blue. The problem was that it was so remote.

Michael hadn't quite finished his contract when his parents and Aldo arrived and the few days they had to wait turned into a real treat. The station manager flew them around, showing off the three sister stations – a grand way to see one of the last remaining wildernesses on the planet.

With the Kimberley cattle season finished, Alwyn, Marion, Aldo and Michael took a run over to Mt Isa to pick up Jeff and head back to Woolton for Christmas. It was a run of a mere 1000 miles, for the best part across unforgiving outback highways and byways. Considering that Christmas would be the first time the family had been together for 12 months, however, those 1000 miles of boneshaking travel weren't too hard for Alwyn and his family to take.

Alwyn's boys still wanted to pick up more stock experience in northern climes, so come the new year they were keen to head up north again. Woolton went up for sale and once again workers were difficult to come by. It was clearly time for Alwyn and Marion to move on also.

As the wet season cleared and dry blue skies returned to the north, Shayne, Michael, Jeff, Aldo and family friend Steve Kimber, on his first job and first trip away from home, left for the Kimberley. They'd all fallen under its spell.

Those who work on a vast northern cattle property either love it or hate it. There's no middle ground. And Alwyn's kids loved it. They prized the opportunity to live and work on a property so immense that the boundaries spread from horizon to horizon. The station became their entire world.

After a solid and rewarding seven months they returned to Woolton and brought with them a bloke called Buster – a useful stockman and a good mechanic – and healthy bank accounts.

It was around this time, in 1984, that Brian Bloxsom, a big businessman from Brisbane, sought to increase his interest in the cattle industry. Bloxsom owned Boynedale Station on the Boyne River near Proston and was keen to take on a much larger property. He cast his eye about and came across Woolton. Liking what he saw, the ambitious cattleman put down a firm deposit.

As part of the deal, Alwyn promised Brian he'd stay for three months just to make sure the handover went smoothly. With one thing and another, the sort of delays and interruptions that so often happen in the bush, after five months Alwyn, Marion and their family looked like not getting off Woolton in any great hurry. That was until Alwyn caught up with Brian and told him straight, 'By the end of the week I'm out of here.'

Brian squared up to Alwyn, smiled and said in an equally matter-of-fact manner, 'Okay. Then so am I, but will you come with me? I'll buy a big place elsewhere if you will manage it for me.'

After 14 years at Woolton, Marion and Alwyn were leaving. To find their next home the couple hit the road in their Toyota Hilux, rocking and rolling along outback tracks west to Windorah, Birdsville and Boulia, then north to Mareeba and through to Hughenden, The Lynd, Musgrave, and then to Strathburn Station on the west side of Cape York Peninsula. By the end of it all Planet Downs was their pick. It was first-class cattle country with ample water, and its neglected state meant that the sell price would be relatively low. Moreover, Brian had the capital necessary to make the property a viable concern.

Christmas was close, so the couple headed back to Boynedale only to hear that Marion's mother was very unwell. That meant a detour to Yeppoon on the Capricorn Coast near Rockhampton.

When they eventually drew to a stop outside Marion's mother's place, they discovered that Maude had passed away earlier that morning. She'd died while chatting to a friend on the phone. They'd been talking about this and that when she collapsed, as if her heart had simply had enough. Marion felt her passing deeply – she'd lost her mother and a great confidante. The memories of the wonderful trip that she'd just shared with Alwyn seemed to evaporate instantly. It was a mournful start to their Planet Downs adventure.

Arriving on Planet Downs, Alwyn found the property extremely run-down and was met by a hostile reception. However, he had discussed the challenge with Marion before he left, and they were confident in their knowledge of the country, the extent of their young people's ability and their desire to bring the big property back into production.

Sometimes hauling an agricultural business out of the financial mire brings out a particular sourness in those who oversaw the initial descent into said mire. It's likely that was the case with Patrick Smith, the cattleman-cum-businessman who represented the group of associates who had been running Planet Downs. To say that Smith was less than hospitable and cooperative is to grossly understate how unpleasant he made things for anyone involved in the purchase of Planet Downs, including the Torenbeek family.

Alwyn and Brian Bloxsom took a light-plane flight over Planet Downs to get a bird's-eye view of the state of the property. What they saw would break the heart of anyone who loved the land.

The run-down homestead, yards, water systems, fences, machinery, the whole kit and caboodle, needed drastic attention. There were also a number of cleanskin cattle and scrub bulls to be dealt with. And all the while, as Alwyn and Brian inspected the neglected property, Patrick Smith lurked, doing his best to make them feel uncomfortable.

After the second day on the property, Alwyn had seen enough; Brian and his business associates were ready to negotiate with the bank to settle on a price for the takeover in June 1985. Alwyn promised to have the station working properly within four years; then he'd move on to whatever new adventure presented itself.

Around six weeks before settlement, court orders allowed Alwyn, Raymond, Mike and Buster to move onto the property to start to get fences, water and cattle up to scratch. Alwyn and his team arrived on Planet Downs fully expecting a hostile reception. And they got it. A few layabout stockmen were sitting and standing around by the homestead as mournful as a mob of blistered bandicoots as Alwyn's team drove through the ironbark gateway. Catching sight of them, the bandicoot mob jeered and booed.

'We're good shots,' they sneered.

'Don't get us riled,' Patrick Smith threatened.

'Come on, 'ave a go, I know karate,' one of the layabouts boasted.

Mike, Buster, Alwyn and Raymond bristled, but drove on. They knew they had more important things to do than tussle with any worthless louts. Ignoring the stockmen, they rattled and bounced along one of the sandy station roads towards an old station outbuilding known as the Ten Mile Hut.

The old timber and iron hut would be their base of operations for the next six weeks. Once they had lit a campfire, boiled their billy and unrolled their swags, they got to work resurrecting the derelict building.

Then they got on with knocking the property into shape, always making sure that they travelled in pairs. The court orders insisted that they move about the property in pairs and report to the company receivers every 24 to 48 hours – that's how serious the threats from the unruly mob that met them were.

Meanwhile, Marion stayed on Boynedale 373 miles away, looking after the horses and breeding more dogs – which Alwyn felt he'd well and truly need.

Eventually the takeover day came and went – without serious incident, despite there being a bailiff on hand to sort out any ruckus that might arise. The threat of violence still felt very real, however, and the receivers decided it would be best if Marion arrived under local police escort. It was a ticklish situation that could turn ugly if tempers got out of hand.

As much as possible, Alwyn's men shrugged off the threats and knuckled down to restoring Planet Downs. They were a crew of seven skilled men; all were experienced, all were strong stockmen and all were determined to make this immense property prosper.

The seven worked to pull into shape the 260 station mix horses. Without a horse book, this would have been a daunting task for less-experienced stockmen. However, in the main, each of the seven was a skilled horseman capable of sorting out the equine cohort. The older mares were well bred, so they drafted the rest by eye. They'd look at the shape of each horse's back, legs, face, nose, ears and mouth – watching them closely for hints of their temperament – until they had the entire mob sorted.

R.M. Williams' wife Erica was involved in breeding Arabs and provided Planet with a strong Arabian stallion, which when put with mares that looked as if they were mostly thoroughbred produced Anglo offspring. That combination meant Planet could produce horses that would have the speed and class of both the Arab and thoroughbred breeds, as well as the stamina and toughness of the Arab.

Alwyn's team were in full swing getting the station horses into line when Jeff and Aldo returned from the Kimberley. The mood lifted immediately. Seven became nine capable hands with which to shape and mould Planet into a worthwhile cattle station. Jeff and Aldo stayed on until the end of the northern wet season.

Of the nine stockmen, Aldo, Jeff, Steve Kimber and Alwyn took on the bulk of the responsibility of putting together a good, coherent working plant of 70 horses. Between them, they made a formidable team. Pocket-sized Steve Kimber, who'd known the family since they'd lived on Darling Plains, was very capable and made an ideal head stockman, while Alwyn and his sons had all the skills needed to make a go of the toughest cattle property. And they worked together beautifully to boot. Meanwhile Marion, Shayne and Vonda set about scrubbing the house, cookhouse, men's quarters, kitchen and mess.

Raymond, who had stayed with Alwyn when they moved from Woolton to Planet Downs, took on the job of horse tailer, while his wife Eileen excelled as the station cook. Before long the workforce was 26 strong and working steadily towards making Planet Downs shine. They certainly had plenty to do.

Planet Downs looked a little too civilised to Jeff and his younger brother Aldo. Jeff had an idea that offered them another adventure, back up in the yellow sands of the Great Sandy Desert. Soon after the calendar rolled over to 1986, the two brothers waved good-bye to the Planet Downs mob and headed northwest on a 900cc motorbike. Out there they'd help prepare seismic lines in a grid pattern for the drilling rigs. Although Aldo was only 16 years old, it was the sort of country in which age didn't matter – you were welcome if you could do the job. Jeff and Aldo promised to return when Planet Downs was up to what Alwyn called 'bulk bull efficiency'.

From the first light of sunrise until the last rays of sunset, the work on Planet Downs didn't let up. To move stock across the large distances on Planet, Alwyn had a semi-trailer that carried a stock crate – except the semi wouldn't start. Life in the bush encourages imaginative solutions to problems. In this case they used a grader to tow the semi around the property.

The semi-trailer wasn't the only dysfunctional – or perhaps bush-functional – vehicle. Bush mechanics Michael and Buster worked on an array of machinery in all degrees of dilapidation. The property boasted one functioning D6 dozer among the fleet of three, two trucks in a rather hit-or-miss state, and the grader, which was in almost ready-to-work order.

Meanwhile, the stockmen went about testing the cattle workings. They mustered a mixture of unkempt cattle – despondent cows, fresh-faced calves, a number of ornery scrub bulls and around half a dozen cranky old bullocks – into the homestead yards. Altogether they'd gathered about 80 head.

The old yards had been sturdy in their time, but now they looked tired enough to want to lie down, and it seemed as if they would do so with very little encouragement. Each post and rail rattled like Grandpa's teeth. The yards were old back in the 1950s when Alwyn had used them for a night camp when droving.

He now climbed into the forcing yard to go about splitting the cattle into separate pens, bullocks this way, bush cattle that way, cows here, calves there. It was all going well when one rough bull took a look at Alwyn and decided he didn't like the cut of the stockman's jib. Now this was a bull of considerable size; he'd cast a deep dark shadow even on a cloudy day.

The nasty, sharp-horned beast snorted once, lowered his head and thundered across the yard straight for Alwyn. Alwyn started running. He scrambled across the yard, scaled the fence, then, pushing off with one hand, he hurdled the top rail and landed heavily outside the yard.

The great creature crashed into the fence and demolished three panels, sending shards of timber, large and small, rocketing into the air like sparks on a Catherine wheel. Even then, the beast didn't stop; it just kept running – straight into the bush.

It wasn't surprising that Mike's very next job was to get the only working dozer into the yard and level it – pushing whatever part was still standing into the dirt. Then the whole pile of timber was burnt. There's little that focuses attention to a job more sharply than a rampaging bull.

Using the Ten Mile, Cattle Creek, Fourteen Mile and Tea Tree yards, which were in reasonable condition, the stockmen worked the cattle to cut out a good number of the excess bulls to be sold. At the same time others cleared fence lines, cut posts, built fences, houses and dams, pulled scrub, drilled for water, and cleared roads all the way to the top end of the property 75 miles away. To get it all done, the entire workforce, including contractors, swelled to 54 men.

It wasn't all hard work, though. There were times when they'd settle back and enjoy the simple pleasures of outback life – fresh air, open spaces, good food, even the occasional spot of good-natured larrikinism. One of the highlights of life on Planet Downs was Michael's wedding. He married his girlfriend Karen on 7 January 1986, with Planet Downs providing the backdrop.

By mid-1987, Jeff, Steve, Shayne and Vonda had pulled out to return to the Kimberley, once again chasing their own adventures, but leaving Alwyn short-handed to clear the scrub of wild bulls. The Planet Downs scrub covered an inhospitable area known as the Shotover Range, including an 80-mile-long valley, and without experienced bull catchers it was going to be a formidable task.

Alwyn got to work building a series of staging posts along the valley, each with water and dry or tinned food just in case of a breakdown, lost dog or some other calamity. The staging posts were about 10 miles apart, until the 40-mile camp. The last five camps were stretched a little further apart.

A staging post called Little Foot, approximately 60 miles up the valley, was the main camp and by comparison with the others a veritable five-star hotel. It had a shower and toilet, and a roofed shed complete with a cement floor, table, chairs, gas hot water, refrigerator and shearers' beds.

It was an oasis on the edge of a 20-mile stretch of bulldust, which, for the uninitiated, is soft, dry sand as fine as talcum powder. Beyond that, the stockmen rode into the steep high country to Turpentine Camp, then on to the last camp, known as Don's Camp, which sat by the bottom of a thundering waterfall. If Little Foot was an oasis, then Don's was Valhalla. For all its splendour, the Shotover country was a nightmare when it came to catching bulls – all rough broken creeks and sheer gorges.

By this time they had a new head stockman, Alan Spence, who joined stockman Graham Essy and Aldo, who was 16, to make up the new bull-catching team. Not one of them had ever mixed it with wild bush bulls before.

The basalt country was impossible to work vehicles in for bull catching, so the work had to be done on horseback. Nearly 50 years old, Alwyn was too slow to work on the ground, but his skill and experience made him a marvellous trainer. He taught the youngsters how to catch bulls by the tail, bring them down and strap their legs, restraining them so they can stand because they will die within an hour if they stay on their side.

While the boys were training they rode down the valley into the Ten Mile country. There they came across a big mob, probably 250 head, and mustered them from the Seven Mile. All was going fairly well, they had crossed Planet Creek, when a roan cleanskin bull that they called Spike Jones – because he had a set of horns that the Devil would have been proud to wear – bolted from the mob in top gear. Spence went with him.

All Alwyn could do was watch in horror as Spence and Spike ran full speed downhill for half a mile through the basalt country, charging down through Planet Creek, storming another half-mile almost to the pine scrub when, as if Spike Jones had said, 'Enough. I'll fight but never surrender', the bull turned. Spence had to change from picador to matador, fast.

Rider and bull faced one another, staring each other down. Alwyn could do nothing but hope and pray that Spence would stay on his horse. No sooner had he thought that, Spence climbed down off his saddle and walked into the fray.

Spike Jones charged, picked Spence up between his horns and shoved him through a four-strand barbwire fence. Then he calmly walked off back to what was clearly his home country without touching the defenceless horse. Spence returned to the mob unhurt. 'How do you reckon I went?' he asked Alwyn enthusiastically. 'Not so good,' the old bushman answered. 'That's only round number one.'

Later on a big raw-boned poley bull nominated himself to be Graham Essy's first opponent. He'd drifted out of a mob of around 50. Alwyn rode in and, as usual, he grabbed the great beast by the tail. In that position he had enough leverage to put the bull on the ground, and did. Seeing Alwyn had the beast by the tail, Graham sped in at a half-gallop and strode off his horse as it was still moving; as fast as you like, the new chum had the back straps on the beast.

Aldo was next to encounter a bull. His was a three-year-old red bull with a good set of horns – or racks, as Alwyn calls them. The red bull ran out of a mob and was fairly flying when Alwyn hit him and took him over. That was the cue for Aldo. Aldo tore into the fray at high speed, just as Graham had earlier. The great animal rolled two and a half times and was straight back on his feet and facing Aldo. Fortunately, the bull was very confused and Aldo soon had him under control.

Those encounters turned the boys into bull catchers, every one of them, and left Alwyn bursting with pride.

Although the young bull catchers were working hard, they had only 20 horses at the camps and that meant the best they could do was catch nine bulls in three days. And the bulls they did catch were as mad as hornets waiting in the camp yard, so they were forced to walk them up to the closest set of yards. The whole process was far too slow.

Having foreseen the problem, Michael Torenbeek, ever resourceful, had started to build a bull-catching machine. Nicknamed Pet, the machine was a modified Toyota LandCruiser and big and sturdy enough to carry the men and their dogs through the scrub.

When Michael unveiled Pet, Alwyn sauntered over to the open-top creation, sat in it, grinned, and said, 'This is going to work. The bulls are now ours!'

Once Pet entered the picture the team would start to throw and tie on a Wednesday, hauling in on average 10 bulls per day, and have

40 at the Ten Mile yards by Saturday night to truck off to Murgon on Sunday.

For most people, it's as if the sun rises at their birth and sets for the final time at their death, yet, as Ernest Hemingway wrote, 'Nobody ever lives their life all the way up except bullfighters.' On those long days in the Shotover, Alwyn, Aldo, Graham and Spence were living their lives all the way up.

That was all the more true considering the wild bulls of Planet Downs were large mountain-bred beasts and fearsome by nature. But that was the fun of it. Anyway, no bull catcher worth his salt would ever go after a small one. The bigger, the more dangerous, the better.

The biggest of them was a red beast called Red Simmons. Alwyn first encountered the red bull while working with Michael to get the staging yards and roads ready for bull catching.

Alwyn would often take out a good travelling horse called Penny Farthing to get a better idea of cattle-feeding grounds and bull numbers. While riding through the scrub, he'd often find that two or three young bulls would come close to him, curious to know what he was doing.

One morning, while he was out exploring the Expedition Range side of Planet Creek on Penny Farthing, he came across 'a massive big red bull as tall as my horse with a rack of horns to complement his majestic physique'. The sheer size of the beast inspired Alwyn. He knew this bull had to be caught and he wanted to be there when it happened.

A few weeks later, while the men were catching bulls in Pet, they came face to face with Red Simmons. Cool as you like, Red trotted out of their way into a patch of bush where he was safe from the bull catcher.

The dogs weren't too happy seeing him trot away, and took off after the beast with a barrage of yapping and barking, chasing him into the scrub. Among them was one very cocky bitch called Nicotine. Determined to show Alwyn she could handle the big beast, she rushed into the scrub and straight into the thick of the fracas.

With Nicotine leading the pack, the dogs circled and nipped at the bull. As each came in to draw the creature out from the scrub, the bull would lower its head and lunge at them. All the while the dogs kept yapping and barking.

The minutes went by, each an eternity. Brave, tenacious little Nico wouldn't give up; she had never let a bull beat her before. This time, however, she took one too many chances and an ear-splitting yelp ended the canine hullabaloo. Red Simmons came out of the bush, prancing and trotting about. Dangling from his near-side horn was Nicotine, and the great bull was desperately trying to shake her off. He stomped and shook his head vigorously this way then that way, determined to get the limp dog off his horn. While the snared body of Nicotine had his full attention, the men made their move.

Spence had positioned himself on the bonnet of Pet with two feet pressed on the bull bar and both hands on the top roll bar while Aldo drove at a steady pace and jarred the great beast under the short rib – and boom, they'd laid Red Simmons out.

Now was the real danger. When a bull this large is over, the bull catcher must get him tied and secured, otherwise there'll be bloody hell to pay should the creature get back on his feet. Spence knew it and wasn't about to let that happen. He understood that if they had to knock Red Simmons over a second time, the crafty creature would have their measure and wouldn't be likely to fall as easily.

Before the bull could recover, Spence jumped off the bull bar, strapped the back legs, strapped the front legs, then eased Nico off big Red's horn. The latter was a somewhat delicate piece of work as the horn had gone up the inside of Nico's right leg and shoulder, and just picked the skin up beside her backbone.

Luckily, after a week and a half of loving care, the little dog recovered beautifully. Red Simmons was not so lucky; the almost one-ton bull was off to market by the next Monday.

Nearly as big as Red Simmons was a range-bred, clean-cut brindle bull called Elvis. When the men discovered Elvis down by Big Ben camp, their eyes popped like organ stops at the sheer size of him. Every night that they spent in that camp Elvis, perhaps knowing the catchers were in their swags or sitting safe by the campfire, would start to sing them to sleep. He'd sing with a sort of deep resonant bull roar so that, should they let their imaginations run a little wild, they'd imagine Elvis Presley serenading them with a Top 40 hit.

The four had tried time and again to catch the crooning curmudgeon of a bull, but each time they went after him, he just slipped across Planet Creek where they couldn't follow with Pet. And then later that night he'd sing a bovine 'Are You Lonesome Tonight?' for them.

One day, they spied old Elvis down by Planet Creek. Well, the race was on and they let loose their team of dogs, who bounded out after the great brindle beast. Alan Spence and Aldo raced right behind the dogs.

The hills fairly echoed with the noise of the chase: thundering hooves on basalt rock, yapping hound dogs, and the bellowing of the bull. Eventually, the dogs caught up to the bull and circled him warily, keeping him from running any further until Aldo and Spence caught up.

When the boys arrived, one bolted to the front of the bull and the other to the back where he got a grip on his tail. The front boy put his hat under the bull's nose and he didn't like that; the back boy grabbed the bull's tail and pulled it towards his head and the great beast bucked off his feet. Then the two of them strapped the bull's legs. The job was done.

It wasn't long before Aldo and Spence walked back into camp, proudly announcing that Elvis had, as it were, left the wild. The musical bull was their biggest catch that season.

By now it was Easter and the young stockmen needed a little incentive, so Alwyn said that if Aldo could get two semi loads down to the Ten Mile camp in one day, the four men could take the four Easter days off.

Aldo took off early on Thursday morning with a full load on a 100-mile return trip along a very slow road. Clouds began to gather by three o'clock in the afternoon. When the young bull catcher arrived back, Alwyn knocked together some tucker for him while the boys got busy loading the remaining bulls.

One by one they loaded the bulls, tying each one to the top truck rail to keep them safe and secure. As they worked dark storm clouds rolled over above them, and any chance of the boys enjoying a long weekend seemed to slip away.

Eventually they loaded the last bull. Aldo threw the truck into gear and drove away as the clouds started to grumble overhead. Alwyn knew he had to find time to feed a small number of bulls that were still in the yard, but he chose to follow the truck down in case Aldo ran into trouble on the windy, muddy bush track.

They made it to Little Foot without any worries just as the storm clouds burst. There was no problem reaching the Thirty Mile camp. At the Twenty Mile camp the road was awash. The semi turned the corner to continue up the Twenty Mile flat and sank to the axle on the driver's side.

It was so dark, wet and slippery that Alwyn wouldn't let the boys climb into the back to untie the bulls and let them go – it was too dangerous in the conditions.

As the storm pounded the mountains, the bull catchers climbed out of the truck and into Turtle, their pick-up Toyota. They headed off into the drubbing rain with the intention of getting back to the head station to collect their grader so that they could tow the truck out of the mud. Three miles from the truck the Turtle sank into the road right up to the chassis. It was in the mud up to its virtual mechanical bum.

Shirtless and shoeless, Graham and Alwyn opted to walk back to the truck to let the bulls go at first light, while Spence and Aldo walked the remaining 23 miles via the Ten Mile camp back to the homestead to wake Michael.

Graham and Alwyn trudged back to the cattle. Along the way they forded the swollen Planet Creek, which was now pitch back and belly deep.

Once at the truck, shivering, wet and exhausted, the two men curled up in the truck cabin and slept the best they could, considering the tempest that raged around them. Daylight, when it came, was very welcome as it brought warmth to defrost their icy bodies.

With nothing more than pocketknives the two men cut the wet ropes and let the bulls free. The happiest one of all to receive his freedom was none other than Elvis.

When the bulls were free, Graham and Alwyn then walked to the Ten Mile to meet the others. Spence and Aldo had walked through the night, enlisted Michael's help with the grader and collected another Toyota. As it turned out, Michael left the semi a few days before retrieving it, but was able to get the Turtle back on the road.

Strangely enough, all the bulls they let go at the Twenty Mile ended up at the Ten Mile within a week or two and found themselves in the Ten Mile yards. All except Elvis, who turned up in the horse paddock at the Ten Mile and stayed there, singing the nights away right up until the Torenbeeks left Planet Downs. By the way, the boys got their Easter in Rockhampton, and they made the most of it, celebrating their success as fully-fledged bull catchers. But they kept that story to themselves.

Some time later one of the stockmanship students came across

Elvis in the horse paddock and told Alwyn he was going to have a go at getting him caught. Alwyn smiled at him and told him that he was 'big and only got bigger the closer you got'.

'He'll be all right,' the boy said and rode out after him. Well, old Elvis took the horse clean out from under him. Both survived, but the big brindle bull had made it perfectly clear he wasn't about to be caught again. Luck was on the boy's side; Elvis had put the skids on his horse and that gave the rider the time to climb a tree and get up out of Elvis's reach. The bull kept him there a half-hour or more. Elvis eventually let the boy go and watched him walk home. All the way, the boy kept looking over his shoulder for that big bovine crooner to come at him for an encore.

Season after season, the clearing of the wild bulls carried on, with a break from the action every winter. Eventually, Alwyn's bull-catching team changed as the company insisted that he couldn't employ single men. Alwyn was left having to send married men into the hunt for the wild bulls.

By the end of the 1989 season, Alwyn and his men had caught about 3000 bulls and 4000 mixed head from the scrub on Planet Downs. During that time Alwyn had continued to run stockmanship schools for Aboriginal youth at risk, teaching them horse, cattle and camp management.

Cody was one of the many kids who'd experienced discrimination, lawlessness, poverty, substance abuse or some other tragedy in their young lives. Alwyn had agreed to take him in, although he was Dutch and not Indigenous, because the boy needed help.

Seventeen-year-old Cody travelled 1200 miles from his home in Victoria to Planet Downs to attend Alwyn's school. Though he was as lean as a whip handle, Cody was remarkably sluggish and had very little stamina. It was as if he had no drive.

The school was in the stock camp, where Alwyn could easily keep an eye on everyone, night and day, every day. Each morning

Cody and the other students woke to the bubbling of porridge, the sizzling pop of frying bacon and eggs, and the toasty aroma of homemade damper.

With that sort of breakfast it was little wonder that Cody began to fill out. Still he slept for hours on end. Three weeks later he was starting to get a shine and stoutness to him, yet he remained listless.

One morning, Alwyn stood by Cody's swag and said forcefully, 'Cody, everyone else is up and doing, must be time you joined in.' Cody looked at Alwyn as if he didn't quite know how to join in or what to do.

'Have a look about and tell me what interests you most,' Alwyn insisted. Then he left to help his other students. A few hours later Cody caught up with Alwyn, saying, 'I'd like to learn how to shoe a horse.'

The idea of this young boy running around with a knife, rasp, nail and hammer attacking every horse in sight made the veteran stockman uneasy. Besides the possibility of Cody sending his horses lame, the chance that he might nod off to sleep under a testy horse seemed a little too real. Yet, Alwyn agreed. Within 10 days, the boy was shoeing proficiently. Cody also found he was good at working young horses from the ground.

There wasn't a wholesome breakfast in the world that could have worked as well on Cody as the realisation that he had some skills of his own, the understanding that he had value, and the awareness that he had come across someone who cared enough to help him find his value.

Cody graduated from the Planet Downs Stockmanship School of 1989. Soon after graduation, Alwyn drove him 930 miles to his first job at a place called Wernadinga Station. Wedged between the grasslands and the vast saltpans of the Gulf of Carpentaria, home to good cattle, prickly acacia, feral pigs and western red kangaroos, Wernadinga was Cody's deliverance.

Two years passed and Alwyn was touring some northern properties, checking on former students and the work prospects for future students. He drove in along the rutted tracks from the cattle grid that marks the Wernadinga front gate towards the homestead.

As he stopped in front of the homestead and the cloud of sandy dust settled around his vehicle, he looked about for one man in particular. There by the stockyards, walking in his direction, he saw Cody. His former student was still working, horse-breaking, shoeing and mustering, loving the outback.

Cody smiled at Alwyn from under a tattered, sweat-stained felt hat and the two men shook hands. 'Would you like a cuppa?' Cody offered.

With the billy on to boil, they sat in Cody's kitchen and the young stockman told his mentor how he'd enjoyed outback life; that he'd worked hard, saved and bought his own car and even got his own quarters. There could be no greater thank-you and nothing more satisfying for Alwyn than to have the chance to sit down and enjoy a good cup of tea with a man who had found his worth.

There were times when Alwyn didn't have such fine results. One student, a white teenager from the Northern Territory, was particularly memorable. This boy had so much pent-up anger that he turned on another student, chasing him with a chainsaw while promising to 'cut him to pieces'. The boy, who was thereafter known as Chainsaw, was sent packing the next morning.

The second half of the 1980s was a time of change for the Torenbeek family. Alwyn's eldest daughter Shayne married Rod Irvine on 6 June 1986 and the couple celebrated the birth of their first daughter Emma in November of that year – making Alwyn a grandfather for the first time.

Almost exactly 12 months after Shayne's marriage, her sister Vonda married Steve Kimber at Rolleston on 7 June 1987.

Then, in April 1988, Alwyn had something else, something of an entirely different nature, to celebrate. It was partly the culmination of another man's dream.

Back in 1974, stockman and artist Hugh Sawrey had dreamed of creating a memorial to the explorers, drovers, pioneers and settlers who had helped open up remote Australia. The memorial was to be known as the Stockman's Hall of Fame.

Sawrey's vision was to be Australia's first national hall of fame – a multimillion-dollar complex at Longreach in Queensland. Inside its walls, records, displays, memorabilia, fine Australian art and sculpture would be set up to preserve the history of early settlers great and small: the women, the bushmen, rogues and rascals, saints and sinners.

The bush artist went to see R.M. Williams, who said to his old mate – the two had been drinking mates for years – 'It's going to be a huge thing to take on, but if you're big enough to do it, I'm big enough to stay with you.'

Sawrey, in his own words, 'went round in raptures, urging people on with the look of a wide-eyed bullock'. Between them they pulled together the funds needed to make Sawrey's vision splendid.

In 1979 Sawrey and Williams set up a board of management, dragging into the idea noted Australian pastoralists Sir James Walker and Ranald Chandler, Jim Bailey (the president of the Australian Rough Riders Association and World All-Round Champion Cowboy) and Dame Mary Durack Miller, who wrote the book *Kings in Grass Castles*.

Then Sir James Walker, Ranald Chandler and Jim Bailey headed off to take a gander at the American Cowboy Hall of Fame in Oklahoma City, to get ideas for Australia's own heritage centre.

When they got home, Ranald Chandler spoke to a *Women's Weekly* reporter and said, sounding more larrikin than Chips Rafferty, 'They may have their cowboy film stars, but we have our great Outback.'

Finally, in April 1988, Queen Elizabeth headed Down Under to say hello to the folk of Longreach and to open the Stockman's Hall of Fame. Thousands gathered under the hot sun to hear her speak about Australia's pioneers. Among the first Hall of Fame inductees was a man in his early fifties, whom some had known as the Kokotunga Kid, and others simply as Alwyn.

One of those present to witness Alwyn's induction was job-placement administrator Bob Symonds, who worked in the Shire of Richmond and was keen to have a word with the new Hall of Fame inductee.

Richmond Shire, a roughly rectangular parcel of 10,000 square miles not far off the geographic centre of Queensland, was, like many remote shires, suffering from a declining population. It had been, to a greater or lesser degree, since the early 1930s. So the shire administration was keen to support anything that would staunch the slow but steady population haemorrhage. For Bob, that meant encouraging Alwyn to train stockmen and women in his territory – arguing that he'd be training people closer to the employment market in which they'd be working. Bob's timing was perfect, as Alwyn was at the end of his four-year commitment to Planet Downs.

Marion stayed with Vonda and Steve at Stratford, a property on the Sutton River nearly 200 miles west of Mackay, as Alwyn toured the Shire of Richmond and broader Gulf country with Bob Symonds, taking in Townsville and Mt Isa, Atherton, Normanton and Hughenden. Cattle folk in all those centres showed an interest in Alwyn setting up a school in the area.

So, with that evidence, in 1989 Alwyn took on Villadale Station and leased part of the property for the school. Marion joined her husband there, followed shortly afterwards by Shayne, Rod and their children Emma, Jess and newborn Kelsey, who after living in Brisbane for a couple of years had decided to return to Central Queensland. Of course, things didn't go entirely according to plan.

In April 1990 almost 400,000 square miles of Queensland, New South Wales and Victoria were flooded in separate but extreme events. Floodwaters invaded many towns and graziers were helpless as rivers overflowed and, in some cases, completely submerged properties, killing up to one million livestock.

Immediately before the April floods, cyclones had caused floodwaters to sweep through Central Queensland, threatening to trap the extended Torenbeek family at Villadale homestead on a large wedge of land between the swollen waters of the Flinders and Dutton rivers.

As the waters rose, threatening to cut them off from the closest town, Richmond, the local electricity company set up a flying fox to ferry supplies and people over the Dutton River.

By this time Alwyn had taken over the management of nearby Silver Hills Station, which was less likely to find itself surrounded by floodwaters. Alwyn saw Marion to the flying fox and off to safety at Silver Hills, but Rod and Shayne decided that moving their young family out of the Villadale homestead via flying fox was too risky.

Instead, they stayed put for about three weeks until the Richmond Shire Council found another way of getting them out: they rolled in a large front-end loader and carried the family out in the bucket.

With the flood worsening, Jeff, three stockmanship school students and Alwyn decided to walk their mob of horses off Villadale and travel the 37 miles to Silver Hills. To do that they needed to swim the horses across the swollen Dutton River at a crossing known as the Charcoal, which lies just before the confluence of the Dutton and Flinders rivers.

The Charcoal crossing is easy enough in normal times, but during the 1990 flood it had turned into a wide, sandy quagmire into which the horses were sucked up to their knees as they strode out, battling their way across the swamp.

Before crossing the Charcoal, the men gathered the herd together in a reasonably tight bunch, and then drove them hard into the turbid water. Every step each beast took was a struggle. The hectic mix of rising floodwaters, quicksand and monsoonal rain threatened to turn the entire trek into a calamity.

Still, the stockmen rode on in a chorus of thundering and snorting horses, splashing into the sandy mud, until each pulled up out of the Dutton, stumbling, slipping and sliding, spewing most of their riders into the mud as they scrambled onto the bank.

They had just managed to cross the Dutton and had gathered themselves to make sure everyone was present and in one piece and to catch their breath when a student named Robert, a weedy sort of chap who wasn't made for the bush, refused to go any further.

Alwyn turned to him, looked up and down the bank of the swollen river and then said, with a strong hint of empathy, 'Well, mate, of course you can stay here if you want.'

The boy offered up an uncertain smile and nodded. Alwyn started to turn away to remount his horse and then paused, adding, 'Of course, we don't have very much tucker to leave you – you'd have to go without before we could get back to you.'

Then, mounting his horse, he leant forward and added, 'You'd be okay though. There're not too many crocs along here. And the ones that are here should leave you alone. Of course, it's night before they really start looking for something to eat, so you'll be okay till then.'

As the old stockman spoke his pupil steadily turned a lighter shade of pale, and his eyes grew ever wider – he looked for all the world like a possum in headlights.

'Don't worry, not many crocs here and we'll be back in a few days, perhaps a week, when the flood subsides.'

With that, Alwyn flicked his horse around and led the stockmen and their herd off towards Silver Hills, leaving a reliable horse called

Fred with the young boy. He was not much further along the track when he heard the tell-tale clip clop of hooves as the boy cantered his horse up behind him. Robert had rejoined the crew, but he had made it clear the bushman's life was not for him.

In the end, with a mix of sheer determination and a reasonable dose of good luck, they managed to walk the horses the entire 37 miles to Silver Hills - together. And before dark.

Chapter Fifteen
ALDO: 1991

Alwyn remembers – losing Aldo

We lost Aldo on 22 September 1991 in Darwin. When I saw his body in Darwin Morgue I made a promise. 'I shall live the extra life that you should have had. I'm going to go out and compete again and do the things that you would have done.'

* * *

Darwin is a melting pot of people and cultures, a city full of life and adventure sitting on the edge of a harbour even bigger than Sydney's. Sadly, the Northern Territory capital is also the scene of Aldo Torenbeek's final adventure.

Aldo had been on a run up to the Northern Territory, driving big machinery while basing himself in Darwin. 'He was up there and had just changed his job when he got killed. It was a motorbike accident,' Alwyn recalls. 'He'd promised me no more motorbikes after Christmas, but he only made it to September.'

When Alwyn heard of Aldo's death, he had thought that he and his son Jeff might drive up to reclaim Aldo's body. However, the local Richmond police officer told him he wouldn't allow it. He said he'd lock Alwyn up before he'd allow a distraught, grieving parent to drive the almost 1300 miles to Darwin. He made it clear to them that there was only one choice. Alwyn and Jeff chartered a plane from Richmond to Cairns, then caught the first available Qantas flight to Darwin.

Darwin welcomed them with the unforgiving tropical heat that rolls down across the 12 degrees that separate the city from the equator. After visiting the morgue they made arrangements to have Aldo's body put on the same flight they'd be taking to return to Rockhampton via Brisbane.

As they landed in Brisbane, Alwyn looked solemnly at the flight attendant who had been looking after him and Jeff and said, 'Now, make sure he changes planes.'

Alwyn and Jeff changed planes and flew to Rockhampton. As the plane landed, they looked at each other; both had a feeling that Aldo's body had not arrived on the same flight.

They walked into the airport baggage-collection area and discovered that their fear was a reality. Alwyn recalls, 'We rattled things and said, "Where's our boy?"' Right then Michael arrived to collect his father and brother from the airport.

No sooner had Alwyn explained to Mike that his brother's body had been lost somewhere en route than Mike made a lunge for the counter, with his eyes firmly fixed on the throat of the unfortunate desk attendant.

Alwyn held Michael back, saying, 'You can't do that here. It's not this fellow's fault, the trouble is in Brisbane.'

Well, there's nothing more likely to move a manager into action than the wrath of a grieving family. Alwyn shook that company so hard that it rattled and his son was duly delivered to Rockhampton by ten the following morning.

The Torenbeeks collected the body of their son and brother that morning and later laid him to rest. Despite a bungling airline, despite a mournful funeral, he stays in their hearts and minds, in the make-up of every day, in words and thoughts spoken and unspoken. Always young, out chasing bulls, or driving through the night, or climbing windmills, or riding wild horses – free, active, their Aldo – forever loved.

Chapter Sixteen
ALDO'S BONNIE DOON: 1992–2012

Alwyn remembers – making a home base

We had never lived on the eastern side of the Great Divide before, nor had we ever lived on a place so small. I wasn't very good company for the first year or so, working and wondering how to make a living on such a little bit of country.

Aldo's Bonnie Doon, as we named our new property, had a good home but very little else. We were used to properties having very little on them when we took over – only this time there was just the two of us. Still, we had plenty of building materials, great ironbark trees with which to build sheds, yards, fences, garden edging. This we did post-haste. The advantage of having no buildings save a good house was we could put things where we wanted them.

That done, endurance riding took my attention and in 2000, the need to compete was back under my skin.

Before that I had just been training endurance horses, not intending to ride again. The thing was, I was feeling as fit as a fiddle, and I was tired of riders telling me what they wanted, that they were not happy with the horse they had been allotted – so

I decided to get back in the competition saddle again.

At the same time, along came a big rough horse to be broken. The horse was a tall 16 hands, creamy with black points and as bold as brass. I called him Fearless John.

Also, I had a beautiful bay Anglo mare I called Queen of Diamonds. She got her name because she and her young rider, Vicki Hogan, got on well from the word go – and diamonds are a girl's best friend.

With Vicki on Queen of Diamonds, the other member of our team, Elizabeth Collins, on Same As, and me on Fearless, we had a happy camp, and a happy camp made training a pleasure.

Another one of my horses, Once Only, was in top condition, so he fitted into my Quilty plans, spot on. Queen of Diamonds, Same As and Once Only started at the Boonah Quilty 2000, and that left Fearless for the state championships at Capella.

Our horses travelled perfectly to Boonah and took their short training rides with no worries. We were sitting on our swags around the campfire, enjoying tea and damper with our strapper Harry Smith, when a mobile phone call came through for me from Bill Elwood's sister, with the bad news that Bill had been tragically killed in a tractor rollover in Philadelphia. I had known Bill since our days on Darling Plain when he and his brother Jim had worked with us for two years before taking up work in the Northern Territory. They were fine stockmen, useful rodeo pick-up men and my good mates. Bill had been my strapper for the 1968 Quilty. He was so well respected that there were five former Australian rodeo champions at his funeral.

I had dedicated my 2000 Quilty ride to Aldo so now I also added Bill, as when Aldo was three, Bill was his idol. I hoped Once Only could carry the three of us – and he did, in fine style.

I placed ninth heavyweight, Elizabeth twelfth lightweight and Vicki twenty-first middleweight. To get through the Quilty with three horses has been probably my biggest equestrian achievement to date.

* * *

The first 18 days of 1992 were scorching hot, and with the heat came the promise of a new year with new hope and renewed optimism. Ultimately, however, this promise was not borne out on Silver Hills Station.

Alwyn had taken on a property that, like all the properties he managed, demanded a lot of maintenance. Unfortunately, as they worked to improve the station, to make it the best that it could be, the property owners were not passing on Alwyn's lease payments to the bank, with the inevitable result – foreclosure. The family were forced to stand by as the property went to auction.

There are times when a bushman and his family come to feel that there is something about a station that is not just theirs, but part of them. Silver Hills was never that sort of place to Alwyn and his family. It was a place in which they'd enjoyed living and working, but not a place that they'd really miss. They'd never felt that they wanted to call it home.

The goods and chattels were sold and Alwyn's payout from the sale was respectable thanks to a final wool sale that saw them pick up decent prices – the last for some years. A buoyant cattle market added to their take. They split up the finances among the family members and everyone went their separate ways. In some respects it marked the end of one great Torenbeek family adventure.

Jeff Torenbeek went to work for a horseman called Bill Elwood. Bill had spent his youth on Darling Plain and Banana stations, then travelled to the USA to build a reputation as a quarter horse handler. Jeff joined him in the Lone Star State – Texas. After some time in Texas, he travelled to England and then back to Australia to take up work in Pine Creek goldmine. Rod and Shayne stayed in Richmond managing the swimming pool for the summer. Steve and Vonda became station managers at Benopie Station between Biloela and Gladstone.

Marion and Alwyn bought a small property on Bonnie Doon Creek near Rockhampton two weeks before Christmas 1992. They had come to realise that after living a gypsy life, taking on wild bulls, raising a family, droving and all their other adventures, at 55 years of age they were ready to 'make a home base', as Alwyn put it. They named their new property Aldo's Bonnie Doon after their youngest son, and it became Aldo's resting place forever.

For a home base Aldo's Bonnie Doon had a lot going for it. There was a good creek meandering through the property that made a perfect venue for training young people and young horses. Sheoak cover on either side provided shade for riders to shelter out of the sun, and the gravel bed of the creek was good for horses with shoes; it was also easy on their legs.

A favourable nickel price in 1994 meant growth in the local economy thanks to the nearby Brolga mine. Rod and Shayne capitalised on the opportunity by moving closer so that Rod could work at the mine and help Alwyn. Jeff, who had returned from a world trip, spent his weekends building a massive shed with quarters for stockmanship school students, a machinery shed, cold room, ablution block and milking bail. Between them they also crafted horse-breaking yards and a rodeo arena.

Apart from the work that needed to be done on Aldo's Bonnie Doon, Alwyn took on a lot of outside work to make ends meet. However, the former rodeo champion needed more excitement, and he met that need by tackling the Longreach to Winton endurance ride.

By this stage, Alwyn had around a good half-dozen endurance rides to his name. The 1995 155-mile ride was his next challenge, but not as a jockey. Instead, Alwyn was the trainer, preparing his horse Once Only for the great ride.

Once Only was a good-looking Sarko-Quadir cross gelding, and Alwyn's 64-year-old sister Gwenda was his jockey.

Gwenda was up against some of Australia's best horsemen and women, battling across stony western plains country, through scrub and bulldust, along ridges and dry creek beds for a gold horseshoe worth $1000.

On race day a crowd gathered in the cold darkness. As the start time neared, the crowd quietened. Then the race started and Gwenda rode into the night on the pride of Aldo's Bonnie Doon, Once Only.

Alwyn liked what he saw in Once Only, especially after Gwenda's ride on him. He was convinced that Once Only stood and moved like a horse best suited to the show ring. So he lent him to a dressage rider and got on with training Once Only's brother Same As for the 1997 Longreach to Winton ride. It's safe to say that things were a bit cool between him and Gwenda for a little while after that.

Apart from training horses, Alwyn taught young riders how to ride 'front end' or forward on the saddle and helped to introduce a local riding school's students to riding in the bush. Among his students was a new rider called Elizabeth Collins. Alwyn could see she had promise as a rider, but her chestnut Arab was suffering from a debilitating bone condition called ringbone. Elizabeth's horse's misfortune was her good luck as she got to ride Alwyn's horse Same As to ready him for the 1997 Longreach to Winton endurance ride, and then later in the event itself.

The Longreach to Winton ride came around and Alwyn had his fingers crossed that Elizabeth and Same As were ready to show the endurance fraternity what they were capable of achieving.

Just before the start, Elizabeth wandered over to Alwyn looking as uncomfortable as a rabbit at a greyhound track. She clearly had a good dose of the butterflies. Elizabeth looked at Alwyn and said, 'I don't know anybody here. What if I get lost?'

Alwyn smiled and said to his down-at-the-mouth student, 'Don't worry about that now. They will all know you by Sunday morning.'

The ride was a pitiless mix of exposed plains country, hard, hot gibber, ghostly gidgee forest, desiccated ridges and thirsty creek beds. Yet, Elizabeth and Same As took every mile at a good pace and with an obstinate sense of cunning.

By that Sunday morning Alwyn's words came true. All of the endurance-riding competitors, trainers, strappers and the like knew Elizabeth's name and that of her proud horse. She had won the Queensland lightweight division in fine style, finishing after 22 hours and 17 minutes, to average just under 11 miles per hour over 155 miles. As for Same As, his win meant that he and his brother had produced back-to-back victories.

Although Alwyn enjoyed training, he longed for adventure of his own. The Quilty Gold Cup had not seen much of him as a competitor. He'd ridden in 1967 and 1968, and then life's commitments had kept him away. The new millennium brought with it the chance for Alwyn to compete in the Quilty again. This time on Once Only at a serene country town called Boonah, not far from Brisbane.

Team Torenbeek – Elizabeth on Same As, Vicki Hogan on Queen of Diamonds and Alwyn on Once Only – were three in a field of 270 top horses and riders.

By the time they rode over the finish line, Alwyn had placed ninth heavyweight, Elizabeth twelfth lightweight and Vicki twenty-first middleweight.

After their success in the 2000 Quilty, and with the hope of more to come, Alwyn, Elizabeth and Vicki rolled into Capella, in the heart of coalmining territory 190 miles west of Rockhampton, to take on the Queensland state championships.

The two women had their same mounts from the Quilty; Alwyn

had Fearless. The Capella ride was everything one would expect from a state championship – a field of first-class riders, strong horses and an interesting course.

Alwyn and Fearless crossed the finish line in 11 hours, nine minutes to secure a first in the heavyweight division and a win for best-conditioned horse. Alwyn was now able to add an endurance championship to his string of rodeo wins.

Vicki picked up fourth middleweight on Queen of Diamonds, with Elizabeth taking home fourth lightweight. Once again, the wily horseman had trained three magnificent horses for riders capable of getting the best from them.

That evening, the trio broke open a bottle of rum by way of celebration. It wasn't a very long celebration; just two or three rums and they were looking for their swags.

The morning light had just lit their camp the next day when a well-spoken gentleman hurried over to Alwyn's campfire. He was a nice young chap, an Arab sheik with a hankering to buy Queen of Diamonds and Fearless John. The sheik – inspired by the former president of the United Arab Emirates Sheikh Zayed bin Sultan Al Nahyan, who had started the sport in his home country – was impressed by the two horses and had the wherewithal to buy them. So he did, there and then.

In 2001 endurance riding called Marion and Alwyn to Western Australia for the Quilty Gold Cup, and they travelled with a posse of fellow riders. On the way out, they took the back roads to Birdsville, where they rested on the edge of the Simpson Desert. From Birdsville they followed the Birdsville Track to Maree in South Australia, travelling through places with names that inspired the imagination – Pandie Pandie, Walker's Crossing, Melon Creek Bore and Lake Harry Ruins. Then from South Australia they drove on to Perth, around 3300 miles and more from Aldo's Bonnie Doon.

Alwyn reckoned it was 'a pretty good trip', then thoughtfully added for the benefit of anyone who might have thought it too easy, 'We only had four tyres blow out.'

They'd arrived among a crowd of competitors from New South Wales, Victoria, South Australia and Queensland. Each and every one had travelled the Nullarbor – that great treeless plain framing the southern border of the continent. They had started arriving in mid-May and were all at the Quilty camp by the end of the month – 130 horses and riders.

Mingling with the Australians, there were also horsemen and women from the United Kingdom, the United Arab Emirates, South Africa, New Zealand and Japan.

That Friday night, they rode out from camp, each one hoping to finish and claim a coveted Quilty buckle. They set off at a good pace, climbing the Darling Scarp, the longest fault line in Australia; then it started raining just enough to cool the horses. In the next leg, they climbed the scarp again and again, and the mob still set a cracking pace through the bush, along gravel roads and then a railway line, and across paddocks so lush they invited the riders to canter. Then they rode up the part of the scarp known locally as The Hill, and riders Meg Wade, Kristie McGaffin and Penny Toft started to break away from the pack.

The final leg had the works – thick forest, a mire, rocks and a steep incline. Yet they rode on until Meg Wade crossed the line; then came Kristie McGaffin and third in was Penny Toft. One of the riders, a competitor from the UAE, rode across the finish line after 100 miles wearing a thick jacket, gloves and balaclava – the chilly southern weather was a little too bracing for a desert-hardened Arab rider.

Alwyn had ridden well, although his horse vetted out lame, and he and Marion were heading home to Queensland when the wet arrived. They were travelling with Kay Barbeller, whose horse had also vetted out of the Quilty. It wasn't an easy trip.

Freezing cold storms slowed their progress just south of Perth at Mundijong. Then, after Kay left them at Port Augusta, Marion and Alwyn drove on to face the Birdsville Track. It kept raining until they reached Leigh Creek, days later.

Alwyn got to work changing the tyres on his truck, while Marion scouted around for a spot to camp for the night, including somewhere for their horses.

Fifteen minutes later she returned, saying she'd met a 'nice fella' who'd shown her the way to the pony club ground, where there was ample space for them and their horses. That 'fella' was wiry, quietly spoken Andrew Hoddle. Andrew's help in finding somewhere to camp was a godsend, and when Alwyn and Marion ended up staying in Leigh Creek for four days until the rain-soaked road reopened, they were able to spend some time on his property, riding the Flinders Ranges.

When the road reopened, the Torenbeeks trundled on to Mungerannie. Crossing Dulkananna Creek, north of Mungerannie, was rather daunting. It was the best part of 320 yards across with no flood markers, so it was difficult to gauge the depth. Luckily, they made it through without any trouble – except for the fact that their destination, Birdsville, was another 196 miles away, with night fast approaching.

Every couple of miles there would be 50 yards of water across the road. As night fell, there was so much mud and so many flying insects that Alwyn had to clean the headlamps on the truck every six or seven miles.

The going was tough for everyone travelling along the track. All of them had given in to the conditions and pulled over to camp until the mud dried up a little, except the Torenbeeks. Alwyn and Marion drove through the slush and mud, fellow travellers in makeshift camps cheering them on along the way. They slogged on all the way to Birdsville, rested a little there and then turned their sights to Charleville, a further 500 miles east. Making Charleville meant the chance to enter another endurance ride with their horses Astro, an Anglo, and Pinfeather, a part-Clydesdale that Alwyn had saved from the dog-meat man.

The morning star and a lone truck welcomed them as they drove into Windorah. Windorah rodeo arena was perfect for their leg-weary horses, while Marion and Alwyn camped beside the truck. They planned to sleep for half an hour, but were so tired they gave in to four hours. After a quick food fix, they loaded up and set off again, with still another 300 miles to go until Charleville.

Charleville had a good 50-mile track and Alwyn was keen to find Astro a jockey. He had just sauntered into the vet ring with Pinfeather when a women walked out from the crowd and said, 'My name is Chris King. I'd love to ride your spare horse.' Marion grabbed the chance and whisked Chris away to meet Astro.

Chris was a spirited Kiwi horsewoman and her meeting with Alwyn and Marion in Charleville was the start of a long-lasting friendship. And, for the record, Chris won the heavyweight ride by 10 minutes in front of Alwyn.

By way of thanking the Torenbeeks for the chance to ride in Australia, Chris invited them to New Zealand to take on the national championships there. Of course, they accepted.

So, in 2002, Alwyn and Marion found themselves winging across the Tasman Sea, returning to New Zealand after four decades. They caught up with old friends Fred and Marie McCauley, Keith Green and John Magee and then skipped over to the South Island to stay with Chris and her husband Nelson, 15 miles outside of Christchurch.

Alwyn trained Chris's horse Nasi for the national championships, which would be held among the foothill battlements of the Southern Alps.

The ride set out from the Amberley showground, through paddocks so lush it was as if the horses were cantering across carpet.

They then climbed up into the foothills along an unforgiving track that took its toll on the field.

Above them loomed great craggy natural ramparts, plush with snow; below them, deep gorges and ice-melt creeks in soft watercolour shades of translucent blue, green, gold and amber. And beyond the hungry gorges, the Canterbury Plains – a vast expanse of opulent, luxurious pastures. Sheep grazed across the pastures, generation after generation following the same long lines, leaving deep-rutted tracks in their wakes.

Alwyn and Nasi were in fine form, until Nasi charged into a deep sheep track and got wedged in tight. 'Struth, mate,' said Alwyn, 'that'll be the end of the ride then.' But the horse wasn't finished.

Nasi pushed and dug, flinging clods of mud into the air. No flaming sheep rut was about to stop that strong-minded horse. He just went harder and bulldozed his way through until he was clear on the other side. Perhaps he wanted to finish; perhaps he just wanted to be out of the cold, rain, sleet and hail. It didn't matter, he rode on untroubled by the delay, the finish line ever closer.

Only half of those who rode out that day were able to ride to the finish. Among them were Alwyn and his newfound mate Nasi, who rode across the line in fourth place.

Alwyn and Marion bade Chris, Nelsen and Nasi a warm-hearted farewell and returned to Australia refreshed and triumphant after their second New Zealand adventure.

Back in Central Queensland, Steve and Vonda were managing a property called Hobartville Station. Shortly after returning from New Zealand, Alwyn took the five-hour drive out to Hobartville to spend some time with Vonda and put Dalgangle, his home-bred Anglo-Arab, and Queen of Hearts into training, in preparation for the winter endurance-riding season.

Alwyn had nominated for a 50-mile endurance ride at Jericho, just up the track from Hobartville. On the morning of the ride, just as the first rays of sunlight lit the central highlands, he strode out to get to work with Dalgangle.

He found a very sad and sorry horse. Sometime in the early hours something had spooked Dalgangle; he'd taken fright and run straight into a four-strand barbwire fence. The horse had major injuries where the wire had lacerated his near-side shoulder and around his eye.

Alwyn's son-in-law Steve organised a tetanus shot for Dalgangle, while Alwyn got to work cleaning and repairing the horse's wounds. The shoulder gash was the worst. Alwyn dried it up with flour and mattress-stitched it, and then did the same for the gash below Dalgangle's eye.

With Dalgangle taken care of, Alwyn needed to load Queen of Hearts onto his truck in time to make the start of the Jericho ride. It may have been the smell of Dalgangle's blood, which Alwyn hadn't had time to clean off – nobody will ever know – but the normally reliable horse refused to be loaded onto the truck.

Impatient, Alwyn smacked his horse on the butt and the horse responded with a whopper of a kick that shattered his forearm. Once again, Alwyn was off to a local hospital. He walked up to the nurses' station and announced that he'd broken his arm. The nurse on duty looked at him and asked how he knew it was broken. Alwyn's response was to the point. He said simply, 'Well, it's wobbling.'

The nurse took one look at the hapless horseman's arm and had him whisked off to Rockhampton General in the air-ambulance.

A nurses' strike over pay and conditions was in full swing at the time, which meant slow going in the Rockhampton emergency department, but eventually a doctor assessed Alwyn's injuries.

'Do you have any requests?' the doctor asked in a quiet, professional manner with a tinge of finality about it.

Alwyn, ever the optimist, looked the doctor over and said,

'Please have me out before twelve o'clock or I might turn into a pumpkin.'

'Are you fair dinkum?' the doctor said. Then he looked at the bushman's paperwork and, noting the date, replied, 'We'll do the best we can.' It was the Kokotunga Kid's sixty-fifth birthday.

Alwyn left hospital 10 days later, after his arm had been plated both sides, screwed and stapled. He didn't have enough strength in it even to hold a beer and wish himself a happy belated birthday. Not being a big drinker, Alwyn wasn't too worried. He went on an endurance ride instead.

Queen of Hearts had never kicked before and didn't repeat her bad behaviour. In fact, in 2004 she was Alwyn's top mare, winning the Longreach 100-mile endurance-ride lightweight division with his granddaughter Kelsey as jockey.

In his sixty-sixth year, Alwyn gave the Queensland long-distance heavyweight title a fair dinkum go. A speckled grey mare called Lucille was ready to give him a hand.

Lucille was an Anglo-Arab from Cocklabinda Station near Baralaba. Although initially a tad too spirited, she quietened soon after arriving on Aldo's Bonnie Doon. Even though she didn't get on particularly well with blokes, Alwyn could get her to respond willingly – he had always had a way with cantankerous horses and brought out their better nature. Lucille, despite her initial showing, had a wonderful nature.

Alwyn's 2003 tilt at the Queensland long-distance heavyweight title kicked off when the president of the UAE sponsored an endurance ride in Canberra.

The Canberra ride wound around Lake Burley Griffin, past Parliament House and the Carillon bell tower, beyond the High Court of Australia and the Australian Mint, along bicycle tracks and tunnels, and then up into the western foothills.

Once in the foothills, they travelled through country that, earlier that year, had been ravaged by bushfires. The fires had blasted through the outskirts of Canberra and surrounds, taking in their wake 70 per cent of the Territory's pastures, forests and nature parks, and completely destroying the historic Mount Stromlo Observatory. Charred reminders of the devastation lined the trail. Despite the large field of riders, Alwyn chose to ride solo for 20 miles, just to take it all in.

The grey mare Lucille and her former rodeo champion rider took second place in the 2003 Presidents Cup – a ride never repeated.

With the Presidents Cup done and dusted, Alwyn took Lucille to endurance rides at Roma, Kingaroy and Chinchilla – the three legs of the endurance-riding Masters. For the Masters, competitors are expected to complete three events using the same horse, over a total of 150 miles. Alwyn's runs with Lucille in the Masters and in Canberra boosted his chances for the long-distance heavyweight title.

Alwyn added another 157 miles to his total thanks to a bay part-Arab mare called Fire Queen. In South Australia in 2004 the two won fifth place in the Quilty Gold Cup, and Fire Queen was the third-fittest horse at the end of the 100-mile ride.

Some more solid runs and endurance rides on Fire Queen contributed 160 miles to Alwyn's mileage tally. Then he added 280 miles with Astro, and another 150 miles with Pinfeather, the grey gelding he had saved from the knackery. At the final count the old competitor had a grand total of 920 miles, and the title for which he'd aimed, placing first overall in endurance riding for Australia.

The following year, 2005, saw Alwyn take out a second heavyweight place in the Queensland championship and, making things even sweeter, his granddaughter Kelsey won second place as a junior. The two teamed up again in 2006 at the Quilty Gold Cup held in Boonah.

Kelsey was 15 years old at the time, yet turning 16 in the year of the race, so according to endurance-riding rules she had to join the 'open' ranks. That put her up against some of the world's best riders. Alwyn reckoned the rule was unfair, but the Endurance Riders Association remained unmoved.

Kelsey rode hard at Boonah and came in twelfth. As she rode across the finish line her face looked tired, yet the energy in her eyes betrayed the pride she felt in finishing the most prestigious Australian endurance ride. She'd secured her Quilty buckle. All that was left was for her horse to pass the final vet check – what felt like a mere formality.

The vet checked her horse over and then said the one word no rider wants to hear: 'Lame'. It meant the final leg, the gruelling last few miles, amounted to naught. Her horse needed to cross the line and pass the critical eyes of the vet for the final stage to count. One hundred miles ridden and no result – nothing could be crueller.

Kelsey's initial reaction was to threaten to give up endurance riding. That was Alwyn's fear. But it proved to be unfounded – Kelsey had the same tenacity as her grandfather, and the two teamed up again for the Queensland state championships at Denison Creek.

The Denison Creek ride was 100 miles of harsh terrain spread over five stages. The course was one of the toughest in Australia, in Alwyn's candid opinion, and includes two mountains, the largest of which is known as the Widow Maker – courtesy of its unforgiving nature.

Team Torenbeek started the ride at midnight with both horses running strong, in control in third and fourth position. By the mountainous third leg over the Widow Maker they were about seventh. At the bottom of that terrible descent Alwyn said to Kelsey, 'Off you go. I don't need to see you again today.' Kelsey rode on to win the middleweight title and to become the youngest middleweight champion ever.

In 2006 Alwyn received one last rodeo call. It came from the agricultural town of Warwick on the southern Darling Downs, which had become the hub of rodeo in Australia. The occasion was the opening of the Australian Rodeo Heritage Centre – a hall of fame celebrating the life and times of the very best of the nation's rodeo stars.

Naturally, the Kokotunga Kid, one of the youngest champion riders of the 1950s, was inducted into the hall of fame. Alongside his name on the honour roll are the names of other great rodeo champions, including Alwyn's heroes Lindsay Black, Ray Crawford and Dally Holden.

His inclusion was a great privilege for Alwyn and a highlight of 2006, but he was still on the lookout for another, bigger adventure. It wasn't long before he cooked up a plan to tour Australia with two trucks, six horses, one four-wheel drive, nine people and one dog.

Alwyn tempted Chris King and Trevor Copeland from New Zealand, Jeremy Robinson and a friend from Tasmania, a young rider from Germany called Bridget Stemm, Yukinobu Horiuchi from Japan and Lyn Eather, who helped run a farmstay business on Myella, to join him on the jaunt. The idea was reminiscent of Alwyn's days touring the rodeo circuits. He and Marion would do the entire tour while others dropped in and out of the trip as their work and other commitments allowed.

By 2007, the trip was organised and pretty much ready to go. The trucks were loaded with food and fuel, and Alwyn was just waiting for veterinary clearance to cross the Northern Territory and West Australian borders. Jeremy had already left for Herberton in the misty mountains of the Atherton Tablelands, in Far North Queensland.

One day that August, Alwyn was sitting at the end of his long hardwood table sipping his tea, with a radio tuned to the national broadcaster blabbering away in the background, when the trumpeting call that heralds an ABC newsflash caught his attention.

It was news he didn't expect and certainly didn't want to hear. The exotic disease equine influenza (EI) had been found in Australia. Horse owners were restricted to riding on their own property until further notice.

Trevor and Alwyn did their best to keep the horses in good order for four days, hoping that the disease would be contained by then. It wasn't, and the equine flu outbreak continued to worsen. For Alwyn, the solution was simple – they'd go riding in New Zealand. It was a good decision, considering the epidemic would spread to infect more than 33,000 horses in New South Wales and Queensland by early October. It was seven months before Australia was declared provisionally free of EI in March 2008.

Over in New Zealand, which was free of EI, they spent time on the west coast of the North Island at Gore, where Trevor Copeland had a 400-acre property with cattle, sheep, deer, and 40 horses, at least 10 of which had to be broken. Alwyn and Trevor broke in four horses and then things turned to custard.

Trevor was on a pony that hadn't been out of the yard before. Alwyn was leading the pony, riding a youngster that they'd broken four days earlier. Trevor's pony started to tug on the lead and with one mighty heave pulled Alwyn's shoulder out of joint and Alwyn out of his saddle. Alwyn was knocked unconscious and suffered a collapsed right lung, which in turn led to a tour of duty at the Invercargill hospital followed by a week of convalescence.

Back in the saddle, Alwyn and Trevor pulled off a 50-mile endurance ride, with Alwyn collecting second place to Trevor's first. Then, after a short stay with Chris King in Christchurch, the Torenbeeks headed back to Aldo's Bonnie Doon in time for Alwyn's annual medical checkup – such are the obligations of growing older. This time his blood result brought bad news: prostate cancer.

A biopsy confirmed the need for surgery and a date was set in April. However, an infection postponed the surgery and gave Alwyn time to reconsider. He was convinced that the best place to do some thinking was away from his usual distractions. So he decided to head back to New Zealand.

For Alwyn, coming to grips with cancer was like coming to grips with a wild bull's tail – it seemed simple, yet a bad or mistimed choice meant risking his health or perhaps his life. He was determined to find a way through the cancer that ensured he stayed active. An indolent old age or what he called a few 'fool-envied years' before shuffling off this mortal coil was not for him.

Having taken himself away to New Zealand to think about what the future had in store for him, Alwyn worked some of Chris King's four-year-old horses that badly needed breaking. Then he went endurance riding. The rides gave him time to think about how best to tackle his cancer and, in between, to relax and let his troubles float away on the breeze. And there was great company to cheer him up: Trevor Copeland, Bridget Stemm, a Queenslander called Tarney, Chris King and her husband Nelson.

Before long, however, the old bushman had to head home to Rockhampton. He had made his decision: he wouldn't have an operation. After talking it over, Marion agreed with her husband's decision, as did the rest of the family.

Determined to avoid the knife, Alwyn changed doctors. With all the bravado of his youth, he waltzed into his new doctor's office and started refusing, in no uncertain terms, to go to surgery.

'Hang on, I'm on your side,' responded the specialist. 'I'm sure I can fix you if you follow these steps.' The specialist's prescription was for oral drug therapy initially and then monthly injections. Alwyn followed the doctor's advice, and his blood results improved slowly and steadily.

There's something about being given a clean bill of health after a scare that focuses the mind on living life to the full. Alwyn had always drawn everything he could from every day. He reckoned that 'one should never miss a ride', and, at 72 years of age, he was still keen to ride another Quilty. So, in 2008, he nominated for the Nanango Quilty Cup.

The ABC was there to record the ride, and a reporter approached Alwyn for an interview. Alwyn looked her in the eye and, with the same hint of mischief he had when he was just 16 years old and dreaming of becoming a champion roughrider, said of the Quilty, 'It's virtually like winning the Melbourne Cup.' Although he conceded that endurance riding 'wasn't the same buzz you get riding a bucking bronc', he pointed out what was obvious to all who knew him: he was hooked on it.

In 2008 Alwyn had a formidable team, consisting of himself, his 14-year-old grandson Luke Torenbeek, Japanese rider Yukinobu Horiuchi, and Trevor Copeland from New Zealand. He had high hopes for the Nanango Quilty and dared to dream that he might pick up four of the coveted buckles. He certainly wanted to be upfront at the end.

In the daylight hours before the race he confided to the ABC reporter that 'I'm trying to finish it, but they better not slip too much in front – I'll beat 'em.'

At the striking of four in the morning the 2008 Quilty riders rode into the night. Team Torenbeek started out strong. At the first vet check, Alwyn did his best to raise a smile for the ABC reporter. 'What a ride, a beautiful track!' he said, adding that it was 'a little bit daunting and testing'.

By the second leg the sun was up and there was a 20-mile scramble through bush and some road-riding before the field hit a heart-stopping hill climb just before the vet check. At the end of the hill climb, Alwyn's team was still going strong.

By mid-afternoon the temperature had spiked unexpectedly to

35 degrees; nature was preparing to deliver a blitzkrieg of a storm. As the thunder started rumbling and the humidity climbed, Alwyn thought, 'This might liven things up a bit.' He was right.

The rising heat and humidity took its toll, knocking the completion rate down from an expected 70 per cent to less than 50 per cent. After crossing the finish line and looking after his horse, Alwyn told the ABC reporter that courtesy of the frightening storm that caught about half of the field, 'This Quilty will be spoken about for the next 10 to 15 years as probably one of the toughest rides we had.'

Two members of Team Torenbeek found success at Nanango. Alwyn and his Japanese mate both earned a Quilty buckle. Thinking his grandson Luke might be a bit unhappy, Alwyn caught up with him for a chat. But the young lad was philosophical, saying, 'Well, Pop, I didn't win it this time, but they'll have to watch me next time.' He was proud he'd ridden almost 70 miles in the Quilty and that meant, as far as he was concerned, he couldn't be disappointed.

From 2008 to 2012 Alwyn brought his tally of endurance rides up to about 130 rides, which represented thousands of miles. Taking his rodeo and droving days into account, Alwyn had spent a long time – a lifetime – in the saddle. Those long hours were recognised in 2012 when he was inducted into the Australian Equine Hall of Fame in Toowoomba.

On becoming an inductee, one of only three chosen every second year, he joined a select group of both people and horses who have made an outstanding contribution to the equine industry. His story was put up for permanent display alongside those of legendary racehorses Phar Lap and Bernborough, Olympian Bill Roycroft, and Stockman's Hall of Fame founder and artist Hugh Sawrey, together with the Australian Light Horses' famous breed of warhorses, the Waler.

Not long before his induction, it occurred to Alwyn – who, at 73, was still looking for adventure – that he should try 'a real tough ride' – the Shahzada.

To say the Shahzada is tough is to understate the true grit it takes to complete the 250-mile ride. The very mention of it stirs the hearts and minds of anyone interested in endurance riding – or in this case, marathon endurance riding. The first hint of the difficulty of the course is its motto: 'To Finish is to Win'. This isn't a race, but a test of man and beast, of horsemanship and athleticism.

Every winter hundreds of endurance riders and their support teams roll up at St Albans in the upper Hunter Valley north of Sydney to compete in the Shahzada. In 2010 Alwyn and his horse Belyando made the trip.

By 4 a.m. on 23 August 2010 they and the other 82 riders were primed and ready. The starter waved them off on the first day's ride of 54 miles. Alwyn and Belyando covered it at nearly 7 miles per hour.

They attacked the second day, a 50-mile ride, at the same pace and brought it in to plan. On the third day, they turned the heat down and covered 49 miles at 6 miles per hour. On day four they saw in 50 miles at 6 miles per hour and then tackled the last day at a steady gait of 5.3 miles per hour. All went well.

Alwyn and Belyando rode home in a very respectable second place in the heavyweight division and received a first for the oldest rider and another for the longest distance travelled to the event – Rockhampton to St Albans is a fair distance.

As time passed, Alwyn's memories of the rigours of the Shahzada softened and by the time he turned 75, he was ready to take it on again.

On 24 August 2012, he headed to St Albans, ready to prove he and his horse Dalgangle still had the ticker to endure a 250-mile ride.

Four in the morning, the hills and mountains were crisp with morning dew, and the sun rested below the horizon as Alwyn on Dalgangle and his riding companion Jane Davidson on A Dynamite cantered off.

The first leg ended without too much worry. Then things started to heat up. Jane and A Dynamite were on a single-lane, rough track, doing well, feeling well, when another rider tried to overtake, apparently having forgotten that the rules of the ride call for courteous riding. The rider clipped A Dynamite on the offside front hoof. The injury concerned Alwyn and Jane, yet they finished that day's ride.

The next morning, A Dynamite's injured hoof failed the vet inspection. That left Alwyn facing the next three days without a companion rider.

By the third leg of the Shahzada the ride was taking its toll, as many of the original lead riders vetted out. That put Alwyn higher up the leader board. By this stage, he thought that if he rode cool and calm, taking risks only where warranted, and stayed in touch with the leaders, he might have a chance at finishing – perhaps first. It's hard to remember that finishing is considered a win, when crossing the line first seems like such an achievement.

The third day dawned and carried the field over high and stony mountainous country. Dalgangle was doing it tough on an extremely narrow single-lane track, scrambling over large rocks covered in bracken fern. Yet the horse pushed hard for Alwyn.

Alwyn leant forward and whispered to Dal, telling him not to worry, to take his time. To help Dal, the champion rider dismounted and started to lead the horse through the forest of blue gum and ironbark over the top of the mountain and down into the shale cap forest with its woven understorey of ferns and acacia shrub.

There were only four horses in front of them, yet Alwyn continued to lead his weary mount for quite a while. Then, as the trail improved, he whispered to Dalgangle, 'I'll be getting back on soon.'

There was one last rough and narrow neck of bracken fern for them to negotiate and they'd be off and riding again. The fern thicket tangled around Alwyn's boots and he tripped, falling face-first onto a large sandstone rock.

The fall knocked out three teeth and put one almost completely through his tongue. Covered in blood, his face a shattered mess, Alwyn picked himself up off the ground, collected his thoughts, and after a short walk mounted Dalgangle and rode on, like a true champion.

Despite the blood streaming from his mouth he rode at a good pace; there were other riders to catch and a marathon to finish. Besides, he knew he needed help and his best chance of getting it was to catch the front-runners.

Time, they say, heals all wounds. Certainly the time it took to ride the last 6 miles did the trick and the flow of blood from Alwyn's mouth eased.

Dalgangle vetted through the leg. The question remaining was whether Alwyn would 'vet out' or not. The ride nurse checked him over, and he offered her a half-hearted bloody and toothless smile.

'Well,' she said, as if realising that Alwyn wasn't going to give up easily, 'if you feel okay, you may continue on to the next leg.' So the determined duo took on the final leg for the day. As the day came to an end, the riders' camp couldn't have looked more inviting to the battle-weary horseman.

Morning bird sounds rang across the Hawkesbury as the early hours made way for the dawn. Alwyn woke to find that the soft tissues around his mouth had swollen and the cool night air had made the bleeding increase. In his own words, he looked 'like Dracula coming out of the back door of a slaughterhouse'. He recognised that it was time to give up the Shahzada. It was time to head home.

It took Alwyn a week in total to make it back to Aldo's Bonnie Doon, where Shayne and Marion were waiting to welcome him home.

It was an emotional reunion. Shayne wrapped her arms around her father, looked him over and said, with great relief, 'You look better than I expected, Dad.'

When the initial greetings were over, and after they'd released Dalgangle into the horse yard, Alwyn and Marion strolled back to the station's camp kitchen. Marion put the kettle on, then looked at Alwyn firmly and said, 'So, you're finished now. No more rides?'

Alwyn gave her a gummy smile that, despite his missing teeth, still had its trademark bush charm and cheekiness. 'A man can't miss a ride,' he said, and went on to explain that he'd already begun to think about the next endurance ride. Marion sighed softly, a sort of acquiescence.

For the Kokotunga Kid it's all about being in the saddle – there's always another ride, another chance to win, another adventure.

Acknowledgements

No book comes about in isolation. Over time many help with the process of writing. We need to offer many thanks to Lyn Eather for encouraging Alwyn to tell his story and to Shayne Irvine, Kelsey Irvine, Emma Irvine and Bonnie Torenbeek for helping him to put his thoughts on paper. Thanks to Yvonne Knight and Amanda Stirling for supporting and encouraging a horseman to write his story.

Thank you to Tracey Gilchrist for her continued support of her journalist husband in taking on this book. Thank you to our sons Benjamin and Matthew for always supporting me in my writing.

Great thanks to Lindsay Black for sharing his rodeo memories of his time as a champion rider with Alwyn, and to Erica Williams for sharing her memories of her late husband R.M. Williams and how the Quilty Gold Cup came about.

Every good horseman knows that he can't succeed at endurance riding without a good strapper, so special thanks to Jan MacPherson for providing key support over many years during many of the endurance riding adventures that feature in the book.

Thanks to my agent Benython Oldfield from Zeitgeist Media Group for recognising a first class yarn and being willing to support it.

And for her unwavering professional support, thanks to Andrea McNamara and the team at Penguin Books Australia. Andrea offers the sort of publishing support any writer would thank their stars to have. Special thanks to editor Sonja Heijn.

Thank you to Mark Muller of *R.M. Williams Outback* magazine for commissioning the original magazine story that prompted me to take up the book with Alwyn.